TOTAL
BASIC SKILLS
Grade 2

Copyright © 2004 by School Specialty Publishing. Published by American Education Publishing, an imprint of School Specialty Publishing, a member of the School Specialty Family.

Send all inquiries to:
School Specialty Publishing
8720 Orion Place
Columbus, OH 43240-2111

ISBN 0-7696-3642-X

6 7 8 9 10 11 12 HPS 13 12 11 10 09

Table of Contents

Math

READING

Name _____

All About Me!

Directions: Fill in the blanks to tell all about you!

Name _____
        (First)   (Last)

Address _____

City _____ State _____

Phone number _____

Age _____

Places I have visited: _____

_____

_____

_____

My favorite vacation: _____

_____

_____

_____

Beginning Consonants: b, c, d, f, g, h, j

Directions: Fill in the beginning consonant for each word.

Example: __c__ at

__B__ ox

__J__ acket

__g__ oat

__H__ ouse

__d__ og

__F__ ire

Name _____

Beginning Consonants: k, l, m, n, p, q, r

Directions: Write the letter that makes the beginning sound for each picture.

M_____   B_____   B_____   n_____

M_____   l_____   k_____   r_____

q_____   P_____   S_____   m_____

L_____   k_____   r_____   M_____

Name __ameerah__

Beginning Consonants: s, t, v, w, x, y, z

Directions: Write the letter under each picture that makes the beginning sound.

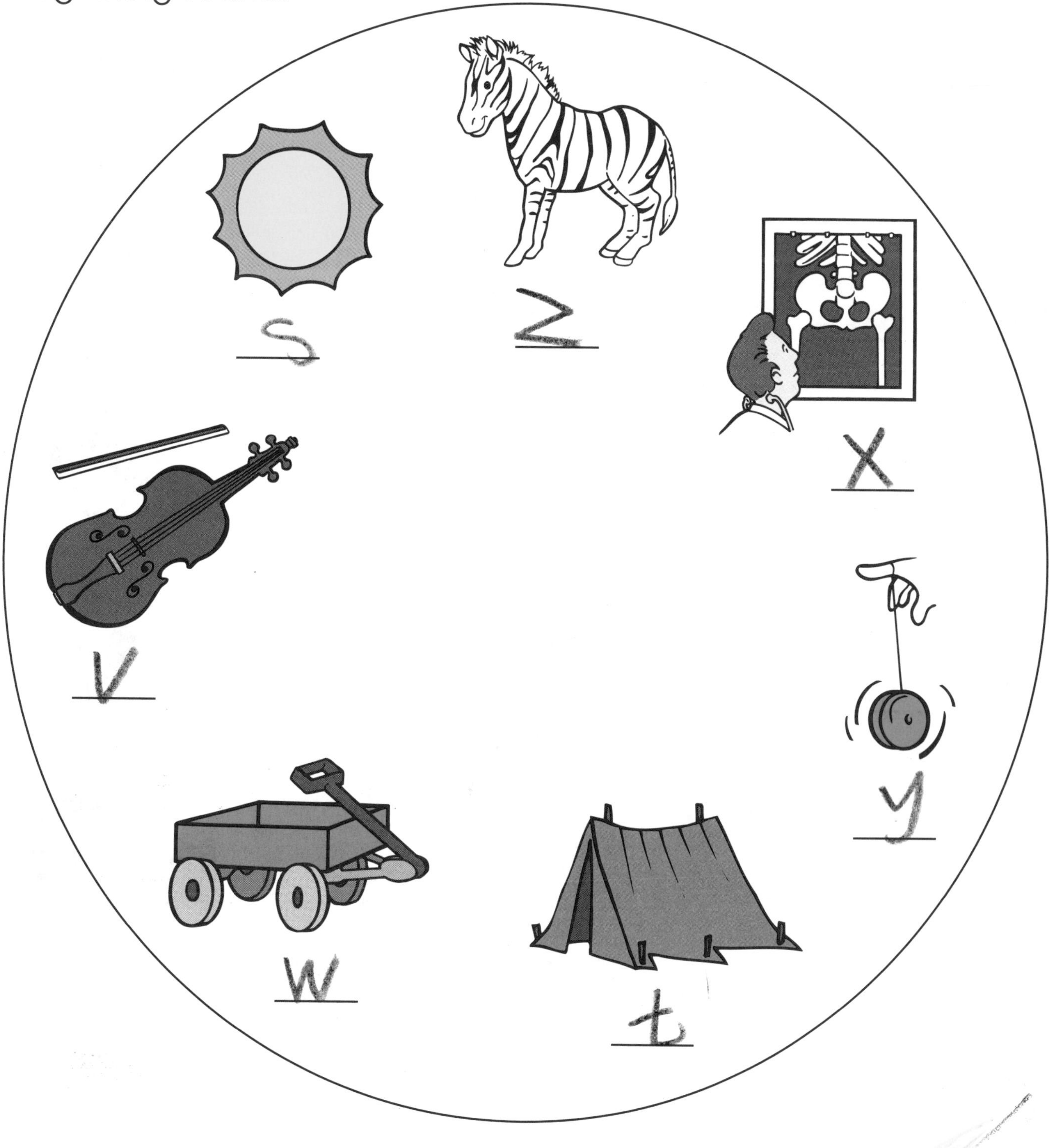

s

z

x

v

y

w

t

Ending Consonants: b, d, f, g

Directions: Fill in the ending consonant for each word.

ma _n_

cu _B_

roo _F_

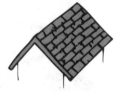

do _g_

be _d_

bi _b_

Name _____

Ending Consonants: k, l, m, n, p, r

Directions: Fill in the ending consonant for each word.

nai __l__

ca __n__

gu __m__

ca __r__

truc __k__

ca __p__

pai_____

Name _____

Ending Consonants: s, t, x

Directions: Fill in the ending consonant for each word.

ca ____

bo ____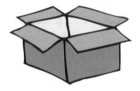

bu ____

fo ____

boa ____

ma ____

Name _____

Consonant Blends

Consonant blends are two or three consonant letters in a word whose sounds combine, or blend. **Examples: br, fr, gr, pr, tr**

Directions: Look at each picture. Say its name. Write the blend you hear at the beginning of each word.

_____   _____   _____

_____   _____   _____

_____   _____   _____

_____   _____   _____

Name _____

Blends: fl, br, pl, sk, sn

Blends are two consonants put together to form a single sound.

Directions: Look at the pictures and say their names. Write the letters for the beginning sound in each word.

14

Blends: bl, sl, cr, cl

Directions: Look at the pictures and say their names. Write the letters for the beginning sound in each word.

_____ own

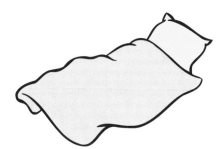

_____ anket

_____ ayon

_____ ock

_____ ide

_____ oud

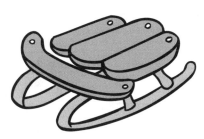

_____ ed

_____ ab

_____ ocodile

Name _____

Consonant Teams

Consonant teams are two or three consonant letters that have a single sound. **Examples: sh** and **tch**

Directions: Write each word from the word box next to its picture. Underline the consonant team in each word. Circle the consonant team in each word in the box.

bench	match	shoe	thimble
shell	brush	peach	watch
whale	teeth	chair	wheel

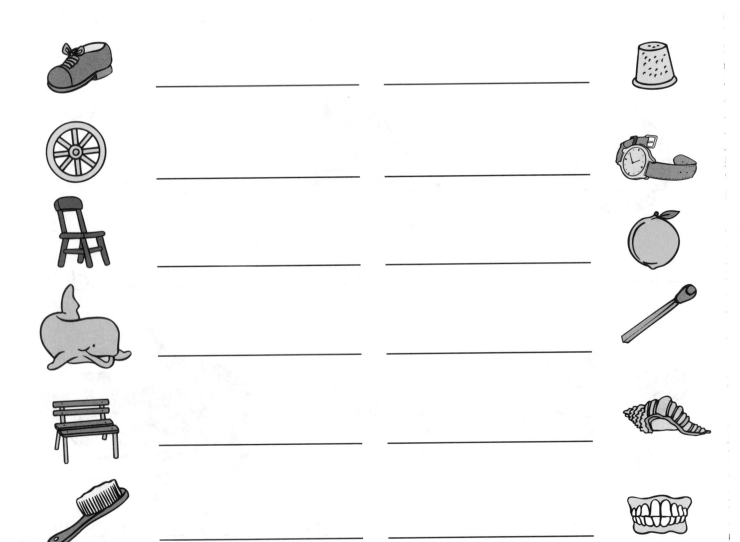

Consonant Teams

Directions: Read the words in the box. Write a word from the word box to finish each sentence. Circle the consonant team in each word. **Hint:** There are three letters in each team!

splash	screen	spray	street	scream
screw	shrub	split	strong	string

1. Another word for a bush is a _____ .

2. I tied a _____ to my tooth to help pull it out.

3. I have many friends who live on my_____ .

4. We always _____ when we ride the roller coaster.

5. A _____ helps keep bugs out of the house.

6. It is fun to _____ in the water.

7. My father uses an ax to _____ the firewood.

8. We will need a _____ to fix the chair.

9. You must be very _____ to lift this heavy box.

10. The firemen _____ the fire with water.

Name _____

Letter Teams: sh, ch, wh, th

Directions: Look at the first picture in each row. Circle the pictures that have the same sound.

whistle

shoe

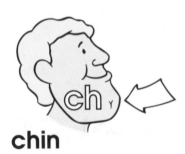
chin

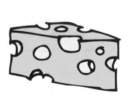

thumb

Name _____

Silent Letters

Some words have letters you can't hear at all, such as the **gh** in **night**, the **w** in **wrong**, the **l** in **walk**, the **k** in **knee**, the **b** in **climb** and the **t** in **listen**.

Directions: Look at the words in the word box. Write the word under its picture. Underline the silent letters.

| knife | light | calf | wrench | lamb | eight |
| wrist | whistle | comb | thumb | knob | knee |

_____   _____   _____   _____

_____   _____   _____   _____

 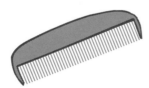  

_____   _____   _____   _____

Hard and Soft c

When **c** is followed by **e**, **i** or **y**, it usually has a **soft** sound. The **soft** **c** sounds like **s**. For example, **c**ircle and fen**c**e. When **c** is followed by **a** or **u**, it usually has a **hard** sound. The **hard c** sounds like **k**.

Example: **c**up and **c**art

Directions: Read the words in the word box. Write the words in the correct lists. One word will be in both. Write a word from the word box to finish each sentence.

Words with soft c

pencil

_____

_____

_____

_____

Words with hard c

_____

_____

_____

_____

_____

pencil	cookie
dance	cent
popcorn	circus
lucky	mice
tractor	card

1. Another word for a penny is a _____.

2. A cat likes to chase _____.

3. You will see animals and clowns at the _____.

4. Will you please sharpen my _____?

Hard and Soft g

When **g** is followed by **e**, **i** or **y**, it usually has a **soft** sound. The **soft g** sounds like **j**. **Example:** chan**g**e and **g**entle. The **hard g** sounds like the **g** in **g**irl or **g**ate.

Directions: Read the words in the word box. Write the words in the correct lists. Write a word from the box to finish each sentence.

engine	glove	cage	magic	frog
giant	flag	large	glass	goose

Words with soft g

engine

_____

_____

_____

_____

Words with hard g

_____

_____

_____

_____

1. Our bird lives in a _____.

2. Pulling a rabbit from a hat is a good _____ trick.

3. A car needs an _____ to run.

4. A _____ is a huge person.

5. An elephant is a very _____ animal.

Name _____

Short Vowels

Vowels can make **short** or **long** sounds. The short **a** sounds like the **a** in cat. The short **e** is like the **e** in leg. The short **i** sounds like the **i** in pig. The short **o** sounds like the **o** in box. The short **u** sounds like the **u** in cup.

Directions: Look at each picture. Write the missing short vowel letter.

p___p

n___t

s ___ ck

___x

l___ps

h___t

f___x

t___nt

p___n

Short Vowels

Vowels can make **short** or **long** sounds. The short **a** sounds like the **a** in **cat**. The short **e** is like the **e** in **leg**. The short **i** sounds like the **i** in **pig**. The short **o** sounds like the **o** in **box**. The short **u** is like the **u** in **cup**.

Directions: Look at the pictures. Their names all have short vowel sounds. But the vowels are missing! Fill in the missing vowels in each word.

a　　　　e　　　　i　　　　o　　　　u

p__pp__t　　　h__mmer　　　p__pcorn　　　__l__ph__nt

t__l__v__sion　　　b__ttle　　　sh__v__l　　　th__mble

c__ndle　　　b__tt__n　　　p__nny　　　l__dder

Name _____

Super Silent e

Long vowel sounds have the same sound as their names. When a **Super Silent e** appears at the end of a word, you can't hear it, but it makes the other vowel have a long sound. For example: **tub** has a **short** vowel sound, and **tube** has a **long** vowel sound.

Directions: Look at the following pictures. Decide if the word has a short or long vowel sound. Circle the correct word. Watch for the **Super Silent e**!

can   cane   tub   tube   rob   robe   rat   rate

pin   pine   cap   cape   not   note   pan   pane

slid   slide   dim   dime   tap   tape   cub   cube

Long Vowels

Long vowel sounds have the same sound as their names. When a **Super Silent e** comes at the end of a word, you can't hear it, but it changes the short vowel sound to a long vowel sound.

Example: rope, skate, bee, pie, cute

Directions: Say the name of the pictures. Listen for the long vowel sounds. Write the missing long vowel sound under each picture.

c ___ ke

h ___ ke

n ___ se

___ pe

c ___ be

gr ___ pe

r ___ ke

b ___ ne

k ___ te

R-Controlled Vowels

When a vowel is followed by the letter **r**, it has a different sound.

Example: he and **her**

Directions: Write a word from the word box to finish each sentence. Notice the sound of the vowel followed by an **r**.

park	chair	horse	bark	bird
hurt	girl	hair	store	ears

1. A dog likes to _____.

2. You buy food at a _____.

3. Children like to play at the _____.

4. An animal you can ride is a _____.

5. You hear with your _____.

6. A robin is a kind of _____.

7. If you fall down, you might get _____.

8. The opposite of a boy is a _____.

9. You comb and brush your _____.

10. You sit down on a _____.

Name _____

R-Controlled Words

R-controlled vowel words are words in which the **r** that comes after the vowel changes the sound of the vowel. **Examples:** bird, star, burn

Directions: Write the correct word in the sentences below.

horse	purple
jar	bird
dirt	turtle

1. Jelly comes in one of these. _____

2. This creature has feathers and can fly. _____

3. This animal lives in a shell. _____

4. This animal can pull wagons. _____

5. If you mix water and this, you will have mud. _____

6. This color starts with the letter **p**. _____

Name _____

Double Vowel Words

Usually when two vowels appear together, the first one says its name and the second one is silent.
Example: b<u>ea</u>n

Directions: Unscramble the double vowel words below. Write the correct word on the line.

 **ocat** _____

 etar _____

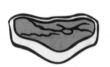 **mtea** _____

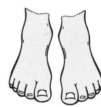 **eetf** _____

 **teas** _____

 **otab** _____

 **ogat** _____

 spea _____

 **atli** _____

 apil _____

Name _____

Vowel Teams

The vowel teams **ou** and **ow** can have the same sound. You can hear it in the words **clown** and **cloud**. The vowel teams **au** and **aw** have the same sound. You hear it in the words **because** and **law**.

Directions: Look at the pictures. Write the correct vowel team to complete the words. The first one is done for you. You may need to use a dictionary to help you with the correct spelling.

au to

cl_____n

h_____se

fl_____er

s_____

_____l

p_____der

m_____th

j_____

p_____

m_____se

cl_____d

Vowel Teams

The vowel team **ea** can have a short **e** sound like in **head**, or a long **e** sound like in **bead**. An **ea** followed by an **r** makes a sound like the one in **ear** or like the one in **heard**.

Directions: Read the story. Listen for the sound **ea** makes in the bold words.

Have you ever **read** a book or **heard** a story about a **bear**? You might have **learned** that bears sleep through the winter. Some bears may sleep the whole **season**. Sometimes they look almost **dead**! But they are very much alive. As the cold winter passes and the spring **weather** comes **near**, they wake up. After such a nice rest, they must be **ready** to **eat** a **really** big **meal**!

words with long **ea**	words with short **ea**	**ea** followed by **r**
_____	_____	_____
_____	_____	_____
_____	_____	_____
_____	_____	_____

Vowel Teams

The vowel team **ie** makes the long **e** sound like in **believe**. The team **ei** also makes the long **e** sound like in **either**. But **ei** can also make a long **a** sound like in **eight**.

Directions: Circle the **ei** words with the long **a** sound.

neighbor   veil

receive   reindeer

reign   ceiling

The teams **eigh** and **ey** also make the long **a** sound.

Directions: Finish the sentences with words from the word box.

chief	sleigh	obey	weigh	thief	field	ceiling

1. Eight reindeer pull Santa's _____ .

2. Rules are for us to _____ .

3. The bird got out of its cage and flew up to the _____ .

4. The leader of an Indian tribe is the _____ .

5. How much do you _____ ?

6. They caught the _____ who took my bike.

7. Corn grows in a _____ .

Name _____

Vowel Teams: oi, oy, ou, ow

Directions: Look at the first picture in each row. Circle the pictures that have the same sound.

oil

toy

couch

howl

Vowel Teams: ai, ee

Directions: Write in the vowel team **ai** or **ee** to complete each word.

r a i n

f o o d

s e e d

p a i l

s a i l

cr e e k

Y as a Vowel

When **y** comes at the end of a word, it is a vowel. When **y** is the only vowel at the end of a one-syllable word, it has the sound of a long **i** (like in **my**). When **y** is the only vowel at the end of a word with more than one syllable, it has the sound of a long **e** (like in **baby**).

Directions: Look at the words in the word box. If the word has the sound of a long **i**, write it under the word **my**. If the word has the sound of a long **e**, write it under the word **baby**. Write the word from the word box that answers each riddle.

| happy | penny | fry | try | sleepy | dry |
| bunny | why | windy | sky | party | fly |

my   **baby**

_____   _____

_____   _____

_____   _____

_____   _____

_____   _____

1. It takes five of these to make a nickel.   _____

2. This is what you call a baby rabbit.   _____

3. It is often blue and you can see it if you look up. _____

4. You might have one of these on your birthday.   _____

5. It is the opposite of wet.   _____

6. You might use this word to ask a question.   _____

Y as a Vowel

Directions: Read the rhyming story. Choose the words from the box to fill in the blanks.

Larry	Mary
money	funny
honey	bunny

_____ and _____ are friends. Larry is

selling _____ . Mary needs _____ to

buy the honey. "I want to feed it to my _____ ," said

Mary. Larry laughed and said, "That is _____ . Everyone

knows that bunnies do not eat honey."

Name _____

Y as a Vowel

Directions: Read the story. Choose the words from the box to fill in the blanks.

| try | my | Why | cry | shy | fly |

Sam is very _____ . Ann asks, "Would you like to

_____ my kite?" Sam starts to _____ .

Ann asks, "_____ are you crying?"

Sam says, "I am afraid to _____ ."

"Oh, _____ ! You are a good kite flyer," cries Ann.

Name _____

Days of the Week

Directions: Write the day of the week that answers each question.

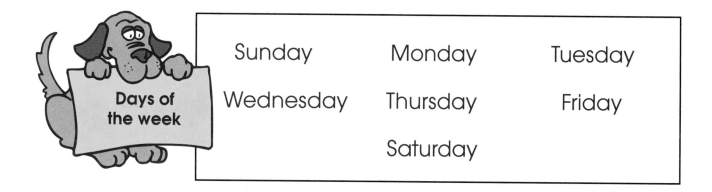

Sunday	Monday	Tuesday
Wednesday	Thursday	Friday
	Saturday	

1. What is the first day of the week?

   _____

2. What is the last day of the week?

   _____

3. What day comes after Tuesday?

   _____

4. What day comes between Wednesday and Friday?

   _____

5. What is the third day of the week?

   _____

6. What day comes before Saturday?

   _____

7. What day comes after Sunday?

   _____

Compound Words

Compound words are formed by putting together two smaller words.

Directions: Help the cook brew her stew. Mix words from the first column with words from the second column to make new words. Write your new words on the lines at the bottom.

grand	brows
snow	light
eye	stairs
down	string
rose	book
shoe	mother
note	ball
moon	bud

1. _____

2. _____

3. _____

4. _____

5. _____

6. _____

7. _____

8. _____

Compound Words

Compound words are two words that are put together to make one new word.

Directions: Read the sentences. Fill in the blank with a compound word from the box.

raincoat	bedroom	lunchbox	hallway	sandbox

1. A box with sand is a

_____.

2. The way through a hall is a

_____.

3. A box for lunch is a

_____.

4. A coat for the rain is a

_____.

5. A room with a bed is a

_____.

Name _____

Compound Words

Directions: Draw a line under the compound word in each sentence. On the line, write the two words that make up the compound word.

1. A firetruck came to help put out the fire.

_____

2. I will be nine years old on my next birthday.

_____

3. We built a treehouse at the back.

_____

4. Dad put a scarecrow in his garden.

_____

5. It is fun to make footprints in the snow.

_____

6. I like to read the comics in the newspaper.

_____

7. Cowboys ride horses and use lassos.

_____

Contractions

Contractions are a short way to write two words, such as **isn't**, **I've** and **weren't**. **Example: it is = it's**

Directions: Draw a line from each word pair to its contraction.

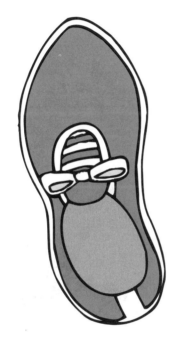 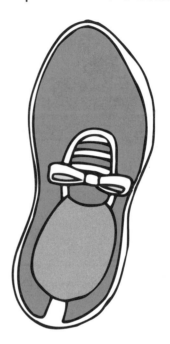

I am	she's
it is	they're
you are	we're
we are	he's
they are	I'm
she is	it's
he is	you're

Name _____

Contractions

Directions: Circle the contraction that would replace the underlined words.

Example: were not = weren't

1. The boy_____was not_____ sad.

      wasn't   weren't

2. We _____were not_____ working.

    wasn't   weren't

3. Jen and Caleb_____have not_____ eaten lunch yet.

     haven't   hasn't

4. The mouse_____has not_____ been here.

    haven't   hasn't

Contractions

Directions: Match the words with their contractions.

would not   I've

was not   he'll

he will   wouldn't

could not   wasn't

I have   couldn't

Directions: Make the words at the end of each line into contractions to complete the sentences.

1. He _____ know the answer.   **did not**

2. _____ a long way home.   **It is**

3. _____ my house.   **Here is**

4. _____ not going to school today.   **We are**

5. _____ take the bus home tomorrow.   **They will**

Name _____

Syllables

Words are made up of parts called **syllables**. Each syllable has a vowel sound. One way to count syllables is to clap as you say the word.

Example: cat   1 clap   1 syllable
             table   2 claps   2 syllables
             butterfly 3 claps   3 syllables

Directions: "Clap out" the words below. Write how many syllables each word has.

movie _____   dog _____

piano _____   basket _____

tree _____   swimmer _____

bicycle _____   rainbow _____

sun _____   paper _____

cabinet _____   picture _____

football _____   run _____

television _____   enter _____

Name _____

Syllables

Dividing a word into syllables can help you read a new word. You also might divide syllables when you are writing if you run out of space on a line.

Many words contain two consonants that are next to each other. A word can usually be divided between the consonants.

Directions: Divide each word into two syllables. The first one is done for you.

kitten   _____ kit   ten _____

lumber   _____

batter   _____

winter   _____

funny   _____

harder   _____

dirty   _____

sister   _____

little   _____

dinner   _____

Name _____

Syllables

One way to help you read a word you don't know is to divide it into parts called **syllables**. Every syllable has a vowel sound.

Directions: Say the words. Write the number of syllables. The first one is done for you.

straw • ber • ry

bird	1	rabbit	_____
apple	_____	elephant	_____
balloon	_____	family	_____
basketball	_____	fence	_____
breakfast	_____	ladder	_____
block	_____	open	_____
candy	_____	puddle	_____
popcorn	_____	Saturday	_____
yellow	_____	wind	_____
understand	_____	butterfly	_____

Name _____

Syllables

When a double consonant is used in the middle of a word, the word can usually be divided between the consonants.

Directions: Look at the words in the word box. Divide each word into two syllables. Leave space between each syllable. One is done for you.

butter	puppy	kitten	yellow
dinner	chatter	ladder	happy
pillow	letter	mitten	summer

but   ter

_____   _____   _____

_____   _____   _____

_____   _____   _____

_____   _____   _____

Many words are divided between two consonants that are not alike.

Directions: Look at the words in the word box. Divide each word into two syllables. One is done for you.

window	doctor	number	carpet
mister	winter	pencil	candle
barber	sister	picture	under

win   dow

_____   _____   _____

_____   _____   _____

_____   _____   _____

Name _____

Syllables

Directions: Write 1 or 2 on the line to tell how many syllables are in each word. If the word has 2 syllables, draw a line between the syllables. **Example: sup|per**

dog _____   timber _____

bedroom _____   cat _____

slipper _____   street _____

tree _____   chalk _____

batter _____   blanket _____

chair _____   marker _____

fish _____   brush _____

master _____   rabbit _____

Name _____

Suffixes

A **suffix** is a syllable that is added at the end of a word to change its meaning.

Directions: Add the suffixes to the root words to make new words. Use your new words to complete the sentences.

help + ful = _____

care + less = _____

build + er = _____

talk + ed = _____

love + ly = _____

loud + er = _____

1. My mother _____ to my teacher about my homework.

2. The radio was _____ than the television.

3. Sally is always _____ to her mother.

4. A _____ put a new garage on our house.

5. The flowers are _____ .

6. It is _____ to cross the street without looking both ways.

Name _____

Suffixes

Adding **ing** to a word means that it is happening now. Adding **ed** to a word means it happened in the past.

Directions: Look at the words in the word box. Underline the root word in each one. Write a word to complete each sentence.

snowing	wished	played	looking	crying
talking	walked	eating	going	doing

1. We like to play. We _____ yesterday.

2. Is that snow? Yes, it is _____.

3. Do you want to go with me? No, I am _____ with my friend.

4. The baby will cry if we leave. The baby is _____.

5. We will walk home from school. We _____ to school this morning.

6. Did you wish for a new bike? Yes, I _____ for one.

7. Who is going to do it while we are away? I am _____ it.

8. Did you talk to your friend? Yes, we are _____ now.

9. Will you look at my book? I am _____ at it now.

10. I like to eat pizza. We are _____ it today.

Name _____

Suffixes

Directions: Write a word from the word box next to its root word.

coming	running	sitting
lived	rained	swimming
visited	carried	racing
hurried		

run _____   come _____

live _____   carry _____

hurry _____   race _____

swim _____   rain _____

visit _____   sit _____

Directions: Write a word from the word box to finish each sentence.

1. I _____ my grandmother during vacation.

2. Mary went _____ at the lake with her cousin.

3. Jim _____ the heavy package for his mother.

4. It _____ and stormed all weekend.

5. Cars go very fast when they are _____ .

Suffixes

Directions: Read the story. Underline the words that end with **est**, **ed** or **ing**. On the lines below, write the root words for each word you underlined.

    The funniest book I ever read was about a girl named Nan. Nan did everything backward. She even spelled her name backward. Nan slept in the day and played at night. She dried her hair before washing it. She turned on the light after she finished her book—which she read from the back to the front! When it rained, Nan waited until she was inside before opening her umbrella. She even walked backward. The silliest part: The only thing Nan did forward was back up!

1. _____

2. _____

3. _____

4. _____

5. _____

6. _____

7. _____

8. _____

9. _____

10. _____

11. _____

12. _____

13. _____

Name _____

Prefixes: The Three R's

Prefixes are syllables added to the beginning of words that change their meaning. The prefix **re** means "again."

Directions: Read the story. Then follow the instructions.

Kim wants to find ways she can save the Earth. She studies the "three R's"—reduce, reuse and recycle. Reduce means to make less. Both reuse and recycle mean to use again.

Add **re** to the beginning of each word below. Use the new words to complete the sentences.

_____ build   _____ fill

_____ read   _____ tell

_____ write   _____ run

1. The race was a tie, so Dawn and Kathy had to _____ it.

2. The block wall fell down, so Simon had to _____ it.

3. The water bottle was empty, so Luna had to _____ it.

4. Javier wrote a good story, but he wanted to _____ it to make it better.

5. The teacher told a story, and students had to _____ it.

6. Toni didn't understand the directions, so she had to

_____ them.

Prefixes

Directions: Read the story. Change Unlucky Sam to Lucky Sam by taking the **un** prefix off of the **bold** words.

Unlucky Sam

Sam was **unhappy** about a lot of things in his life. His parents were **uncaring**. His teacher was **unfair**. His big sister was **unkind**. His neighbors were **unfriendly**. He was **unhealthy**, too! How could one boy be as **unlucky** as Sam?

Lucky Sam

Sam was _____ about a lot of things in his life. His parents were _____ . His teacher was _____ . His big sister was _____ . His neighbors were _____ . He was _____, too! How could one boy be as _____ as Sam?

Name _____

Prefixes

Directions: Change the meaning of the sentences by adding the prefixes to the **bold** words.

The boy was **lucky** because he guessed the answer **correctly**.

The boy was (un)_____ because he guessed the

answer (in)_____ .

When Mary **behaved**, she felt **happy**.

When Mary (mis) _____ ,

she felt (un)_____ .

Mike wore his jacket **buttoned** because the dance was **formal**.

Mike wore his jacket (un) _____ because the dance

was (in)_____ .

Tim **understood** because he was **familiar** with the book.

Tim (mis) _____ because he was

(un)_____ with the book.

READING COMPREHENSION

Name _____

Parts of a Book

A book has many parts. The title is the name of the book. The author is the person who wrote the words. The illustrator is the person who drew the pictures. The table of contents is located at the beginning to list what is in the book. The glossary is a little dictionary in the back to help you with unfamiliar words. Books are often divided into smaller sections of information called chapters.

Directions: Look at one of your books. Write the parts you see below.

The title of my book is _____

The author is _____

The illustrator is _____

My book has a table of contents.   Yes or No

My book has a glossary.   Yes or No

My book is divided into chapters.   Yes or No

Name _____

Recalling Details: Nikki's Pets

Directions: Read about Nikki's pets. Then answer the questions.

Nikki has two cats, Tiger and Sniffer, and two dogs, Spot and Wiggles. Tiger is an orange striped cat who likes to sleep under a big tree and pretend she is a real tiger. Sniffer is a gray cat who likes to sniff the flowers in Nikki's garden. Spot is a Dalmatian with many black spots. Wiggles is a big furry brown dog who wiggles all over when he is happy.

1. Which dog is brown and furry? _____

2. What color is Tiger? _____

3. What kind of dog is Spot? _____

4. Which cat likes to sniff flowers? _____

5. Where does Tiger like to sleep? _____

6. Who wiggles all over when he is happy? _____

Nikki's Garden

Name _____

Reading for Details

Directions: Read the story about baby animals. Answer the questions with words from the story.

   Baby cats are called kittens. They love to play and drink lots of milk. A baby dog is a puppy. Puppies chew on old shoes. They run and bark. A lamb is a baby sheep. Lambs eat grass. A baby duck is called a duckling. Ducklings swim with their wide, webbed feet. Foals are baby horses. A foal can walk the day it is born! A baby goat is a kid. Some people call children kids, too!

1. A baby cat is called a _____.

2. A baby dog is a _____.

3. A _____ is a baby sheep.

4. _____ swim with their webbed feet.

5. A _____ can walk the day it is born.

6. A baby goat is a _____.

Name _____

Reading for Details

Directions: Read the story about bike safety. Answer the questions below the story.

Mike has a red bike. He likes his bike. Mike wears a helmet. Mike wears knee pads and elbow pads. They keep him safe. Mike stops at signs. Mike looks both ways. Mike is safe on his bike.

1. What color is Mike's bike? _____

2. Which sentence in the story tells why Mike wears pads and a helmet? Write it here.

   _____

3. What else does Mike do to keep safe?

   He _____ at signs and _____
   both ways.

Following Directions

Directions: Read the story. Answer the questions. Try the recipe.

Cows Give Us Milk

Cows live on a farm. The farmer milks the cow to get milk. Many things are made from milk. We make ice cream, sour cream, cottage cheese and butter from milk. Butter is fun to make! You can learn to make your own butter. First, you need cream. Put the cream in a jar and shake it. Then you need to pour off the liquid. Next, you put the butter in a bowl. Add a little salt and stir! Finally, spread it on crackers and eat!

1. What animal gives us milk? _____

2. What 4 things are made from milk?

_____ _____ _____ _____

3. What did the story teach you to make? _____

4. Put the steps in order. Place 1, 2, 3, 4 by the sentence.

_____ Spread the butter on crackers and eat!

_____ Shake cream in a jar.

_____ Start with cream.

_____ Add salt to the butter.

Name _____

Following Directions: How to Treat a Ladybug

Directions: Read about how to treat ladybugs. Then follow the instructions.

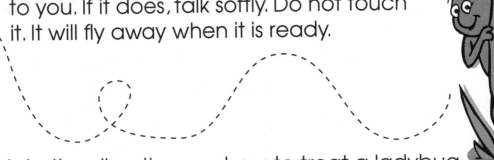

Ladybugs are shy. If you see a ladybug, sit very still. Hold out your arm. Maybe the ladybug will fly to you. If it does, talk softly. Do not touch it. It will fly away when it is ready.

1. Complete the directions on how to treat a ladybug.

   a. Sit very still.

   b. _____

   c. Talk softly.

   d. _____

2. Ladybugs are red. They have black spots. Color the ladybug.

Sequencing: Packing Bags

Directions: Read about packing bags. Then number the objects in the order they should be packed.

Cans are heavy. Put them in first. Then put in boxes. Now, put in the apple. Put the bread in last.

Name _____

Sequencing: Story Events

Spencer likes to make new friends. Today, he made friends with the dog in the picture.

Directions: Number the sentences in order to find out what Spencer did today.

____ Spencer kissed his mother good-bye.

____ Spencer saw the new dog next door.

____ Spencer went outside.

____ Spencer said hello.

____ Spencer got dressed and ate breakfast.

____ Spencer woke up.

Name _____

Sequencing: Yo-Yo Trick

Directions: Read about the yo-yo trick.

Wind up the yo-yo string. Hold the yo-yo in your hand. Now, hold your palm up. Throw the yo-yo downward on the string. Hold your palm down. Now, swing the yo-yo forward. Make it "walk." This yo-yo trick is called "walk the dog."

Directions: Number the directions in order.

_____ Swing the yo-yo forward and make it "walk."

_____ Hold your palm up and drop the yo-yo.

_____ Turn your palm down as the yo-yo reaches the ground.

Name _____

Sequencing: Follow a Recipe

Here is a recipe for chocolate peanut butter cookies. When you use a recipe, you must follow the directions carefully. The sentences below are not in the correct order.

Directions: Write number 1 to show what you would do first. Then number each step to show the correct sequence.

_____ Melt the chocolate almond bark in a microsafe bowl.

_____ Eat!

_____ While the chocolate is melting, spread peanut butter on a cracker and place another cracker on top.

_____ Let the melted candy drip off the cracker into the bowl before you place it on wax paper.

_____ Let it cool!

_____ Carefully use a fork or spoon to dip the crackers into the melted chocolate.

Try the recipe with an adult.

Do you like to cook? _____

Name _____

Sequencing: Story Events

Mari was sick yesterday.

Directions: Number the events in 1, 2, 3 order to tell the story about Mari.

_____ She went to the doctor's office.

_____ Mari felt much better.

_____ Mari felt very hot and tired.

_____ Mari's mother went to the drugstore.

_____ The doctor wrote down something.

_____ The doctor looked in Mari's ears.

_____ Mari took a pill.

_____ The doctor gave Mari's mother the piece of paper.

_____ Mari drank some water with her pill.

Name _____

Sequencing: Making Clay

Directions: Read about making clay. Then follow the instructions.

It is fun to work with clay. Here is what you need to make it:

1 cup salt
2 cups flour
3/4 cup water

Mix the salt and flour. Then add the water. DO NOT eat the clay. It tastes bad. Use your hands to mix and mix. Now, roll it out. What can you make with your clay?

1. Circle the main idea:

   Do not eat clay.

   Mix salt, flour and water to make clay.

2. Write the steps for making clay.

   a. _____

   b. _____

   c. Mix the clay.

   d. _____

3. Write why you should not eat clay. _____

   _____

Name _____

Sequencing: A Visit to the Zoo

Directions: Read the story. Then follow the instructions.

One Saturday morning in May, Gloria and Anna went to the zoo. First, they bought tickets to get into the zoo. Second, they visited the Gorilla Garden and had fun watching the gorillas stare at them. Then they went to Tiger Town and watched the tigers as they slept in the sunshine. Fourth, they went to Hippo Haven and laughed at the hippos cooling off in their pool. Next, they visited Snake Station and learned about poisonous and nonpoisonous snakes. It was noon, and they were hungry, so they ate lunch at the Parrot Patio.

Write **first**, **second**, **third**, **fourth**, **fifth** and **sixth** to put the events in order.

_____ They went to Hippo Haven.

_____ Gloria and Anna bought zoo tickets.

_____ They watched the tigers sleep.

_____ They ate lunch at Parrot Patio.

_____ The gorillas stared at them.

_____ They learned about poisonous and nonpoisonous snakes.

Name _____

Same/Different: Stuffed Animals

Kate and Oralia like to collect and trade stuffed animals.

Directions: Draw two stuffed animals that are alike and two that are different.

Alike

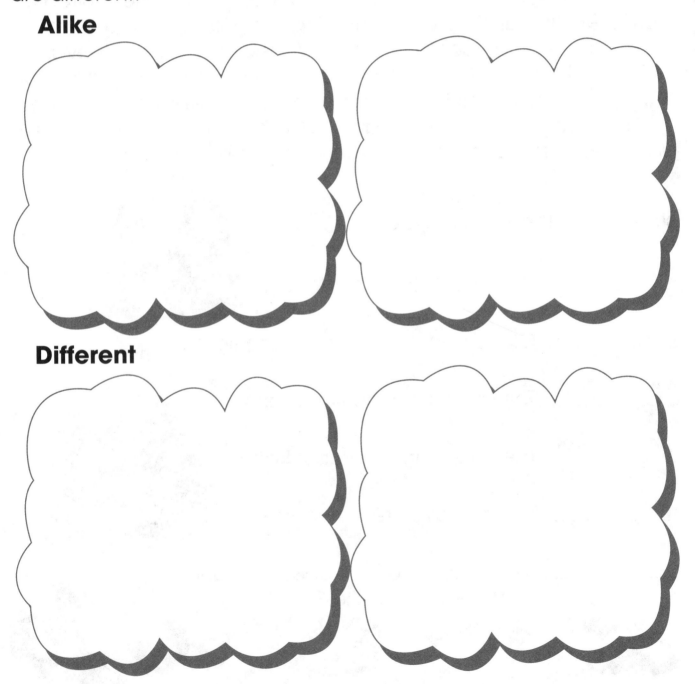

Different

Name _____

Same/Different: Shell Homes

Directions: Read about shells. Then answer the questions.

Shells are the homes of some animals. Snails live in shells on the land. Clams live in shells in the water. Clam shells open. Snail shells stay closed. Both shells keep the animals safe.

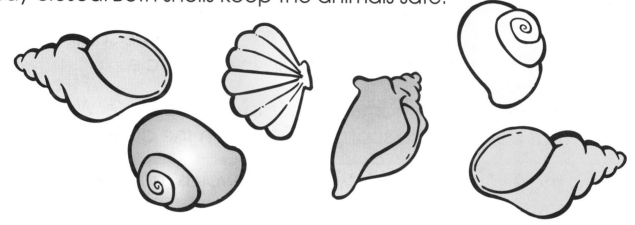

1. (Circle the correct answer.) Snails live in shells on the

   water.   land.

2. (Circle the correct answer.)
   Clam shells are different from snail shells because

   they open.

   they stay closed.

3. Write one way all shells are the same. _____

   _____

Same/Different: Venn Diagram

A **Venn diagram** is a diagram that shows how two things are the same and different.

Directions: Choose two outdoor sports. Then follow the instructions to complete the Venn diagram.

1. Write the first sport name under the first circle. Write some words that describe the sport. Write them in the first circle.

2. Write the second sport name under the second circle. Write some words that describe the sport. Write them in the circle.

3. Where the 2 circles overlap, write some words that describe both sports.

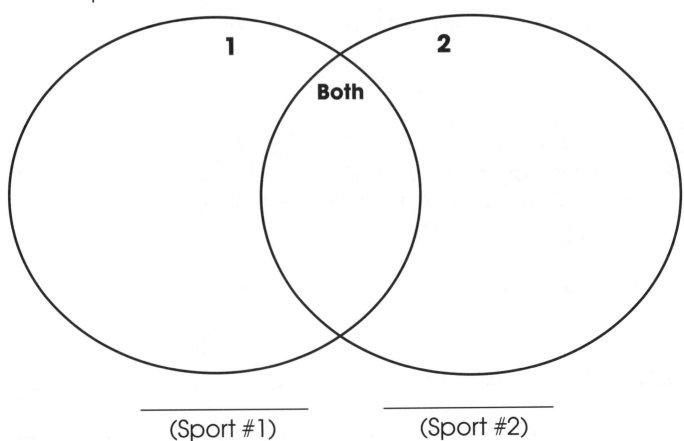

(Sport #1)   (Sport #2)

Name _____

Same/Different: Dina and Dina

Directions: Read the story. Then complete the Venn diagram, telling how Dina, the duck, is the same or different than Dina, the girl.

One day in the library, Dina found a story about a duck named Dina!

My name is Dina. I am a duck, and I like to swim. When I am not swimming, I walk on land or fly. I have two feet and two eyes. My feathers keep me warm. Ducks can be different colors. I am gray, brown and black. I really like being a duck. It is fun.

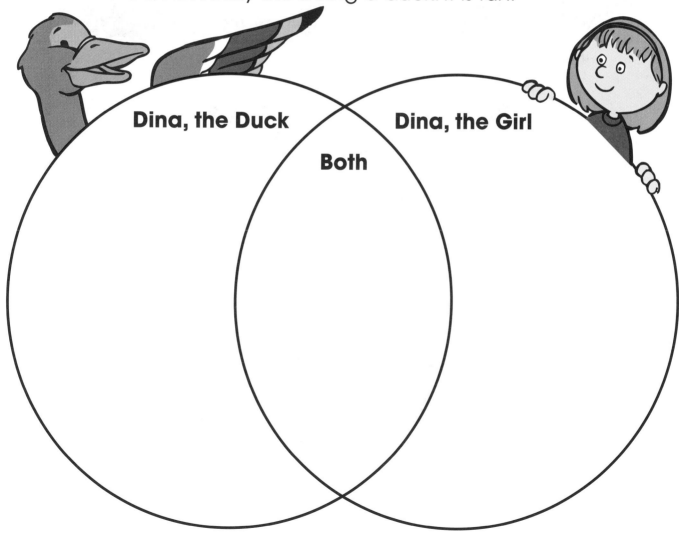

Dina, the Duck

Dina, the Girl

Both

Same/Different: Cats and Tigers

Directions: Read about cats and tigers. Then complete the Venn diagram, telling how they are the same and different.

Tigers are a kind of cat. Pet cats and tigers both have fur. Pet cats are small and tame. Tigers are large and wild.

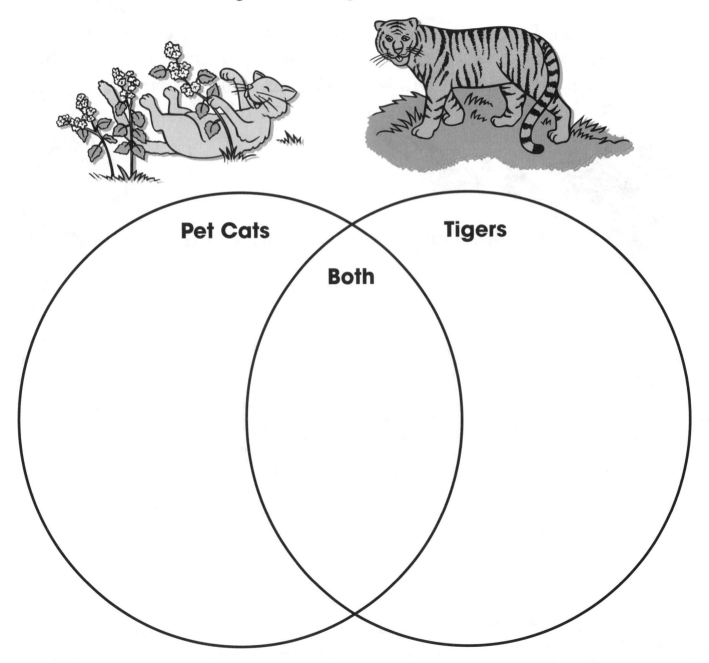

Pet Cats   **Both**   **Tigers**

Name _____

Same/Different: Bluebirds and Parrots

Directions: Read about parrots and bluebirds. Then complete the Venn diagram, telling how they are the same and different.

Bluebirds and parrots are both birds. Bluebirds and parrots can fly. They both have beaks. Parrots can live inside a cage. Bluebirds must live outdoors.

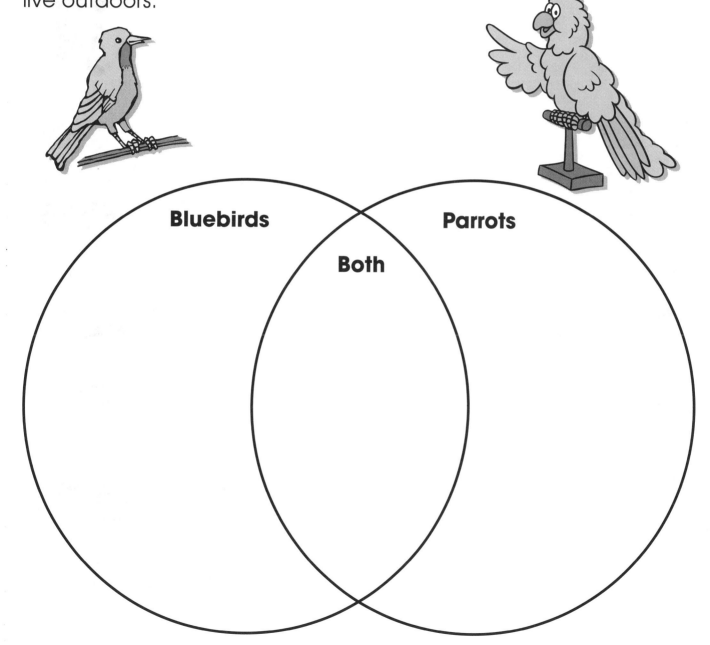

Bluebirds

Both

Parrots

Name _____

Similes

A **simile** is a figure of speech that compares two different things. The words **like** or **as** are used in similes.

Directions: Draw a line to the picture that goes with each set of words.

as hard as a

as hungry as a

as quiet as a

as soft as a

as easy as

as light as a

as tiny as an

Name _____

Classifying: Outdoor/Indoor Games

Classifying is putting things that are alike into groups.

Directions: Read about games. Draw an **X** on the games you can play indoors. Circle the objects used for outdoor games.

Some games are outdoor games. Some games are indoor games. Outdoor games are active. Indoor games are quiet.

Which do you like best? _____

Name _____

Classifying

Classifying is putting similar things into groups.

Directions: Write each word from the word box on the correct line.

baby	donkey	whale	family	fox
uncle	goose	grandfather	kangaroo	policeman

people   animals

 _____    _____

 _____   _____

 _____    _____

 _____

 _____    _____

Name _____

Classifying: Animals

Directions: Use a red crayon to circle the names of three animals that would make good pets. Use a blue crayon to circle the names of three wild animals. Use an orange crayon to circle the two animals that live on a farm.

BEAR	CAT	LION	SHEEP	BIRD	DOG	COW	TIGER

```
A  M  E  O  W  W  N  L  I  O  N
B  M  D  O  G  G  X  I  I  S  O
A  B  E  A  R  R  V  L  M  H  R
R  M  R  M  O  O  U  S  E  E  K
K  C  A  B  B  I  R  D  S  E  M
I  O  T  T  I  G  E  R  M  P  Q
B  W  N  O  W  W  R  Q  N  E  N
D  N  C  P  H  H  I  D  U  D  N
F  K  C  A  T  T  R  O  A  R  M
```

Name _____

Classifying: Words

Dapper Dog is going camping.

Directions: Draw an **X** on the word in each row that does not belong in that group.

1.	flashlight	candle	radio	fire
2.	shirt	pants	coat	bat
3.	cow	car	bus	train
4.	beans	hot dog	ball	bread
5.	gloves	hat	book	boots
6.	fork	butter	cup	plate
7.	book	ball	bat	milk
8.	dogs	bees	flies	ants

Name _____

Classifying: Animal Habitats

Directions: Read the story. Then write each animal's name under **Water** or **Land** to tell where it lives.

Animals live in different habitats. A habitat is the place of an animal's natural home. Many animals live on land and others live in water. Most animals that live in water breathe with gills. Animals that live on land breathe with lungs.

fish	shrimp	giraffe	dog
cat	eel	whale	horse
bear	deer	shark	jellyfish

WATER

1. _____   4. _____

2. _____   5. _____

3. _____   6. _____

LAND

1. _____   4. _____

2. _____   5. _____

3. _____   6. _____

Name _____

Comprehension: Ladybugs

Directions: Read about ladybugs. Then answer the questions.

Have you ever seen a ladybug? Ladybugs are red. They have black spots. They have six legs. Ladybugs are pretty!

1. What color are ladybugs? _____

2. What color are their spots? _____

3. How many legs do ladybugs have? _____

Comprehension: Types of Tops

The **main idea** is the most important point or idea in a story.

Directions: Read about tops. Then answer the questions.

Tops come in all sizes. Some tops are made of wood. Some tops are made of tin. All tops do the same thing. They spin! Do you have a top?

1. Circle the main idea:

   There are many kinds of tops.

   Some tops are made of wood.

2. What are some tops made of? _____

3. What do all tops do? _____

Name _____

Comprehension: Singing Whales

Directions: Read about singing whales. Then follow the instructions.

Some whales can sing! We cannot understand the words. But we can hear the tune of the humpback whale. Each season, humpback whales sing a different song.

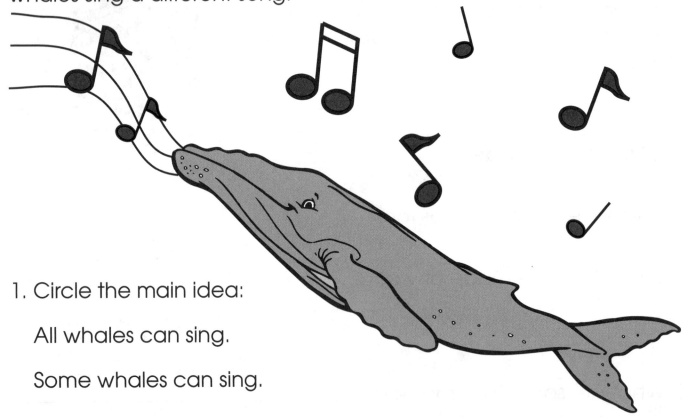

1. Circle the main idea:

   All whales can sing.

   Some whales can sing.

2. Name the kind of whale that sings.

   _____

3. How many different songs does the humpback whale sing each year?

   1   2   3   4

Name _____

Comprehension: Sea Horses Look Strange!

Directions: Read about sea horses. Then answer the questions.

Sea horses are fish, not horses. A sea horse's head looks like a horse's head. It has a tail like a monkey's tail. A sea horse looks very strange!

1. (Circle the correct answer.)
   A sea horse is a kind of

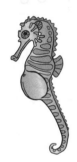

   horse.

   monkey.

   fish.

2. What does a sea horse's head look like?

   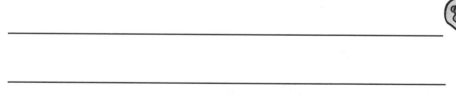

   _____

3. What makes a sea horse look strange?

   a. _____

   b. _____

Name _____

Comprehension: How to Stop a Dog Fight

Directions: Read about how to stop a dog fight. Then answer the questions.

Sometimes dogs fight. They bark loudly. They may bite. Do not try to pull apart fighting dogs. Turn on a hose and spray them with water. This will stop the fight.

1. Name some things dogs may do if they are mad.

_____

_____

2. Why is it unwise to pull on dogs that are fighting?

_____

_____

3. Do you think dogs like to get wet?

_____

Name _____

Comprehension: How to Meet a Dog

Directions: Read about how to meet a dog. Then follow the instructions.

Do not try to pet a dog right away. First, let the dog sniff your hand. Do not move quickly. Do not talk loudly. Just let the dog sniff.

1. Predict what the dog will let you do if it likes you.

_____

_____

2. What should you let the dog do?_____

_____

3. Name three things you should not do when you meet a dog.

1) _____

2) _____

3) _____

Name _____

Comprehension: Pretty Parrots

Directions: Read about parrots. Then follow the instructions.

Big parrots are pretty. Their feet have four toes each. Two toes are in front. Two toes are in back. Parrots use their feet to climb. They use them to hold food.

1. (Circle the correct answer.)
   A parrot's foot has

   four toes.

   two toes.

2. Name two things a parrot does with its feet.

   1) _____

   _____

   2) _____

   _____

3. Color the parrot.

Name _____

Comprehension: The Puppet Play

Directions: Read the play out loud with a friend. Then answer the questions.

Pip: Hey, Pep. What kind of turkey eats very fast?

Pep: Uh, I don't know.

Pip: A gobbler!

Pep: I have a good joke for you, Pip. What kind of burger does a polar bear eat?

Pip: Uh, a cold burger?

Pep: No, an iceberg-er!

Pip: Hey, that was a great joke!

1. Who are the characters in the play? _____

_____

2. Who are the jokes about? _____

_____

3. What are the characters in the play doing? _____

_____

Name _____

Comprehension: Snakes!

Directions: Read about snakes. Then answer the questions.

There are many facts about snakes that might surprise someone. A snake's skin is dry. Most snakes are shy. They will hide from people. Snakes eat mice and rats. They do not chew them up. Snakes' jaws drop open to swallow their food whole.

1. How does a snake's skin feel? _____

2. Most snakes are _____.

3. What do snakes eat?

    a. _____

    b. _____

Name _____

Comprehension: Sean's Basketball Game

Directions: Read about Sean's basketball game. Then answer the questions.

Sean really likes to play basketball. One sunny day, he decided to ask his friends to play basketball at the park, but there were six people—Sean, Aki, Lance, Kate, Zac and Oralia. A basketball team only allows five to play at a time. So, Sean decided to be the coach. Sean and his friends had fun.

1. How many kids wanted to play basketball? _____

2. Write their names in ABC order:

_____   _____   _____

_____   _____   _____

3. How many players can play on a basketball team

   at a time? _____

4. Where did they play basketball? _____

5. Who decided to be the coach? _____

Comprehension: Amazing Ants

Directions: Read about ants. Then answer the questions.

Ants are insects. Ants live in many parts of the world and make their homes in soil, sand, wood and leaves. Most ants live for about 6 to 10 weeks. But the queen ant, who lays the eggs, can live for up to 15 years!

The largest ant is the bulldog ant. This ant can grow to be 5 inches long, and it eats meat! The bulldog ant can be found in Australia.

1. Where do ants make their homes? _____

_____

2. How long can a queen ant live? _____

_____

3. What is the largest ant? _____

4. What does it eat? _____

Name _____

Comprehension: Fish

Directions: Read about fish. Then follow the instructions.

Some fish live in warm water. Some live in cold water. Some fish live in lakes. Some fish live in oceans. There are 20,000 kinds of fish!

1. Name two types of water in which fish live.

a. _____

b. _____

2. Name another place fish live _____

Some fish live in lakes and some live in _____ .

3. There are _____ kinds of fish.

Name _____

Predicting: A Rainy Game

Predicting is telling what is likely to happen based on the facts.

Directions: Read the story. Then check each sentence below that tells how the story could end.

One cloudy day, Juan and his baseball team, the Bears, played the Crocodiles. It was the last half of the fifth inning, and it started to rain. The coaches and umpires had to decide what to do.

_____ They kept playing until nine innings were finished.

_____ They ran for cover and waited until the rain stopped.

_____ Each player grabbed an umbrella and returned to the field to finish the game.

_____ They canceled the game and played it another day.

_____ They acted like crocodiles and slid around the wet bases.

_____ The coaches played the game while the players sat in the dugout.

Name _____

Predicting: Dog Derby

Directions: Read the story. Then answer the questions.

Marcy had a great idea for a game to play with her dogs, Marvin and Mugsy. The game was called "Dog Derby." Marcy would stand at one end of the driveway and hold on to the dogs by their collars. Her friend Mitch would stand at the other end of the driveway. When he said, "Go!" Marcy would let go of the dogs and they would race to Mitch. The first one there would get a dog biscuit. If there was a tie, both dogs would get a biscuit.

1. Who do you think will win the race?

_____

Why? _____

_____

2. What do you think will happen when they race again?

_____

_____

Predicting: Dog-Gone!

Directions: Read the story. Then follow the instructions.

Scotty and Simone were washing their dog, Willis. His fur was wet. Their hands were wet. Willis did NOT like to be wet. Scotty dropped the soap. Simone picked it up and let go of Willis. Uh-oh!

1. Write what happened next.

_____

_____

_____

2. Draw what happened next.

Name _____

Predicting Outcome

Directions: Read the story. Complete the story in the last box.

1. "Look at that elephant! He sure is big!"

3. "Stop, Amy! Look at that sign!"

2. "I'm hungry." "I bet that elephant is, too."

4. _____

_____

_____

Predicting Outcomes

Directions: Complete the story. Then draw pictures to match the four parts.

1. Sylvia and Marge are flying a kite.

Beginning

3. _____

_____

Middle

2. The kite gets stuck in a tree.

Middle

4. _____

_____

End

Name _____

Predicting Outcome

Kelly and Gina always have fun at the fair.

Directions: Read the sentences.
Write what you think will happen next.

1. Kelly and Gina are riding the Ferris wheel. It stops when they are at the top.

   _____

   _____

   _____

2. As they walk into the animal barn, a little piglet runs towards them.

   _____

   _____

   _____

3. Snow cones are their favorite way to cool off. The ones they bought are made from real snow.

   _____

   _____

   _____

4. They play a "toss the ring over the bottle" game, but when the ring goes around the bottle, it disappears.

   _____

   _____

   _____

Name _____

Fact and Opinion: Games!

A **fact** is something that can be proven. An **opinion** is a feeling or belief about something and cannot be proven.

Directions: Read these sentences about different games. Then write **F** next to each fact and **O** next to each opinion.

_____ 1. Tennis is cool!

_____ 2. There are red and black markers in a Checkers game.

_____ 3. In football, a touchdown is worth six points.

_____ 4. Being a goalie in soccer is easy.

_____ 5. A yo-yo moves on a string.

_____ 6. June's sister looks like the queen on the card.

_____ 7. The six kids need three more players for a baseball team.

_____ 8. Table tennis is more fun than court tennis.

_____ 9. Hide-and-Seek is a game that can be played outdoors or indoors.

_____ 10. Play money is used in many board games.

Name _____

Fact and Opinion: Recycling

Directions: Read about recycling. Then follow the instructions.

What do you throw away every day? What could you do with these things? You could change an old greeting card into a new card. You could make a puppet with an old paper bag. Old buttons make great refrigerator magnets. You can plant seeds in plastic cups. Cardboard tubes make perfect rockets. So, use your imagination!

1. Write **F** next to each fact and **O** next to each opinion.

_____ Cardboard tubes are ugly.

_____ Buttons can be made into refrigerator magnets.

_____ An old greeting card can be changed into a new card.

_____ Paper-bag puppets are cute.

_____ Seeds can be planted in plastic cups.

_____ Rockets can be made from cardboard tubes.

2. What could you do with a cardboard tube? _____

_____

Name _____

Fact and Opinion: An Owl Story

Directions: Read the story. Then follow the instructions.

My name is Owen Owl, and I am a bird. I go to Nocturnal School. Our teacher is Mr. Screech Owl. In his class I learned that owls are birds and can sleep all day and hunt at night. Some of us live in nests in trees. In North America, it is against the law to harm owls. I like being an owl!

Write **F** next to each fact and **O** next to each opinion.

_____ 1. No one can harm owls in North America.

_____ 2. It would be great if owls could talk.

_____ 3. Owls sleep all day.

_____ 4. Some owls sleep in nests.

_____ 5. Mr. Screech Owl is a good teacher.

_____ 6. Owls are birds.

_____ 7. Owen Owl would be a good friend.

_____ 8. Owls hunt at night.

_____ 9. Nocturnal School is a good school for smart owls.

_____ 10. This story is for the birds.

Name _____

Fact and Opinion: Henrietta the Humpback

Directions: Read the story. Then follow the instructions.

My name is Henrietta, and I am a humpback whale. I live in cold seas in the summer and warm seas in the winter. My long flippers are used to move forward and backward. I like to eat fish. Sometimes, I show off by leaping out of the water. Would you like to be a humpback whale?

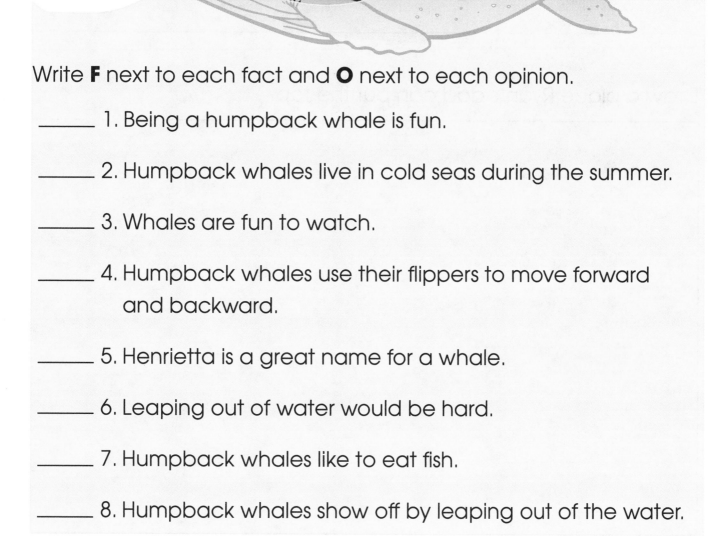

Write **F** next to each fact and **O** next to each opinion.

_____ 1. Being a humpback whale is fun.

_____ 2. Humpback whales live in cold seas during the summer.

_____ 3. Whales are fun to watch.

_____ 4. Humpback whales use their flippers to move forward and backward.

_____ 5. Henrietta is a great name for a whale.

_____ 6. Leaping out of water would be hard.

_____ 7. Humpback whales like to eat fish.

_____ 8. Humpback whales show off by leaping out of the water.

Name _____

Making Inferences: Ryan's Top

Directions: Read about Ryan's top. Then follow the instructions.

Ryan got a new top. He wanted to place it where it would be safe. He asked his dad to put it up high. Where can his dad put the top?

1. Write where Ryan's dad can put the top. _____

_____

Draw a place Ryan's dad can put the top.

Reading Comprehension

Making Inferences: Down on the Ant Farm

Directions: Read about ant farms. Then answer the questions.

Ants are busy on the farm. They dig in the sand. They make roads in the sand. They look for food in the sand. When an ant dies, other ants bury it.

1. Where do you think ants are buried? _____

_____

2. Is it fair to say ants are lazy? _____

3. Write a word that tells about ants. _____

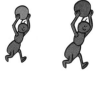

Name _____

Making Inferences

Directions: Read the story. Then answer the questions.

Jeff is baking cookies. He wears special clothes when he bakes. He puts flour, sugar, eggs and butter into a bowl. He mixes everything together. He puts the cookies in the oven at 11:15 A.M. It takes 15 minutes for the cookies to bake. Jeff wants something cold and white to drink when he eats his cookies.

1. Is Jeff baking a cake?   Yes   No

2. What are two things Jeff might wear when he bakes?
   hat   boots   apron   tie   raincoat   roller skates

3. What didn't Jeff put in the cookies?
   flour   eggs   milk   butter   sugar

4. What do you think Jeff does after he mixes the cookies but before he bakes them?_____
   _____
   _____

5. What time will the cookies be done? _____

6. What will Jeff drink with his cookies? _____

7. Why do you think Jeff wanted to bake cookies? _____
   _____
   _____

Name _____

Making Inferences

Directions: Read the story. Then answer the questions.

Mrs. Sweet looked forward to a visit from her niece, Candy. In the morning, she cleaned her house. She also baked a cherry pie. An hour before Candy was to arrive, the phone rang. Mrs. Sweet said, "I understand." When she hung up the phone, she looked very sad.

1. Who do you think called Mrs. Sweet?

_____

_____

2. How do you know that?

_____

_____

3. Why is Mrs. Sweet sad?

_____

_____

Making Inferences: Using Pictures

Directions: Draw a picture for each idea. Then write two sentences that tell about it.

You and a friend are playing your favorite game.

_____

_____

You and a friend are sharing your favorite food.

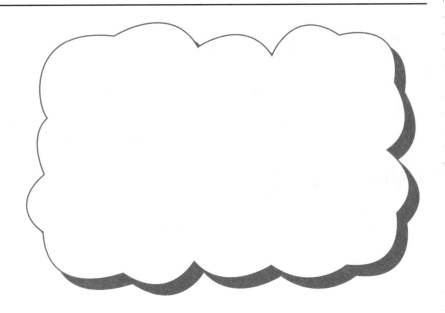

_____

_____

Name _____

Making Inferences: Visualizing

Directions: Read the story about Melinda. Then draw pictures that describe each part of the story.

Beginning: It was Halloween. Melinda's costume was a black cat with super-duper, polka-dot sunglasses.

Middle: Her little brown dog, Marco, yelped and ran under a big red chair when he saw her come into the room.

End: Melinda took off her black cat mask and sunglasses. Then she held out a dog biscuit. She picked Marco up and hugged him. Then he was happy.

Making Inferences: Point of View

Juniper has three problems to solve. She needs your help.

Directions: Read each problem. Write what you think she should do.

1. Juniper is watching her favorite TV show when the power goes out.

_____

_____

_____

_____

2. Juniper is riding her bike to school when the front tire goes flat.

_____

_____

_____

_____

3. Juniper loses her father while shopping in the supermarket.

_____

_____

_____

_____

Name _____

Making Inferences: Sequencing

Directions: Draw three pictures to tell a story about each topic.

1. Feeding a pet

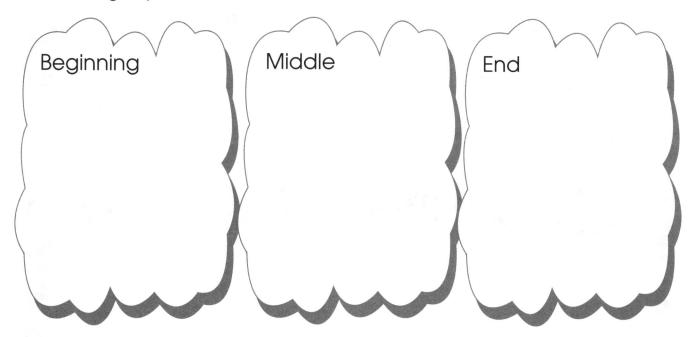

Beginning   Middle   End

2. Playing with a friend

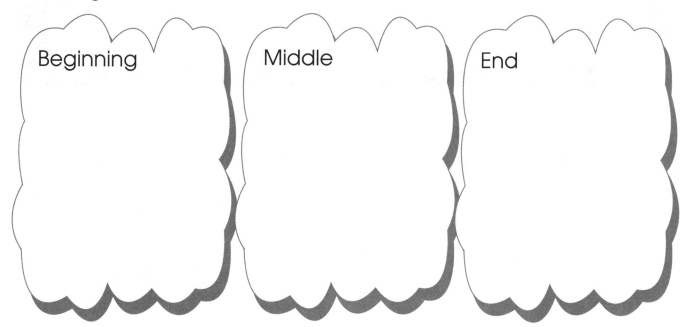

Beginning   Middle   End

Making Deductions: Find the Books

Directions: Use the clues to help the children find their books. Draw a line from each child's name to the correct book.

Brett   Aki   Lorenzo   Kate   Zac   Oralia

CHILDREN	BOOKS
Brett	jokes
Aki	cakes
Lorenzo	monsters
Kate	games
Zac	flags
Oralia	space

Clues

1. Lorenzo likes jokes.

2. Kate likes to bake.

3. Oralia likes far away places.

4. Aki does not like monsters or flags.

5. Zac does not like space or monsters.

6. Brett does not like games, jokes or cakes.

Name _____

Making Deductions: Sports

Children all over the world like to play sports. They like many different kinds of sports: football, soccer, basketball, softball, in-line skating, swimming and more.

Directions: Read the clues. Draw dots and **X**'s on the chart to match the children with their sports.

	swimming	football	soccer	basketball	baseball	in-line skating
J.J.						
Zoe						
Andy						
Amber						
Raul						
Sierra						

Clues
1. Zoe hates football.
2. Andy likes basketball.
3. Raul likes to pitch in his favorite sport.
4. J.J. likes to play what Zoe hates.
5. Amber is good at kicking the ball to her teammates.
6. Sierra needs a pool for her favorite sport.

Fiction/Nonfiction: Heavy Hitters

Fiction is a make-believe story. **Nonfiction** is a true story.

Directions: Read the stories about two famous baseball players. Then write **fiction** or **nonfiction** in the baseball bats.

In 1998, Mark McGwire played for the St. Louis Cardinals. He liked to hit home runs. On September 27, 1998, he hit home run number 70, to set a new record for the most home runs hit in one season. The old record was set in 1961 by Roger Maris, who later played for the St. Louis Cardinals (1967 to 1968), when he hit 61 home runs.

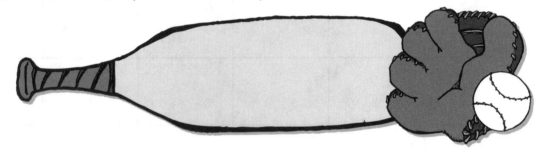

The Mighty Casey played baseball for the Mudville Nine and was the greatest of all baseball players. He could hit the cover off the ball with the power of a hurricane. But, when the Mudville Nine was behind 4 to 2 in the championship game, Mighty Casey struck out with the bases loaded. There was no joy in Mudville that day, because the Mudville Nine had lost the game.

Name _____

Nonfiction: Tornado Tips

Directions: Read about tornadoes. Then follow the instructions.

A tornado begins over land with strong winds and thunderstorms. The spinning air becomes a funnel. It can cause damage. If you are inside, go to the lowest floor of the building. A basement is a safe place. A bathroom or closet in the middle of a building can be a safe place, too. If you are outside, lie in a ditch. Remember, tornadoes are dangerous.

Write five facts about tornadoes.

1. _____

_____

2. _____

_____

3. _____

_____

4. _____

_____

5. _____

_____

Name _____

Fiction: Hercules

The setting is where a story takes place. The characters are the people in a story or play.

Directions: Read about Hercules. Then answer the questions.

Hercules was born in the warm Atlantic Ocean. He was a very small and weak baby. He wanted to be the strongest hurricane in the world. But he had one problem. He couldn't blow 75-mile-per-hour winds. Hercules blew and blew in the ocean, until one day, his sister, Hola, told him it would be more fun to be a breeze than a hurricane. Hercules agreed. It was a breeze to be a breeze!

1. What is the setting of the story? _____

2. Who are the characters? _____

3. What is the problem? _____

4. How does Hercules solve his problem? _____

_____

Name _____

Fiction/Nonfiction: The Fourth of July

Directions: Read each story. Then write whether it is fiction or nonfiction.

One sunny day in July, a dog named Stan ran away from home. He went up one street and down the other looking for fun, but all the yards were empty. Where was everybody? Stan kept walking until he heard the sound of band music and happy people. Stan walked faster until he got to Central Street. There he saw men, women, children and dogs getting ready to walk in a parade. It was the Fourth of July!

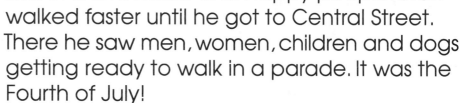

Fiction or Nonfiction?_____

Americans celebrate the Fourth of July every year, because it is the birthday of the United States of America. On July 4, 1776, the United States got its independence from Great Britain. Today, Americans celebrate this holiday with parades, picnics and fireworks as they proudly wave the red, white and blue American flag.

Fiction or Nonfiction?_____

Name _____

Fiction and Nonfiction: Which Is It?

Directions: Read about fiction and nonfiction books. Then follow the instructions.

There are many kinds of books. Some books have make-believe stories about princesses and dragons. Some books contain poetry and rhymes, like Mother Goose. These are fiction.

Some books contain facts about space and plants. And still other books have stories about famous people in history like Abraham Lincoln. These are nonfiction.

Write **F** for fiction and **NF** for nonfiction.

_____ 1. nursery rhyme

_____ 2. fairy tale

_____ 3. true life story of a famous athlete

_____ 4. Aesop's fables

_____ 5. dictionary entry about foxes

_____ 6. weather report

_____ 7. story about a talking tree

_____ 8. story about how a tadpole becomes a frog

_____ 9. story about animal habitats

_____ 10. riddles and jokes

ENGLISH

TALL

TALLEST

TALLER

Name _____

ABC Order

Directions: Put the words in ABC order on the bags.

grapes _____

bread _____

soup _____

apples _____

napkins _____

rolls _____

ice cream _____

pizza _____

milk _____

carrots _____

treats _____

potatoes _____

meat _____

soda _____

cups _____

rice _____

Name _____

ABC Order

Directions: Write these words in order. If two words start with the same letter, look at the second letter in each word.

Example: **lamb**   Lamb comes first because **a** comes before **i**
                light   in the alphabet.

tree   _____

branch   _____

leaf   _____

dish   _____

dog   _____

bone   _____

rain   _____

umbrella _____

cloud   _____

mail   _____

stamp   _____

slot   _____

Sequencing: ABC Order

If the first letters of two words are the same, look at the second letters in both words. If the second letters are the same, look at the third letters.

Directions: Write 1, 2, 3 or 4 on the lines in each row to put the words in ABC order.

Example:

1. __1__ candy   __2__ carrot   __4__ duck   __3__ dance

2. _____ cold   _____ hot   _____ carry   _____ hit

3. _____ flash   _____ fan   _____ fun   _____ garden

4. _____ seat   _____ sun   _____ saw   _____ sit

5. _____ row   _____ ring   _____ rock   _____ run

6. _____ truck   _____ turn   _____ twin   _____ talk

7. _____ seven   _____ shoe   _____ soup   _____ smell

Name _____

Sequencing: ABC Order

Kwan likes to make rhymes. Help Kwan think of rhyming words.

Directions: Write three words in ABC order that rhyme with each word Kwan wrote.

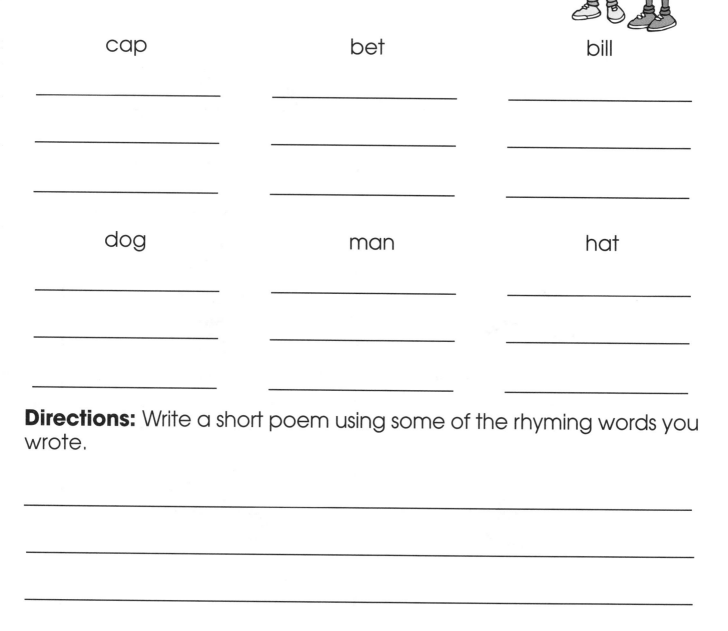

cap   bet   bill

_____   _____   _____

_____   _____   _____

_____   _____   _____

dog   man   hat

_____   _____   _____

_____   _____   _____

_____   _____   _____

Directions: Write a short poem using some of the rhyming words you wrote.

_____

_____

_____

_____

Name _____

Synonyms

Words that mean the same or nearly the same are called **synonyms**.

Directions: Read the sentence that tells about the picture. Draw a circle around the word that means the same as the **bold** word.

The child is **unhappy**.

sad   hungry

The flowers are **lovely**.

pretty   green

The baby was very **tired**.

sleepy   hurt

The **funny** clown made us laugh.

silly   glad

The ladybug is so **tiny**.

small   red

We saw a **scary** tiger.

frightening   ugly

Name _____

Synonyms

Synonyms are words that have almost the same meaning.

Directions: Read the story. Then fill in the blanks with the synonyms.

funny	unhappy
windy	little

A New Balloon

It was a breezy day. The wind blew the small child's balloon away. The child was sad. A silly clown gave him a new balloon.

1. It was a _____ day.

2. The wind blew the _____ child's balloon away.

3. The child was _____ .

4. A _____ clown gave him a new balloon.

Synonyms

Directions: Read each sentence. Fill in the blanks with the synonyms.

friend	tired	story
presents	little	

I want to go to bed because
I am very <u>sleepy</u>.   _____

On my birthday I like to open
my <u>gifts</u>.   _____

My <u>pal</u> and I like to play
together.   _____

My favorite <u>tale</u> is *Cinderella*. _____

The mouse was so <u>tiny</u> that it
was hard to catch him.   _____

Name _____

Antonyms

Antonyms are words that mean the opposite of another word.

Examples:
    hot and **cold**
    short and **tall**

Directions: Draw a line from each word on the left to its antonym on the right.

sad   white

bottom   stop

black   fat

tall   top

thin   hard

little   found

cold   short

lost   hot

go   big

soft   happy

Name _____

Antonyms

Antonyms are words that are opposites.

Directions: Read the words next to the pictures. Draw a line to the antonyms.

   dark   empty

     hairy   dry

   closed   happy

   dirty   bald

     sad   clean

     full   light

   wet   open

Name _____

Antonyms

Words that mean the opposite are called **antonyms**.

Directions: Read the sentence. Write the word from the word box that means the opposite of the **bold** word.

bottom	outside	black	summer	after
light	sister	clean	last	evening

1. Lisa has a new baby **brother**. _____

2. The class went **inside** for recess. _____

3. There is a **white** car in the driveway. _____

4. We went to the park **before** dinner. _____

5. Joe's puppy is **dirty**. _____

6. My name is at the **top** of the list. _____

7. I like to play outside in the **winter**. _____

8. I like to take walks in the **morning**. _____

9. The sky was **dark** after the storm. _____

10. Our team is in **first** place. _____

Name _____

Homophones

Homophones are words that sound the same but are spelled differently and mean different things.

Directions: Write the homophone from the box next to each picture.

so	see	blew	pear

sew _____

pair _____

sea _____

blue _____

Name _____

Homophones

Directions: Look at each picture. Circle the correct homophone.

deer   dear

blue   blew

two   to

hi   high

by   bye

new   knew

ate   eight

red   read

Name _____

Homophones

Directions: Match each word with its homophone.

eight   blew

buy   whole

pail   ate

red   pale

hole   read

blue   hour

our   by

Directions: Choose 3 homophone pairs and write sentences using them.

1. _____

2. _____

3. _____

Name _____

Nouns

A **noun** is the name of a person, place or thing.

Directions: Read the story and circle all the nouns. Then write the nouns next to the pictures below.

Our family likes to go to the park.

_____

_____

We play on the swings.

_____

We eat cake.

_____

We drink lemonade.

_____

We throw the ball to our dog.

_____

_____

Then we go home.

_____

Name _____

Nouns

Directions: Look through a magazine. Cut out pictures of nouns and glue them below. Write the name of the noun next to the picture.

Proper Nouns

Proper nouns are the names of specific people, places and pets. Proper nouns begin with a capital letter.

Directions: Write the proper nouns on the lines below. Use capital letters at the beginning of each word.

logan, utah

mike smith

_____

_____

lynn cramer

buster

_____

_____

fluffy

chicago, illinois

_____

_____

Name _____

Proper Nouns

The days of the week and the months of the year are always capitalized.

Directions: Circle the words that are written correctly. Write the words that need capital letters on the lines below.

sunday	July	Wednesday	may	december
friday	tuesday	june	august	Monday
january	February	March	Thursday	April
September	saturday	October		

Days of the Week   **Months of the Year**

1. _____   1. _____

2. _____   2. _____

3. _____   3. _____

4. _____   4. _____

5. _____

Name _____

Capitalization

The first word and all of the important words in a title begin with a capital letter.

Directions: Write the book titles on the lines below. Use capital letters.

1. _____

2. _____

3. _____

4. _____

5. _____

6. _____

Name _____

Plural Nouns

Plural nouns name more than one person, place or thing.

Directions: Read the words in the box. Write the words in the correct column.

hats	girl	cows	kittens	cake
spoons	glass	book	horse	trees

_____   _____

_____   _____

_____   _____

_____   _____

Plurals

Plurals are words that mean more than one. You usually add an **s** or **es** to the word. In some words ending in **y**, the **y** changes to an **i** before adding **es**. For example, **baby** changes to **babies**.

Directions: Look at the following lists of plural words. Write the word that means one next to it. The first one has been done for you.

foxes	**fox**	balls	_____
bushes	_____	candies	_____
dresses	_____	wishes	_____
chairs	_____	boxes	_____
shoes	_____	ladies	_____
stories	_____	bunnies	_____
puppies	_____	desks	_____
matches	_____	dishes	_____
cars	_____	pencils	_____
glasses	_____	trucks	_____

Name _____

Pronouns

Pronouns are words that can be used instead of nouns. **She**, **he**, **it** and **they** are pronouns.

Directions: Read the sentence. Then write the sentence again, using **she**, **he**, **it** or **they** in the blank.

1. Dan likes funny jokes. _____ likes funny jokes.

2. Peg and Sam went to the zoo. _____ went to the zoo.

3. My dog likes to dig in the yard. _____ likes to dig in the yard.

4. Sara is a very good dancer. _____ is a very good dancer.

5. Fred and Ted are twins. _____ are twins.

Name _____

Subjects

The **subject** of a sentence is the person, place or thing the sentence is about.

Directions: Underline the subject in each sentence.

Example: Mom read a book.

(Think: Who is the sentence about? <u>Mom</u>)

1. The bird flew away.

2. The kite was high in the air.

3. The children played a game.

4. The books fell down.

5. The monkey climbed a tree.

Name _____

Compound Subjects

Two similar sentences can be joined into one sentence if the predicate is the same. A **compound subject** is made up of two subjects joined together by the word **and**.

Example: Jamie can sing.
Sandy can sing.

Jamie **and** Sandy can sing.

Directions: Combine the sentences. Write the new sentence on the line.

1. The cats are my pets.
   The dogs are my pets.

_____

2. Chairs are in the store.
   Tables are in the store.

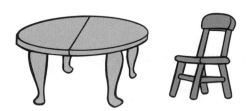

_____

3. Tom can ride a bike.
   Jack can ride a bike.

_____

Verbs

A **verb** is the action word in a sentence. Verbs tell what something does or that something exists.

Example: Run, **sleep** and **jump** are verbs.

Directions: Circle the verbs in the sentences below.

1. We play baseball everyday.

2. Susan pitches the ball very well.

3. Mike swings the bat harder than anyone.

4. Chris slides into home base.

5. Laura hit a home run.

Verbs

We use verbs to tell when something happens. Sometimes we add an **ed** to verbs that tell us if something has already happened.

Example: Today, we will **play**. Yesterday, we **played**.

Directions: Write the correct verb in the blank.

1. Today, I will _____ my dog, Fritz.

                      wash   washed

2. Last week, Fritz _____when we said, "Bath time, Fritz."

                             cry   cried

3. My sister likes to _____ wash Fritz.

                          help   helped

4. One time she _____ Fritz by herself.

                       clean   cleaned

5. Fritz will _____ a lot better after his bath.

               look   looked

Name _____

Predicates

The **predicate** is the part of the sentence that tells about the action.

Directions: Circle the predicate in each sentence.

Example: The boys ran on the playground.

(Think: The boys did what? (Ran))

1. The woman painted a picture.

2. The puppy chases his ball.

3. The students went to school.

4. Butterflies fly in the air.

5. The baby wants a drink.

Name _____

Subjects and Predicates

The **subject** part of the sentence is the person, place or thing the sentence is about. The **predicate** is the part of the sentence that tells what the subject does.

Directions: Draw a line between the subject and the predicate. Underline the noun in the subject and circle the verb.

Example: The furry <u>cat</u> | food.

1. Mandi walks to school.

2. The bus drove the children.

3. The school bell rang very loudly.

4. The teacher spoke to the students.

5. The girls opened their books.

Name _____

Parts of a Sentence

Directions: Draw a circle around the noun, the naming part of the sentence. Draw a line under the verb, the action part of the sentence.

Example: John drinks juice every morning.

1. Our class skates at the roller-skating rink.

2. Mike and Jan go very fast.

3. Fred eats hot dogs.

4. Sue dances to the music.

5. Everyone likes the skating rink.

Parts of a Sentence

Directions: Look at the pictures. Draw a line from the naming part of the sentence to the action part to complete the sentence.

The boy   delivered the mail.

A small dog   threw a football.

The mailman   fell down.

The goalie   chased the ball.

Name _____

Adjectives

Adjectives are words that tell more about a person, place or thing.

Examples: cold, fuzzy, dark

Directions: Circle the adjectives in the sentences.

1. The juicy apple is on the plate.

2. The furry dog is eating a bone.

3. It was a sunny day.

4. The kitten drinks warm milk.

5. The baby has a loud cry.

Name _____

Adjectives

Directions: Choose an adjective from the box to fill in the blanks.

hungry	sunny	busy	funny
fresh	deep	pretty	cloudy

1. It is a _____ day on Farmer Brown's farm.

2. Farmer Brown is a very _____ man.

3. Mrs. Brown likes to feed the _____ chickens.

4. Every day she collects the _____ eggs.

5. The ducks swim in the _____ pond.

Adjectives

Directions: Think of your own adjectives. Write a story about Fluffy the cat.

1. Fluffy is a _____ cat.

2. The color of his fur is _____ .

3. He likes to chew on my _____ shoes.

4. He likes to eat _____ cat food.

5. I like Fluffy because he is so _____ .

Name _____

Articles

Articles are small words that help us to better understand nouns. **A** and **an** are articles. We use **an** before a word that begins with a vowel. We use **a** before a word that begins with a consonant.

Example: We looked in **a** nest. It had **an** eagle in it.

Directions: Read the sentences. Write **a** or **an** in the blank.

1. I found _____ book.

2. It had a story about _____ ant in it.

3. In the story, _____ lion gave three wishes to _____ ant.

4. The ant's first wish was to ride _____ elephant.

5. The second wish was to ride _____ alligator.

6. The last wish was _____ wish for three more wishes.

Name _____

Sentences and Non-Sentences

A **sentence** tells a complete idea. It has a noun and a verb. It begins with a capital letter and has punctuation at the end.

Directions: Circle the group of words if it is a sentence.

1. Grass is a green plant.

2. Mowing the lawn.

3. Grass grows in fields and lawns.

4. Tickle the feet.

5. Sheep, cows and horses eat grass.

6. We like to play in.

7. My sister likes to mow the lawn.

8. A picnic on the grass.

9. My dog likes to roll in the grass.

10. Plant flowers around.

Name _____

Sentences and Non-Sentences

Directions: Circle the group of words if it tells a complete idea.

1. A secret is something you know.

2. My mom's birthday gift is a secret.

3. No one else.

4. If you promise not to.

5. I'll tell you a secret.

6. Something nobody knows.

Name _____

Statements

Statements are sentences that tell us something. They begin with a capital letter and end with a period.

Directions: Write the sentences on the lines below. Begin each sentence with a capital letter and end it with a period.

1. we like to ride our bikes

_____

2. we go down the hill very fast

_____

3. we keep our bikes shiny and clean

_____

4. we know how to change the tires

_____

Surprising Sentences

Surprising sentences tell a strong feeling and end with an exclamation point. A surprising sentence may be only one or two words showing fear, surprise or pain. **Example: Oh, no!**

Directions: Put a period at the end of the sentences that tell something. Put an exclamation point at the end of the sentences that tell a strong feeling. Put a question mark at the end of the sentences that ask a question.

1. The cheetah can run very fast

2. Wow

3. Look at that cheetah go

4. Can you run fast

5. Oh, my

6. You're faster than I am

7. Let's run together

8. We can run as fast as a cheetah

9. What fun

10. Do you think cheetahs get tired

Commands

Commands tell someone to do something. **Example: "Be careful."**
It can also be written as "Be careful!" if it tells a strong feeling.

Directions: Put a period at the end of the command sentences.
Use an exclamation point if the sentence tells a strong feeling. Write
your own commands on the lines below.

1. Clean your room

2. Now

3. Be careful with your goldfish

4. Watch out

5. Be a little more careful

_____

_____

Questions

Questions are sentences that ask something. They begin with a capital letter and end with a question mark.

Directions: Write the questions on the lines below. Begin each sentence with a capital letter and end it with a question mark.

1. will you be my friend

_____

2. what is your name

_____

3. are you eight years old

_____

4. do you like rainbows

_____

Making Inferences: Writing Questions

Tommy likes to answer questions. He knows the answers, but you need to write the questions.

Directions: Write two questions for each answer.

Answer: It has four legs.

1. _____?

_____?

Answer: It lives on a farm.

2. _____?

_____?

Answer: It is soft.

3. _____?

_____?

Name _____

Making Inferences: Writing Questions

Toban and Sean use many colors when they paint.

Directions: Write two questions for each answer.

Answer: It is red.

1. _____ ?

_____ ?

Answer: It is purple.

2. _____ ?

_____ ?

Answer: It is green.

3. _____ ?

_____ ?

Making Inferences: Point of View

Chelsea likes to pretend she will meet famous people someday. She would like to ask them many questions.

Directions: Write a question you think Chelsea would ask if she met these people.

1. an actor in a popular, new film _____

_____?

2. an Olympic gold medal winner _____

_____?

3. an alien from outer space _____

_____?

Directions: Now, write the answers these people might have given to Chelsea's questions.

4. an actor in a popular, new film _____

_____

5. an Olympic Gold medal winner _____

_____

6. an alien from outer space _____

_____

Name _____

Making Inferences: Point of View

Ellen likes animals. Someday she might want to be an animal doctor.

Directions: Write one question you think Ellen would ask each of these animals if she could speak their language.

1. a giraffe _____?

2. a mouse _____?

3. a shark _____?

4. a hippopotamus _____?

5. a penguin _____?

6. a gorilla _____?

7. an eagle _____?

Directions: Now, write the answers you think these animals might have given Ellen.

9. a giraffe _____

10. a mouse _____

11. a shark _____

12. a hippopotamus _____

13. a penguin _____

14. a gorilla _____

15. an eagle _____

Creative Writing

Directions: Look at the picture below. Write a story about the picture.

_____

_____

_____

_____

_____

_____

Ownership

We add **'s** to nouns (people, places or things) to tell who or what owns something.

Directions: Read the sentences. Fill in the blanks to show ownership.

Example: The doll belongs to **Sara**.

It is **Sara's** doll.

1. Sparky has a red collar.

_____ collar is red.

2. Jimmy has a blue coat.

_____ coat is blue.

3. The tail of the cat is short.

The _____ tail is short.

4. The name of my mother is Karen.

My _____ name is Karen.

Name _____

Ownership

Directions: Read the sentences. Choose the correct word and write it in the sentences below.

Hal's

1. The _____ lunchbox is broken.   boys   boy's

2. The _____ played in the cage.   gerbil's   gerbils

3. _____ hair is brown.   Anns   Ann's

4. The _____ ran in the field.   horse's   horses

5. My _____ coat is torn.   sister's   sisters

6. The _____ fur is brown.   cats   cat's

7. Three _____ flew past our window.   birds   bird's

8. The _____ paws are muddy.   dogs   dog's

9. The _____ neck is long.   giraffes   giraffe's

10. The _____ are big and powerful.   lion's   lions

Is, Are and Am

Is, **are** and **am** are special action words that tell us something is happening now.

Use **am** with **I**. **Example: I am**.
Use **is** to tell about one person or thing. **Example: He is**.
Use **are** to tell about more than one. **Example: We are**.
Use **are** with **you**. **Example: You are**.

Directions: Write **is**, **are** or **am** in the sentences below.

1. My friends _____ helping me build a tree house.

2. It _____ in my backyard.

3. We _____ using hammers, wood and nails.

4. It_____ a very hard job.

5. I _____ lucky to have good friends.

Was and Were

Was and **were** tell us about something that already happened.

Use **was** to tell about one person or thing. **Example:** I **was**, he **was**.
Use **were** to tell about more than one person or thing or when using
the word you. **Example:** We **were**, you **were**.

Directions: Write **was** or **were** in each sentence.

1. Lily_____ eight years old on her birthday.

2. Tim and Steve _____ happy to be at the party.

3. Megan _____ too shy to sing "Happy Birthday."

4. Ben_____ sorry he dropped his cake.

5. All of the children _____ happy to be invited.

Go, Going and Went

We use **go** or **going** to tell about now or later. Sometimes we use **going** with the words **am** or **are**. We use **went** to tell about something that already happened.

Directions: Write **go**, **going** or **went** in the sentences below.

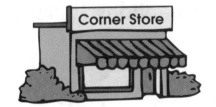

1. Today, I will _____ to the store.

2. Yesterday, we _____ shopping.

3. I am _____ to take Muffy to the vet.

4. Jan and Steve _____ to the party.

5. They are _____ to have a good day.

Name _____

Have, Has and Had

We use **have** and **has** to tell about now. We use **had** to tell about something that already happened.

Directions: Write **has**, **have** or **had** in the sentences below.

1. We _____ three cats at home.

2. Ginger _____ brown fur.

3. Bucky and Charlie _____ gray fur.

4. My friend Tom _____ one cat, but he died.

5. Tom _____ a new cat now.

Name _____

See, Saw and Sees

We use **see** or **sees** to tell about now. We use **saw** to tell about something that already happened.

Directions: Write **see**, **sees** or **saw** in the sentences below.

1. Last night, we _____ the stars.

2. John can _____ the stars from his window.

3. He _____ them every night.

4. Last week, he _____ the Big Dipper.

5. Can you _____ it in the night sky, too?

6. If you _____ it, you would remember it!

7. John _____ it often now.

8. How often do you _____ it?

Eat, Eats and Ate

We use **eat** or **eats** to tell about now. We use **ate** to tell about what already happened.

Directions: Write **eat**, **eats** or **ate** in the sentences below.

1. We like to _____ in the lunchroom.

2. Today, my teacher will _____ in a different room.

3. She _____ with the other teachers.

4. Yesterday, we _____ pizza, pears and peas.

5. Today, we will _____ turkey and potatoes.

Name _____

Leave, Leaves and Left

We use **leave** and **leaves** to tell about now. We use **left** to tell about what already happened.

Directions: Write **leave**, **leaves** or **left** in the sentences below.

1. Last winter, we _____ seeds in the bird feeder everyday.

2. My mother likes to _____ food out for the squirrels.

3. When it rains, she _____ bread for the birds.

4. Yesterday, she _____ popcorn for the birds.

Name _____

Learning Dictionary Skills

A dictionary is a book that gives the meaning of words. It also tells how words sound. Words in a dictionary are in ABC order. That makes them easier to find. A picture dictionary lists a word, a picture of the word and its meaning.

Directions: Look at this page from a picture dictionary. Then answer the questions.

baby

A very young child.

band

A group of people who play music.

bank

A place where money is kept.

bark

The sound a dog makes.

berry

A small, juicy fruit.

board

A flat piece of wood.

1. What is a small, juicy fruit? _____

2. What is a group of people who play music? _____

3. What is the name for a very young child? _____

4. What is a flat piece of wood called? _____

Name ____________________

Learning Dictionary Skills

Directions: Look at this page from a picture dictionary. Then answer the questions.

safe

A metal box.

sea

A body of water.

seed

The beginning of a plant.

---

sheep

An animal that has wool.

store

A place where items are sold.

skate

A shoe with wheels or a blade on it.

---

snowstorm

A time when much snow falls.

squirrel

A small animal with a bushy tail.

stone

A small rock.

1. What kind of animal has wool? ____________________
2. What do you call a shoe with wheels on it? ____________________
3. When a lot of snow falls, what is it called? ____________________
4. What is a small animal with a bushy tail? ____________________
5. What is a place where items are sold? ____________________
6. When a plant starts, what is it called? ____________________

Name _____

Learning Dictionary Skills

Directions: Look at this page from a picture dictionary. Then answer the questions.

table

Furniture with legs and a flat top.

tail

A slender part that is on the back of an animal.

teacher

A person who teaches lessons.

telephone

A machine that sends and receives sounds.

ticket

A paper slip or card.

tiger

An animal with stripes.

1. Who is a person who teaches lessons? _____

2. What is the name of an animal with stripes? _____

3. What is a piece of furniture with legs and a flat top? _____

4. What is the definition of a ticket?

_____

5. What is a machine that sends and receives sounds?

_____

Learning Dictionary Skills

Directions: Write each word from the box in ABC order between each pair of guide words.

fierce	fix	fight	first	few
fish	fill	flush	flat	finish

few   **flush**

_____   _____

_____   _____

_____   _____

_____   _____

_____   _____

SPELLING

Name _____

Number Words

Directions: Write the correct number words in the blanks.

| one   two   three   four   five   six   seven   eight   nine   ten |

Add a letter to each of these words to make a number word.

Example:

even   on   tree

seven   _____   _____

Change a letter to make these words into number words.

Example:

live   fix   line

five   _____   _____

Write the number words that sound the same as these:

Example:

ate   to   for

eight   _____   _____

Write the number word you did not use: _____

Number Words: Sentences

Directions: Change the telling sentences into asking sentences. Change the asking sentences into telling sentences. Begin each one with a capital letter and end it with a period or a question mark.

Examples:

Is she eating three cookies?

She is eating three cookies.

He is bringing one truck.

Is he bringing one truck?

1. Is he painting two blue birds?

_____

2. Did she find four apples?

_____

3. She will be six on her birthday.

_____

Short a Words: Rhyming Words

Short a is the sound you hear in the word **math**.

Directions: Use the **short a** words in the box to write rhyming words.

lamp	fat	bat	van
path	can	cat	Dan
math	stamp	fan	sat

1. Write four words that rhyme with **mat**.

_____   _____

_____   _____

2. Write two words that rhyme with **bath**.

_____   _____

3. Write two words that rhyme with **damp**.

_____   _____

4. Write four words that rhyme with **pan**.

_____   _____

_____   _____

Short a Words: Sentences

Directions: Use a word from the box to complete each sentence.

fat	path	lamp	can
van	stamp	Dan	math
sat	cat	fan	bat

Example:

1. The _____ lamp _____ had a pink shade.

2. The bike _____ led us to the park.

3. I like to add in _____ class.

4. The cat is very _____.

5. The _____ of beans was hard to open.

6. The envelope needed a _____.

7. He swung the _____ and hit the ball.

8. The _____ blew air around.

9. My mom drives a blue _____.

10. I _____ in the backseat.

Long a Words

Long a is the vowel sound which says its own name. **Long a** can be spelled **ai** as in the word **mail, ay** as in the word **say** and **a** with a **silent e** at the end of a word as in the word **same**.

Directions: Say each word and listen for the **long a** sound. Then write each word and underline the letters that make the **long a** vowel sound.

mail	bake	train
game	day	sale
paint	play	name
made	gray	tray

1. _____

2. _____

3. _____

4. _____

5. _____

6. _____

7. _____

8. _____

9. _____

10. _____

11. _____

12. _____

Name _____

Long a Words: Sentence Order

Directions: Write the words in order so that each sentence tells a complete idea. Begin each sentence with a capital letter and end it with a period or a question mark.

1. plate was on the cake a

_____

2. like you would to play a game

_____

3. gray around the a corner train came

_____

4. was on mail Bob's name the

_____

5. sail for on day we went a nice a

_____

Name _____

Short o Words

Short o is the vowel sound you hear in the word **pot**.

Directions: Say each word and listen for the **short o** sound. Then write each word and underline the letter that makes the **short o** sound.

hot	box	sock	mop
stop	not	fox	cot
Bob	rock	clock	lock

1. _____

2. _____

3. _____

4. _____

5. _____

6. _____

7. _____

8. _____

9. _____

10. _____

11. _____

12. _____

Name _____

Short o Words: Rhyming Words

Short o is the vowel sound you hear in the word **got**.

Directions: Use the **short o** words in the box to write rhyming words.

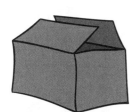

hot	rock	lock	cot
stop	sock	fox	mop
box	mob	clock	Bob

1. Write the words that rhyme with **dot**.

_____   _____

2. Write the words that rhyme with **socks**.

_____   _____

3. Write the words that rhyme with **hop**.

_____   _____

4. Write the words that rhyme with **dock**.

_____   _____

_____   _____

5. Write the words that rhyme with **cob**.

_____   _____

Name _____

Long o Words

Long o is the vowel sound which says its own name. **Long o** can be spelled **oa** as in the word **float** or **o** with a **silent e** at the end as in **cone**.

Directions: Say each word and listen for the **long o** sound. Then write each word and underline the letters that make the **long o** sound.

rope	coat	soap	wrote
note	hope	boat	cone
bone	pole	phone	hole

1. _____

2. _____

3. _____

4. _____

5. _____

6. _____

7. _____

8. _____

9. _____

10. _____

11. _____

12. _____

Long o Words: Sentences

Directions: Draw a line from the first part of the sentence to the part which completes the sentence.

1. Do you know

in the water.

2. The dog

was in the tree.

3. The boat floats

who wrote the note?

4. I hope the phone

has a bone.

5. Carol's ice-cream cone

rings soon for me!

6. The rope swing

a coat in the cold.

7. I had to wear

was melting.

Name _____

Animal Words

Directions: Write the animal names twice beside each picture.

| fox | rabbit | bear | squirrel | mouse | deer |

Example:

squirrel   squirrel

_____

_____

_____

_____

_____

Animal Words: More Than One

To show more than one of something, we add **s** to most words.

Example: one dog – **two dogs**   one book – **two books**

But some words are different. For words that end with **x**, use **es** to show two.

Example: one fox – **two foxes**   one box – **two boxes**

The spelling of some words changes a lot when there are two.

Example: one mouse – **two mice**

Some words stay the same, even when you mean two of something.

Example: one deer – **two deer**   one fish – **two fish**

Directions: Complete the sentences below with the correct word.

1. The  run fast.   _____

2. The  are eating.   _____

3. Have you seen any  today?   _____

4. Where do the  live?   _____

5. Did you ever have  for pets? _____

Animal Words: Kinds of Sentences

Another name for an asking sentence is a **question**.

Directions: Use the words in the box to write a telling sentence. Then use the words to write a question.

Example:

a	mouse	I	see
the	bed	under	do

Telling sentence:

I see a mouse under the bed.

Question:

Do I see a mouse under the bed?

in	live
these	woods
bears	do

Telling sentence: _____

_____

Question: _____

_____

Name _____

Animal Words: Sentences

Directions: Read the sentences on each line and draw a line between them. Then write each sentence again on the lines below. Begin each one with a capital letter and put a period or question mark at the end.

Example:

why do squirrels hide nuts | they eat them in the winter

Why do squirrels hide nuts?
They eat them in the winter.

1. bears sleep in the winter they don't need food then

_____

_____

2. he said he saw a fox do you think he did

_____

Family Words

Directions: This is Andy's **family tree**. It shows all the people in his family. Use the words in the box to finish writing the names in Andy's family tree.

grandmother	mother
grandfather	father
aunt	uncle
brother	sister

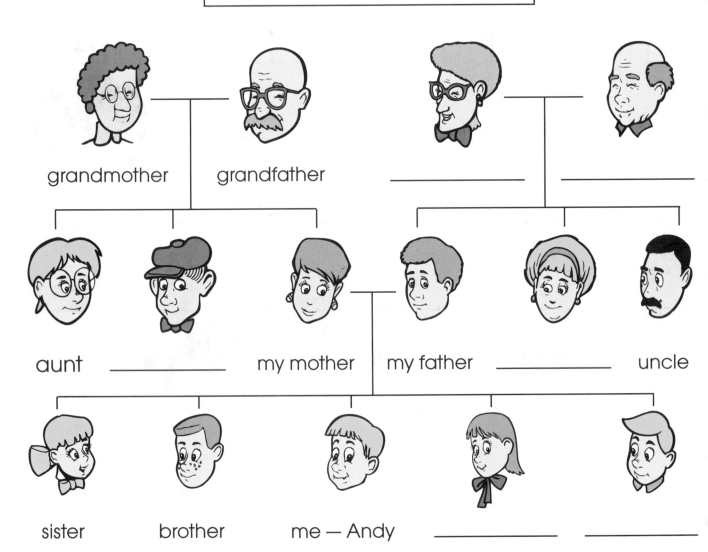

grandmother   grandfather   _____ _____

aunt _____   my mother   my father _____ uncle

sister   brother   me — Andy   _____   _____

Family Words

Some words tell how a person looks or feels. These are called **describing** words or **adjectives**.

Directions: Help Andy write about the people in his family. Cross out the **describing** word that does not tell about each picture. Write a sentence that uses the other two describing words.

Example:

asleep
funny
tall

My aunt

is tall and funny.

fast
happy
smiling

1. My grandmother

_____

hot
broken
tired

2. My uncle

_____

thirsty
hungry
hard

3. My little brother

_____

Name _____

Family Words: Joining Words

Joining words join two ideas to make one long sentence. Three words help do this:

and — if both sentences are much the same.
Example: I took my dog for a walk, **and** I played with my cat.

but — if the second sentence says something different than the first sentence. Sometimes the second sentence tells why you can't do the first sentence.
Example: I want to play outside, **but** it is raining.

or — if each sentence names a different thing you could do.
Example: You could eat your cookie, **or** you could give it to me.

Directions: Use the word given to join the two short sentences into one longer sentence.

(but)
My aunt lives far away. She calls me often.

My aunt lives far away, but she calls me often.

1. **(and)**
My sister had a birthday. She got a new bike.

_____

_____

2. **(or)**
We can play outside. We can play inside.

_____

_____

Name _____

Family Words: Joining Words

Directions: Read each pair of sentences. Then join them with **and**, **but** or **or**.

1. My uncle likes popcorn.
   He does not like peanuts.

_____

_____

2. He could read a book.
   He could tell me his own story.

_____

_____

3. My little brother is sleepy.
   He wants to go to bed.

_____

_____

Name _____

Short e Words

Short e is the vowel sound you hear in the word **pet**.

Directions: Say each word and listen for the **short e** sound. Then write each word and underline the letter that makes the **short e** sound.

get	Meg	rest	tent
red	spent	test	help
bed	pet	head	best

1. _____

2. _____

3. _____

4. _____

5. _____

6. _____

7. _____

8. _____

9. _____

10. _____

11. _____

12. _____

Short e Words: Rhyming Words

Short e is the vowel sound you hear in the word **egg**.

Directions: Use the **short e** words in the box to write rhyming words.

get	test	pet	help
let	head	spent	red
best	tent	rest	bed

1. Write the words that rhyme with **fed**.

_____   _____   _____

2. Write the words that rhyme with **bent**.

_____   _____

3. Write the words that rhyme with **west**.

_____   _____   _____

4. Write the words that rhyme with **bet**.

_____   _____   _____

Name _____

Short e Words: Sentences

Directions: Write the correct **short e** word in each sentence.

get	Meg	rest	bed	spent	best
test	help	head	pet	red	tent

1. Of all my crayons, I like the color _____

the _____ !

2. I always make my _____ when I _____ up.

3. My new hat keeps my _____ warm.

4. _____ wanted a dog for a _____ .

5. When we go camping, my job is to _____ put up

the _____ .

6. I have a _____ in math tomorrow, so I want to get

a good night's _____ .

Name _____

Long e Words

Long e is the vowel sound which says its own name. **Long e** can be spelled **ee** as in the word **teeth**, **ea** as in the word **meat** or **e** as in the word **me**.

Directions: Say each word and listen for the **long e** sound. Then write the words and underline the letters that make the **long e** sound.

street	neat	treat	feet
sleep	keep	deal	meal
mean	clean	beast	feast

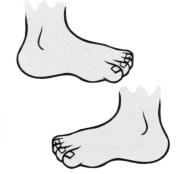

1. _____

2. _____

3. _____

4. _____

5. _____

6. _____

7. _____

8. _____

9. _____

10. _____

11. _____

12. _____

Name _____

Long e Words: Rhyming Words

Long e is the vowel sound you hear in the word **meet**.

Directions: Use the **long e** words in the box to write rhyming words.

street	feet	neat	treat
keep	deal	sleep	meal
mean	beast	clean	feast

1. Write the words that rhyme with **beat**.

_____   _____

_____   _____

2. Write the words that rhyme with **deep**.

_____   _____

3. Write the words that rhyme with **feel**.

_____   _____

4. Write the words that rhyme with **bean**.

_____   _____

5. Write the words that rhyme with **least**.

_____   _____

Name _____

Long e Words: Sentences

Directions: Write a word from the box to complete each sentence.

street	feet	neat	treat
keep	deal	sleep	meal
mean	beast	clean	feast

1. I went to _____ late last night.

2. One of my favorite stories is "Beauty and

the _____ ."

3. Look both ways when you cross the _____ .

4. It would be _____ to kick someone.

5. I wear socks and shoes on my _____ .

6. The most important _____ of the day

is breakfast.

Name _____

Verbs

Verbs are words that tell the action in the sentence.

Directions: Draw a line from each sentence to its picture. Then finish the sentence with the verb or action word that is under each picture.

Example:
He will ___**help**___ the baby.

help

carry

1. I can _____ my book.

2. It is time to _____ up.

cut

3. That chair might _____ .

build

4. They _____ houses.

clean

5. I _____ this out myself.

fix

6. Is that too heavy to _____ ?

break

Name _____

Verbs: Sentences

Directions: Read the two sentences in each story below. Then write one more sentence to tell what happened next. Use the verbs from the box.

| break | build | fix | clean | cut | carry |

Today is Mike's birthday.

Mike asked four friends to come.

Edith's dog walked in the mud.

He got mud in the house.

_____

Verbs: Sentences

Directions: Join each pair of sentences to make one longer sentence. Use one of the **joining** words: **and**, **but** or **or**. In the second part of the sentence, use **he**, **she** or **they** in place of the person's name.

Example: I asked Tim to help me. Tim wanted to play.

I asked Tim to help me, but he wanted to play.

1. Kelly dropped a glass. Kelly cut her finger.

_____

_____

2. Linda and Allen got a new dog. Linda and Allen named it Baby.

_____

_____

Verbs: Word Endings

Most **verbs** end with **s** when the sentence tells about one thing. The **s** is taken away when the sentence tells about more than one thing.

Example:

One dog walks.　　　　　One boy runs.
Two dogs **walk**.　　　　Three boys **run**.

The spelling of some **verbs** changes when the sentence tells about only one thing.

Example:

One girl carries her lunch.　　　The boy fixes his car.
Two girls **carry** their lunches.　Two boys **fix** their cars.

Directions: Write the missing verbs in the sentences.

Example:

Pam works hard. She and Peter __work__ all day.

1. The father bird builds a nest.

   The mother and father _____ it together.

2. The girls clean their room. Jenny _____ under her bed.

3. The children cut out their pictures. Henry _____ his slowly.

4. These workers fix things. This man _____ televisions.

5. Two trucks carry horses. One truck _____ pigs.

Name _____

Short i Words

Short i is the vowel sound you hear in the word **pig**.

Directions: Say each word and listen for the **short i** sound. Then write each word and underline the letter that makes the **short i** sound.

pin	fin	dip	dish
kick	rich	ship	wish
win	fish	sick	pitch

1. _____

2. _____

3. _____

4. _____

5. _____

6. _____

7. _____

8. _____

9. _____

10. _____

11. _____

12. _____

Name _____

Short i Words: Sentences

Directions: Complete the sentences by matching the words to the correct sentence.

1. I made a _____ on a star.   fin

2. All we could see was the shark's _____
   above the water.   fish

3. I like to eat vegetables with _____ .   kick

4. We saw lots of _____ in the water.   win

5. The soccer player will_____the   dish
   ball and score a goal.

6. If you feel _____ , see a doctor.   dip

7. Did Bob _____ the race?   wish

8. The_____ was full of candy.   sick

Name _____

Long i Words

Long i is the vowel sound which says its own name. **Long i** can be spelled **igh** as in **sight**, **i** with a **silent e** at the end as in **mine** and **y** at the end as in **fly**.

Directions: Say each word and listen for the **long i** sound. Then write each word and underline the letters that make the **long i** sound.

bike	hike	ride	line
glide	ripe	nine	pipe
fight	high	light	sigh

1. _____

2. _____

3. _____

4. _____

5. _____

6. _____

7. _____

8. _____

9. _____

10. _____

11. _____

12. _____

Name _____

Long i Words: Rhyming Words

Long i is the sound you hear in the word **fight**.

Directions: Use the **long i** words in the box to write rhyming words.

hide	ride	line	my
by	nine	high	light
sight	fly		

1. Write the words that rhyme with **sigh**.

_____ _____ _____ _____

2. Write the words that rhyme with **side**.

_____ _____

3. Write the words that rhyme with **fine**.

_____ _____

4. Write the words that rhyme with **fight**.

_____ _____

Name _____

Location Words

Directions: Use one of the location words from the box to complete each sentence.

between	around	inside	outside	beside	across

Example:

She will hide ___**under**___ the basket.

1. In the summer, we like to play _____.

2. She can swim _____ the lake.

3. Put the bird _____ its cage so it won't fly away.

4. Sit _____ Bill and me so we can all work together.

5. Your picture is right _____ mine on the wall.

6. The fence goes _____ the house.

Name _____

Location Words

Directions: Draw a line from each sentence to its picture. Then complete each sentence with the word under the picture.

Example:

He is walking **behind** the tree.

outside

1. We stay _____ when it rains.

behind

between

2. She drew a dog _____ his house.

3. She stands _____ her friends.

across

4. They walked _____ the bridge.

around

5. Let the cat go _____ .

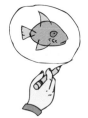
beside

6. Draw a circle _____ the fish.

inside

Name _____

Short u Words

Short u is the sound you hear in the word **bug**.

Directions: Say each word and listen for the **short u** sound. Then write each word and underline the letter that makes the **short u** sound.

dust	must	nut	bug
bump	pump	tub	jump
cut	hug	rug	cub

1. _____

2. _____

3. _____

4. _____

5. _____

6. _____

7. _____

8. _____

9. _____

10. _____

11. _____

12. _____

Name _____

Short u Words: Sentences

Directions: Circle the words in each sentence which are not correct. Then write the correct **short u** words from the box on the lines.

tub	cub	bump	pump
bug	dust	cut	must
nut	jump	rug	hug

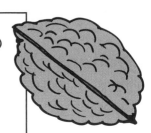

1. The crust made me sneeze. _____

2. I need to take a bath in the cub. _____

3. The mug bite left a big pump on my arm.

_____   _____

4. It is time to get my hair hut. _____

5. The mother bear took care of her shrub. _____

6. We need to jump more gas into the car. _____

Name _____

Long u Words

Long u is the vowel sound which says its own name. **Long u** is spelled **u** with a silent **e** at the end as in **cute**. The letters **oo** make a sound very much like long **u**. They make the sound you hear in the word **zoo**. The letters **ew** also make the **oo** sound as in the word **grew**.

Directions: Say the words and listen for the **u** and **oo** sounds. Then write each word and underline the letters that make the **long u** and **oo** sounds.

choose	blew	moon	fuse
cube	Ruth	tooth	use
flew	loose	goose	noon

1. _____

2. _____

3. _____

4. _____

5. _____

6. _____

7. _____

8. _____

9. _____

10. _____

11. _____

12. _____

Name _____

Long u Words: Sentences

Directions: Write the words in the sentences below in the correct order. Begin each sentence with a capital letter and end it with a period or a question mark.

1. the pulled dentist tooth my loose

_____

2. ice cubes I choose in my drink to put

_____

3. a Ruth fuse blew yesterday

_____

4. loose the got in garden goose the

_____

5. flew the goose winter for the south

_____

6. is full there a moon tonight

_____

Name _____

Opposite Words

Directions: Opposites are words which are different in every way.
Use the opposite word from the box to complete these sentences.

hard	hot	bottom	quickly	happy
sad	slowly	cold	soft	top

Example:

My new coat is blue on ___top___ and

red on the ___bottom___ .

1. Snow is _____ , but fire is _____ .

2. A rabbit runs _____ , but a turtle

    moves _____ .

3. A bed is _____ , but a floor is _____ .

4. I feel _____ when my friends come

    and _____ when they leave.

Opposite Words

Directions: Draw a line from each sentence to its picture. Then complete each sentence with the word under the picture.

Example:

She bought a __new__ bat.

hard

new

1. I like my _____ pillow.

2. Birthdays make me _____.

top

3. Put that book on _____.

sad

4. Jenny runs _____.

slowly

5. A rock makes a _____ seat.

quickly

6. I feel _____ when it rains.

happy

7. He eats _____.

soft

Opposite Words: Sentences

Directions: Cross out the word in each box that does not tell about the picture. Write a sentence about the picture using the other two words.

Example:

~~teeth~~	garden	digs

She digs in her garden.

swims	quickly	five

_____

_____

soft	fly	happy

_____

_____

popcorn	bottom	sad

_____

_____

Name _____

Opposite Words: Sentences

Directions: Look at each picture. Then write a sentence that uses the word under the picture and tells how something is the same as the picture.

Example:

cold

My hands are as cold as ice.

hard

_____

_____

slow

_____

_____

soft

_____

_____

happy

_____

_____

Name _____

Opposite Words: Completing a Story

Directions: Write opposite words in the blanks to complete the story.

hot	hard	top	cold	bottom
soft	quickly	happy	slowly	sad

One day, Grandma came for a visit. She gave my sister Jenny and me a box of chocolate candy. We said, "Thank you!" Then Jenny _____ took the _____ off the box. The pieces all looked the same! I couldn't tell which pieces were _____ inside and which were _____ ! I only liked the _____ ones. Jenny didn't care. She was _____ to get any kind of candy!

I _____ looked at all the pieces. I didn't know which one to pick. Just then Dad called us. Grandma was going home. He wanted us to say good-bye to her. I hurried to the front door where they were standing. Jenny came a minute later.

I told Grandma I hoped I would see her soon. I always feel _____ when she leaves. Jenny stood behind me and didn't say anything. After Grandma went home, I found out why. Jenny had most of our candy in her mouth! Only a few pieces were left in the _____ of the box! Then I was _____ ! That Jenny!

Name _____

Time Words

The time between breakfast and lunch is **morning**.

The time between lunch and dinner is **afternoon**.

The time between dinner and bedtime is **evening**.

Directions: Write a time word from the box to complete each sentence. Use each word only once.

evening	morning	today	tomorrow	afternoon

1. What did you eat for breakfast

   this _____?

2. We came home from school in the _____ .

3. I help wash the dinner dishes in

   the _____ .

4. I feel a little tired _____ .

5. If I rest tonight, I will feel better _____ .

Name _____

Time Words: Sentences

Directions: Write a sentence for these time words. Tell something you do at that time.

Example:

day

Every day I walk to school.

morning

_____

_____

afternoon

_____

_____

evening

_____

_____

MATH

Less Than, Greater Than

Directions: The open mouth points to the larger number. The small point goes to the smaller number. Draw the symbol **<** or **>** to the correct number.

Example: 5 3

This means that 5 is greater than 3, and 3 is less than 5.

12 ◯ 2   16 ◯ 6

16 ◯ 15   1 ◯ 2

7 ◯ 1   19 ◯ 5

9 ◯ 6   11 ◯ 13

Name _____

Counting

Directions: Write the numbers that are:

next in order	one less	one greater
22, 23, _____ , _____	_____ , 16	6, _____
674, _____ , _____	_____ , 247	125, _____
227, _____ , _____	_____ , 550	499, _____
199, _____ , _____	_____ , 333	750, _____
329, _____ , _____	_____ , 862	933, _____

Directions: Write the missing numbers.

Name _____

Counting by 2's

Directions: Each basket the players make is worth 2 points. Help your team win by counting by 2's to beat the other team's score.

2

___

___

8

___

___

16

20

___

___

28

___

32

Final Score	
Home	Visitor
	30

Winner!

Name _____

Counting: 2's, 5's, 10's

Directions: Write the missing numbers.

Count by 2's:

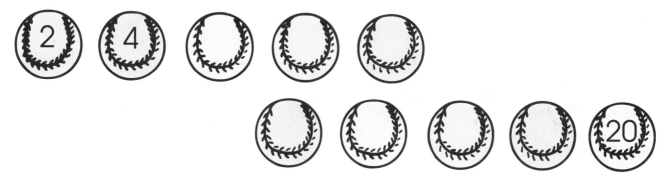

Count by 5's:

Count by 10's:

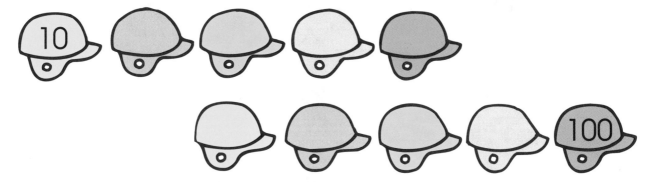

Name _____

Patterns

Directions: Write or draw what comes next in the pattern.

Example: **1, 2, 3, 4,** __5__

1.

2. A, 1, B, 2, C _____

3. 2, 4, 6, 8, _____

4. A, C, E, G, _____

5. 5, 10, 15, 20, _____

Name _____

Finding Patterns: Numbers

Mia likes to count by twos, threes, fours, fives, tens and hundreds.

Directions: Complete the number patterns.

1. 5, ____, ____, 20, ____, ____, 35, ____, ____, 50

2. 100, ____, ____, 400, ____, ____, ____, 800, ____

3. ____, 4, 6, ____, ____, 12, ____, 16, ____, ____

4. 10, ____, ____, 40, ____, ____, 70, ____, 90

5. 4, ____, 12, ____, ____, 24, ____, 32, ____, 40

6. ____, 6, 9, ____, ____, 18, ____, 24, ____, 30

Directions: Make up two of your own number patterns.

____, ____, ____, ____, ____, ____, ____, ____

____, ____, ____, ____, ____, ____, ____, ____

Name _____

Finding Patterns: Shapes

Directions: Complete each row by drawing the correct shape.

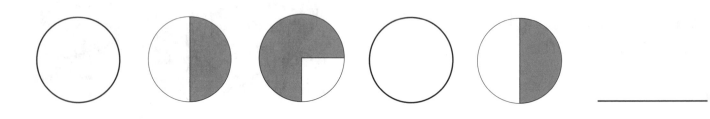 _____

 _____

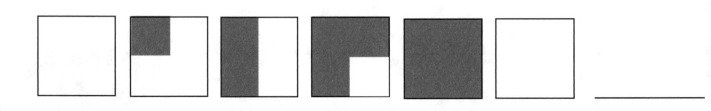 _____

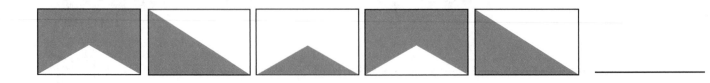 _____

Name _____

Ordinal Numbers

Ordinal numbers indicate order in a series, such as **first**, **second** or **third**.

Directions: Follow the instructions to color the train cars. The first car is the engine.

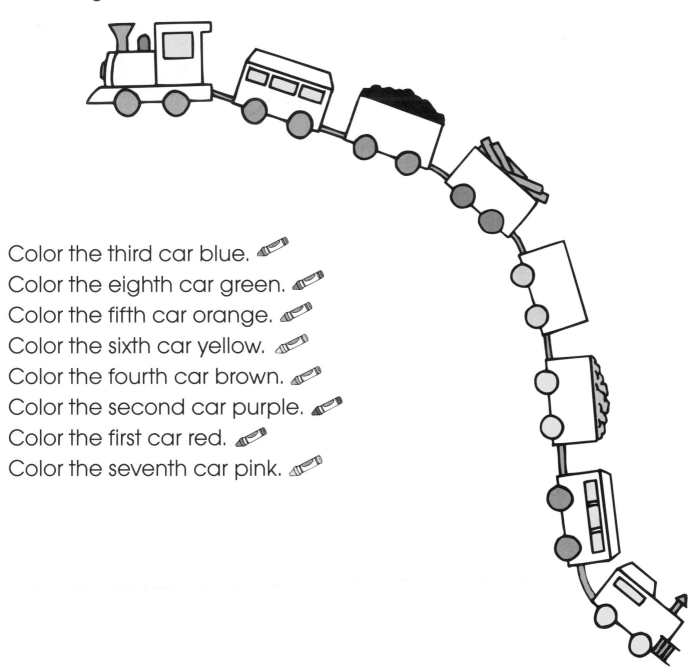

Color the third car blue.
Color the eighth car green.
Color the fifth car orange.
Color the sixth car yellow.
Color the fourth car brown.
Color the second car purple.
Color the first car red.
Color the seventh car pink.

Name _____

Ordinal Numbers

Directions: Follow the instructions.

Draw glasses on the second one.

Put a hat on the fourth one.

Color blonde hair on the third one.

Draw a tie on the first one.

Draw ears on the fifth one.

Draw black hair on the seventh one.

Put a bow on the head of the sixth one.

Addition

Addition is "putting together" or adding two or more numbers to find the sum.

Directions: Add.

Example:

```
   2
 + 5
 ___
   7
```

```
   3        6        7        8        5        3
 + 4      + 2      + 1      + 2      + 4      + 1
 ___      ___      ___      ___      ___      ___
```

```
   8        9       10        6        4        7
 + 2      + 5      + 3      + 6      + 9      + 7
 ___      ___      ___      ___      ___      ___
```

```
   9        8        6        7        7        9
 + 3      + 7      + 5      + 9      + 6      + 9
 ___      ___      ___      ___      ___      ___
```

Name _____

Addition: Commutative Property

The commutative property of addition states that even if the order of the numbers is changed in an addition sentence, the sum will stay the same.

Example: **2 + 3 = 5**
3 + 2 = 5

Directions: Look at the addition sentences below. Complete the addition sentences by writing the missing numerals.

5 + 4 = 9   3 + 1 = 4   2 + 6 = 8
4 + __ = 9   1 + __ = 4   6 + __ = 8

6 + 1 = 7   4 + 3 = 7   1 + 9 = 10
1 + __ = 7   3 + __ = 7   9 + __ = 10

Now try these:

6 + 3 = 9   10 + 2 = 12   8 + 3 = 11
__ + __ = 9   __ + __ = 12   __ + __ = 11

Look at these sums. Can you think of two number sentences that would show the commutative property of addition?

__ + __ = 7   __ + __ = 11   __ + __ = 9

__ + __ = 7   __ + __ = 11   __ + __ = 9

Adding 3 or More Numbers

Directions: Add all the numbers to find the sum. Draw pictures to help or break up the problem into two smaller problems.

Example:

```
1 ○
2 ○○
+3 ○○○
 6
```

```
 2
+5  >  7
 2
+4  > +6
      13
```

```
 3
 6
+2
```

```
 8
 5
+4
```

```
 3
 1
+5
```

```
 8
 2
+9
```

```
 2
 8
 4
+3
```

```
 3
 6
 5
+2
```

```
 4
 1
 2
+5
```

```
 6
 7
 3
+1
```

Subtraction

Subtraction is "taking away" or subtracting one number from another to find the difference.

Directions: Subtract.

Example:

$$\begin{array}{r} 4 \\ -3 \\ \hline 1 \end{array}$$

$$\begin{array}{r} 5 \\ -3 \\ \hline \end{array} \qquad \begin{array}{r} 6 \\ -1 \\ \hline \end{array} \qquad \begin{array}{r} 4 \\ -3 \\ \hline \end{array} \qquad \begin{array}{r} 3 \\ -1 \\ \hline \end{array} \qquad \begin{array}{r} 2 \\ -0 \\ \hline \end{array} \qquad \begin{array}{r} 1 \\ -1 \\ \hline \end{array}$$

$$\begin{array}{r} 9 \\ -2 \\ \hline \end{array} \qquad \begin{array}{r} 7 \\ -4 \\ \hline \end{array} \qquad \begin{array}{r} 10 \\ -5 \\ \hline \end{array} \qquad \begin{array}{r} 14 \\ -6 \\ \hline \end{array} \qquad \begin{array}{r} 15 \\ -9 \\ \hline \end{array} \qquad \begin{array}{r} 12 \\ -3 \\ \hline \end{array}$$

$$\begin{array}{r} 18 \\ -8 \\ \hline \end{array} \qquad \begin{array}{r} 13 \\ -5 \\ \hline \end{array} \qquad \begin{array}{r} 14 \\ -7 \\ \hline \end{array} \qquad \begin{array}{r} 11 \\ -4 \\ \hline \end{array} \qquad \begin{array}{r} 17 \\ -9 \\ \hline \end{array} \qquad \begin{array}{r} 16 \\ -8 \\ \hline \end{array}$$

Name _____

Addition and Subtraction

Addition is "putting together" or adding two or more numbers to find the sum. Subtraction is "taking away" or subtracting one number from another to find the difference.

Directions: Add or subtract. Circle the answers that are less than 10.

Examples:

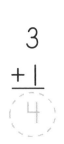

$$\begin{array}{r} 3 \\ +1 \\ \hline 4 \end{array}$$

$$\begin{array}{r} 3 \\ -1 \\ \hline 2 \end{array}$$

9 +3	6 −2	12 − 1	18 +1	15 −6
7 + 6	16 − 9	10 − 3	14 + 5	16 − 8
8 +7	12 + 2	13 − 4	17 + 2	9 +9

Place Value: Ones, Tens

The place value of a digit or numeral is shown by where it is in the number. For example, in the number **23**, **2** has the place value of **tens,** and **3** is **ones**.

Directions: Add the tens and ones and write your answers in the blanks

Example:

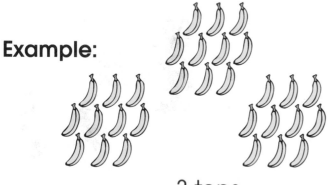

= _33_

3 tens + 3 ones = _33_

	tens ones		tens ones
7 tens + 5 ones =	_____	4 tens + 0 ones =	_____
2 tens + 3 ones =	_____	8 tens + 1 one =	_____
5 tens + 2 ones =	_____	1 ten + 1 one =	_____
5 tens + 4 ones =	_____	6 tens + 3 ones =	_____
9 tens + 5 ones =	_____		

Directions: Draw a line to the correct number.

6 tens + 7 ones ————————— 73
4 tens + 2 ones —————→ 67
8 tens + 0 ones   51
7 tens + 3 ones   80
5 tens + 1 one   42

Name _____

Place Value: Ones, Tens

Directions: Write the numbers for the tens and ones. Then add.

Example:

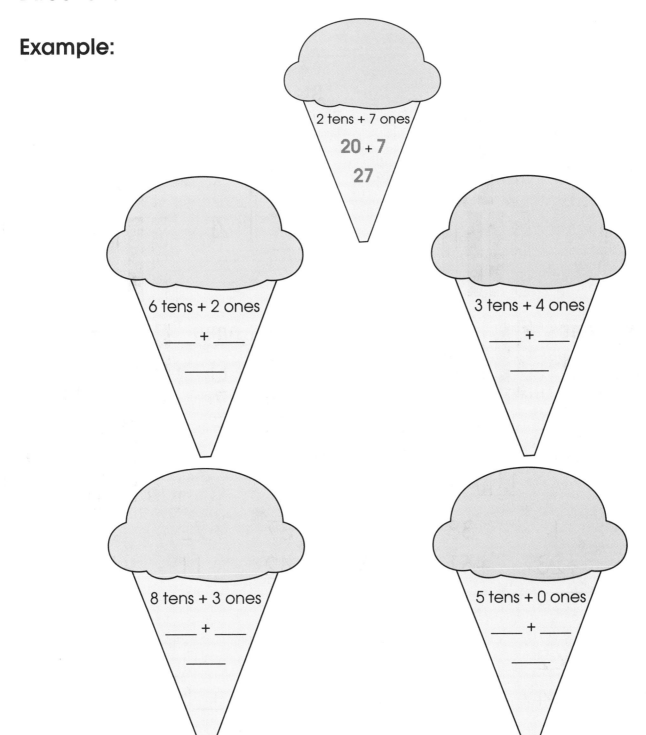

2 tens + 7 ones

20 + 7

27

6 tens + 2 ones

___ + ___

___

3 tens + 4 ones

___ + ___

___

8 tens + 3 ones

___ + ___

___

5 tens + 0 ones

___ + ___

___

Name _____

2-Digit Addition

Directions: Study the example. Follow the steps to add.

Example: 33
            +41

Step 1: Add the ones.

tens	ones
3	3
+4	1
4	4

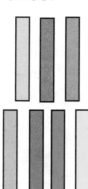 

Step 2: Add the tens.

tens	ones
3	3
+4	1
7	4

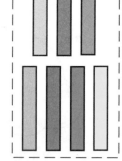

tens	ones
4	2
+ 2	4
6	6

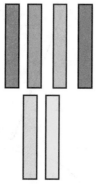 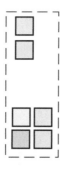

tens	ones
5	0
+ 4	7
9	7

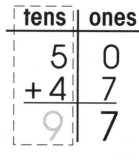 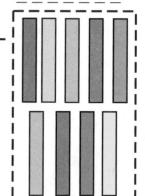

24	15	38	11	37	72	33	10
+62	+23	+61	+26	+42	+11	+51	+30

25	62	32	25	82	91	16	55
+42	+14	+44	+13	+ 6	+ 5	+71	+ 3

2-Digit Addition

Directions: Add the total points scored in each game. Remember to add **ones** first and **tens** second.

Example:

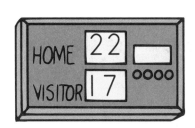

HOME 22
VISITOR 17

Total __39__

HOME 28
VISITOR 30

Total _____

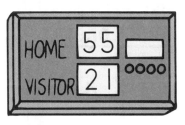

HOME 55
VISITOR 21

Total _____

HOME 14
VISITOR 33

Total _____

HOME 24
VISITOR 13

Total _____

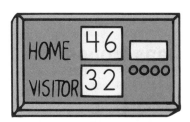

HOME 46
VISITOR 32

Total _____

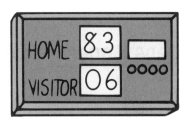

HOME 83
VISITOR 06

Total _____

HOME 30
VISITOR 20

Total _____

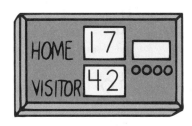

HOME 17
VISITOR 42

Total _____

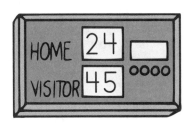

HOME 24
VISITOR 45

Total _____

Name _____

2-Digit Addition: Regrouping

Addition is "putting together" or adding two or more numbers to find the sum. Regrouping is using **ten ones** to form **one ten, ten tens** to form **one 100, fifteen ones** to form **one ten** and **five ones** and so on.

Directions: Study the examples. Follow the steps to add.

Example:

$$\begin{array}{r} 14 \\ +\ 8 \\ \hline \end{array}$$

Step 1: Add the ones.

tens	ones
1	4
+	8
	12

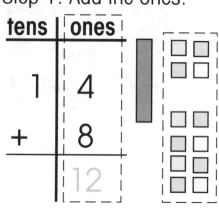

Step 2: Regroup the tens.

tens	ones
1	4
+	8
	2

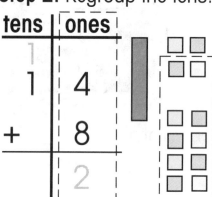

Step 3: Add the tens.

tens	ones
1	4
+	8
2	2

tens	ones
1	
1	6
+3	7
5	3

tens	ones
1	
3	8
+5	3
9	1

tens	ones
1	
2	4
+4	7
7	1

$$\begin{array}{r} 28 \\ +17 \\ \hline \end{array} \qquad \begin{array}{r} 32 \\ +38 \\ \hline \end{array} \qquad \begin{array}{r} 54 \\ +25 \\ \hline \end{array} \qquad \begin{array}{r} 19 \\ +55 \\ \hline \end{array} \qquad \begin{array}{r} 44 \\ +48 \\ \hline \end{array} \qquad \begin{array}{r} 25 \\ +64 \\ \hline \end{array} \qquad \begin{array}{r} 29 \\ +33 \\ \hline \end{array} \qquad \begin{array}{r} 79 \\ +15 \\ \hline \end{array}$$

Name _____

2-Digit Addition: Regrouping

Directions: Add the total points scored in the game.
Remember to add the ones, regroup, and then add the tens.

Example:

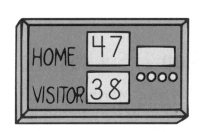

Total __85__

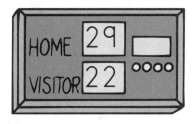

Total _____

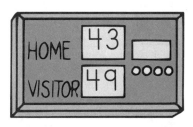

Total _____

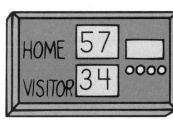

Total _____

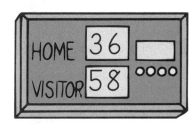

Total _____

Total _____

Total _____

Total _____

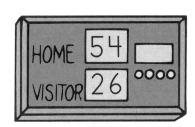

Total _____

Name _____

2-Digit Subtraction

Directions: Study the example. Follow the steps to subtract.

Example:

$$\begin{array}{r} 28 \\ -14 \\ \hline \end{array}$$

Step 1: Subtract the ones.

tens	ones
2	8
-1	4
	4

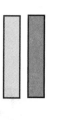
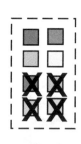

Step 2: Subtract the tens.

tens	ones
2	8
-1	4
1	4

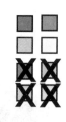

tens	ones
2	4
-1	2
1	2

tens	ones
3	8
-1	5
2	3

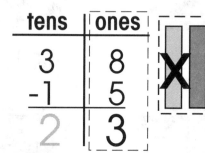
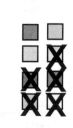

24	61	77	85	57	87	59	96
− 12	− 30	− 44	− 24	− 23	− 33	− 34	− 16

29	74	46	69	95	33	78	22
− 15	− 51	− 32	− 35	− 32	− 33	− 26	− 11

2-Digit Subtraction: Regrouping

Subtraction is "taking away" or subtracting one number from another to find the difference. Regrouping is using **one ten to form ten ones, one 100 to form ten tens** and so on.

Directions: Study the examples. Follow the steps to subtract.

Example: 37
             -19

Step 1: Regroup.   **Step 2:** Subtract the ones.   **Step 3:** Subtract the tens.

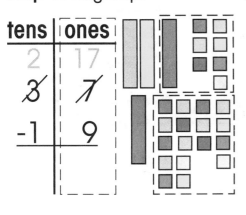

tens	ones
0	12
1̸	2̸
-	9
3	

tens	ones
2	14
3̸	4̸
-1	6
1	8

tens	ones
3	15
4̸	5̸
-2	9
1	6

28	46	12	30	52	47	21	45
− 19	− 18	− 8	− 12	− 25	− 35	− 13	− 25

Name _____

2-Digit Subtraction: Regrouping

Directions: Study the steps for subtracting. Solve the problems using the steps.

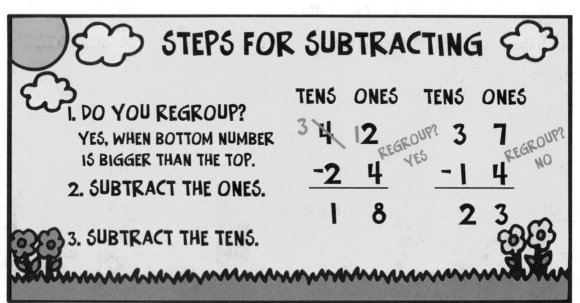

STEPS FOR SUBTRACTING

1. DO YOU REGROUP?
   YES, WHEN BOTTOM NUMBER IS BIGGER THAN THE TOP.
2. SUBTRACT THE ONES.
3. SUBTRACT THE TENS.

TENS	ONES		TENS	ONES	
3 4̸	12	REGROUP? YES	3	7	REGROUP? NO
- 2	4		- 1	4	
1	8		2	3	

tens	ones		tens	ones		tens	ones
4	7		6	4		5	3
- 2	8		- 3	4		- 3	9

56	83	43	75	91
− 27	− 47	− 39	− 53	− 18

73	35	67	26	68
− 66	− 14	− 58	− 7	− 45

Name _____

Review

Directions: Add or subtract. Use regrouping when needed. Always do ones first and tens last.

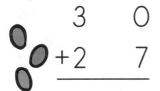

tens	ones
9	3
−2	5

tens	ones
3	0
+2	7

tens	ones
6	5
+1	7

tens	ones
7	1
−3	6

7	6
−2	8

8	2
+1	9

5	6
−2	8

2	5
−1	6

4	3
−1	4

5	3
−1	5

2	4
+5	7

4	8
+2	8

$$33 + 47$$

$$52 + 29$$

$$46 - 37$$

$$97 - 68$$

Name _____

2-Digit Addition and Subtraction

Addition is "putting together" or adding two or more numbers to find the sum. Subtraction is "taking away" or subtracting one number from another to find the difference. Regrouping is using **one ten** to form **ten ones**, **one 100** to form **ten tens**, and so on.

Directions: Add or subtract using regrouping.

Example:

tens ones

$$
\begin{array}{cc}
2 & 15 \\
\cancel{3} & 5 \\
-2 & 7 \\
\hline
 & 8
\end{array}
$$

$$
\begin{array}{r}
56 \\
-27 \\
\hline
\end{array}
\quad
\begin{array}{r}
40 \\
-16 \\
\hline
\end{array}
\quad
\begin{array}{r}
35 \\
+27 \\
\hline
\end{array}
\quad
\begin{array}{r}
42 \\
-14 \\
\hline
\end{array}
\quad
\begin{array}{r}
53 \\
+38 \\
\hline
\end{array}
\quad
\begin{array}{r}
97 \\
-48 \\
\hline
\end{array}
\quad
\begin{array}{r}
44 \\
+27 \\
\hline
\end{array}
\quad
\begin{array}{r}
93 \\
-39 \\
\hline
\end{array}
$$

$$
\begin{array}{r}
56 \\
-17 \\
\hline
\end{array}
\quad
\begin{array}{r}
44 \\
+28 \\
\hline
\end{array}
\quad
\begin{array}{r}
68 \\
-49 \\
\hline
\end{array}
\quad
\begin{array}{r}
73 \\
-24 \\
\hline
\end{array}
\quad
\begin{array}{r}
33 \\
+18 \\
\hline
\end{array}
\quad
\begin{array}{r}
49 \\
+32 \\
\hline
\end{array}
\quad
\begin{array}{r}
77 \\
-68 \\
\hline
\end{array}
\quad
\begin{array}{r}
27 \\
+19 \\
\hline
\end{array}
$$

Name _____

2-Digit Addition and Subtraction

Directions: Add or subtract using regrouping.

$$
\begin{array}{r} 23 \\ +48 \\ \hline \end{array}
\qquad
\begin{array}{r} 84 \\ -56 \\ \hline \end{array}
\qquad
\begin{array}{r} 69 \\ +29 \\ \hline \end{array}
\qquad
\begin{array}{r} 41 \\ -17 \\ \hline \end{array}
$$

$$
\begin{array}{r} 52 \\ -28 \\ \hline \end{array}
\qquad
\begin{array}{r} 73 \\ +18 \\ \hline \end{array}
\qquad
\begin{array}{r} 84 \\ -27 \\ \hline \end{array}
\qquad
\begin{array}{r} 57 \\ -39 \\ \hline \end{array}
$$

$$
\begin{array}{r} 33 \\ -15 \\ \hline \end{array}
\qquad
\begin{array}{r} 64 \\ +17 \\ \hline \end{array}
\qquad
\begin{array}{r} 37 \\ +58 \\ \hline \end{array}
\qquad
\begin{array}{r} 36 \\ -19 \\ \hline \end{array}
$$

$$
\begin{array}{r} 65 \\ -28 \\ \hline \end{array}
\qquad
\begin{array}{r} 48 \\ -30 \\ \hline \end{array}
\qquad
\begin{array}{r} 33 \\ +18 \\ \hline \end{array}
\qquad
\begin{array}{r} 25 \\ +35 \\ \hline \end{array}
$$

Place Value: Hundreds

The place value of a digit or numeral is shown by where it is in the number. For example, in the number **123**, **1** has the place value of **hundreds**, **2** is **tens** and **3** is **ones.**

Directions: Study the examples. Then write the missing numbers in the blanks.

Examples:

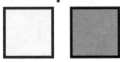

2 hundreds + 3 tens + 6 ones =   1 hundreds + 4 tens + 9 ones =

hundreds	tens	ones
2	3	6	= 236

hundreds	tens	ones
1	4	9	= 149

	hundreds	tens	ones	total
3 hundreds + 4 tens + 8 ones =	3	4	8	= _____
_ hundreds + _ ten + _ ones =	2	1	7	= _____
_ hundreds + _ tens + _ ones =	6	3	5	= _____
_ hundreds + _ tens + _ ones =	4	7	9	= _____
_ hundreds + _ tens + _ ones =	2	9	4	= _____
_ hundreds + 5 tens + 6 ones =	4	____	____	= _____
3 hundreds + 1 ten + 3 ones =	____	____	____	= _____
3 hundreds + _ tens + 7 ones =	____	5	____	= _____
6 hundreds + 2 tens + _ ones =	____	____	8	= _____

Name _____

Place Value: Hundreds

Directions: Write the numbers for hundreds, tens and ones. Then add.

Example:

1 hundred + 4 tens + 6 ones

100 + 40 + 6

146

7 hundreds + 3 tens + 5 ones

_____ + _____ + _____

_____

3 hundreds + 1 ten + 9 ones

_____ + _____ + _____

_____

5 hundreds + 8 tens + 0 ones

_____ + _____ + _____

_____

9 hundreds + 0 tens + 7 ones

_____ + _____ + _____

_____

Name _____

3-Digit Addition: Regrouping

Directions: Study the examples. Follow the steps to add.

Example:

Step 1: Add the ones.

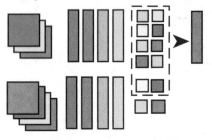

Do you regroup? Yes

Step 2: Add the tens.

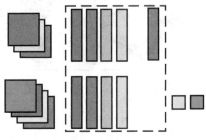

Do you regroup? No

Step 3: Add the hundreds.

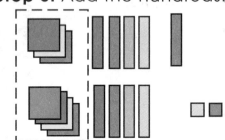

hundreds	tens	ones
	1	
3	4	8
+4	4	4
		2

hundreds	tens	ones
	1	
3	4	8
+4	4	4
	9	2

hundreds	tens	ones
	1	
3	4	8
+4	4	4
7	9	2

hundreds	tens	ones
	1	
2	1	4
+2	3	8
4	5	2

hundreds	tens	ones
	1	
3	6	8
+2	1	3
	8	1

hundreds	tens	ones
	1	
1	1	9
+5	6	5
		4

$$\begin{array}{r} 418 \\ +323 \\ \hline \end{array} \quad \begin{array}{r} 471 \\ +319 \\ \hline \end{array} \quad \begin{array}{r} 334 \\ +528 \\ \hline \end{array} \quad \begin{array}{r} 659 \\ +127 \\ \hline \end{array} \quad \begin{array}{r} 736 \\ +145 \\ \hline \end{array} \quad \begin{array}{r} 426 \\ +165 \\ \hline \end{array} \quad \begin{array}{r} 567 \\ +228 \\ \hline \end{array} \quad \begin{array}{r} 327 \\ +354 \\ \hline \end{array}$$

Name _____

3-Digit Addition: Regrouping

Directions: Study the example. Follow the steps to add. Regroup when needed.

Step 1: Add the ones.
Step 2: Add the tens.
Step 3: Add the hundreds.

hundreds	tens	ones
3	4	8
+4	5	4
8	0	2

$10 = 1$ ten $+ 0$ ones

$$
\begin{array}{r} 348 \\ +214 \\ \hline \end{array}
\qquad
\begin{array}{r} 172 \\ +418 \\ \hline \end{array}
\qquad
\begin{array}{r} 575 \\ +329 \\ \hline \end{array}
\qquad
\begin{array}{r} 623 \\ +268 \\ \hline \end{array}
\qquad
\begin{array}{r} 369 \\ +533 \\ \hline \end{array}
\qquad
\begin{array}{r} 733 \\ +229 \\ \hline \end{array}
$$

$$
\begin{array}{r} 411 \\ +299 \\ \hline \end{array}
\qquad
\begin{array}{r} 423 \\ +169 \\ \hline \end{array}
\qquad
\begin{array}{r} 639 \\ +177 \\ \hline \end{array}
\qquad
\begin{array}{r} 624 \\ +368 \\ \hline \end{array}
\qquad
\begin{array}{r} 272 \\ +469 \\ \hline \end{array}
\qquad
\begin{array}{r} 393 \\ +418 \\ \hline \end{array}
$$

Name _____

3-Digit Subtraction: Regrouping

Directions: Study the example. Follow the steps to subtract.

Step 1: Regroup ones.
Step 2: Subtract ones.
Step 3: Subtract tens.
Step 4: Subtract hundreds.

Example:

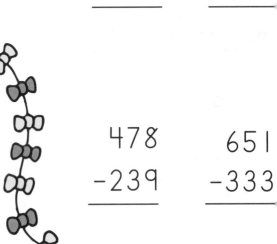

hundreds	tens	ones
	5	12
4	6̸	2̸
-2	5	3
2	0	9

$$423 \atop -114$$ $$562 \atop -349$$

$$478 \atop -239$$ $$651 \atop -333$$

Directions: Draw a line to the correct answer. Color the kites.

$$347 \atop -218$$ $$144 \atop -135$$ $$963 \atop -748$$ $$762 \atop -553$$ $$287 \atop -179$$ $$427 \atop -398$$

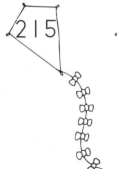

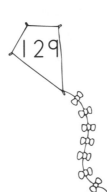
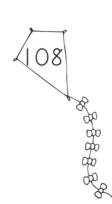
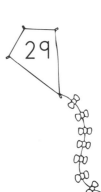
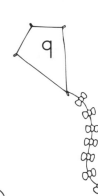

Name _____

3-Digit Subtraction: Regrouping

Directions: Subtract. Circle the **7**'s that appear in the **tens place**.

```
  492          184
 -221         -129
 ─────        ─────
  2⑦1
```

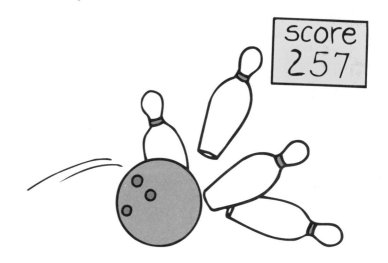

score
257

```
  358          765          584          693          921
 -238         -326         -435         -314         -362
 ─────        ─────        ─────        ─────        ─────
```

```
  128          744          835          248          635
 -109         -674         -217         -199         -428
 ─────        ─────        ─────        ─────        ─────
```

Name _____

Place Value: Thousands

Directions: Study the example. Write the missing numbers.

Example:

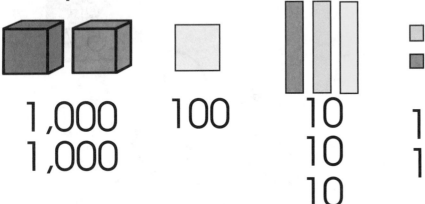

1,000
1,000

100

10
10
10

1
1

2 thousands + 1 hundred + __3__ tens + 2 ones = __2,132__

5,286 = ____ thousands + ____ hundreds + ____ tens + ____ ones

1,831 = ____ thousands + ____ hundreds + ____ tens + ____ ones

8,972 = ____ thousands + ____ hundreds + ____ tens + ____ ones

4,528 = ____ thousands + ____ hundreds + ____ tens + ____ ones

3,177 = ____ thousands + ____ hundreds + ____ tens + ____ ones

Directions: Draw a line to the number that has:

8 hundreds	7,103
5 ones	2,862
9 tens	5,996
7 thousands	1,485

Name _____

Place Value: Thousands

6 , 4 3 1

thousands | hundreds | tens | ones

Directions: Tell which number is in each place.

 Thousands place:

2,456   4,621   3,456

_____   _____   _____

 Tens place:

4,286   1,234   5,678

_____   _____   _____

 Hundreds place:

6,321   3,210   7,871

_____   _____   _____

 Ones place:

5,432   6,531   9,980

_____   _____   _____

Place Value: Thousands

Directions: Use the code to color the fan.

If the answer has:

9 thousands, color it pink.
6 thousands, color it green.
5 hundreds, color it orange.

8 tens, color it red.
3 ones, color it blue.

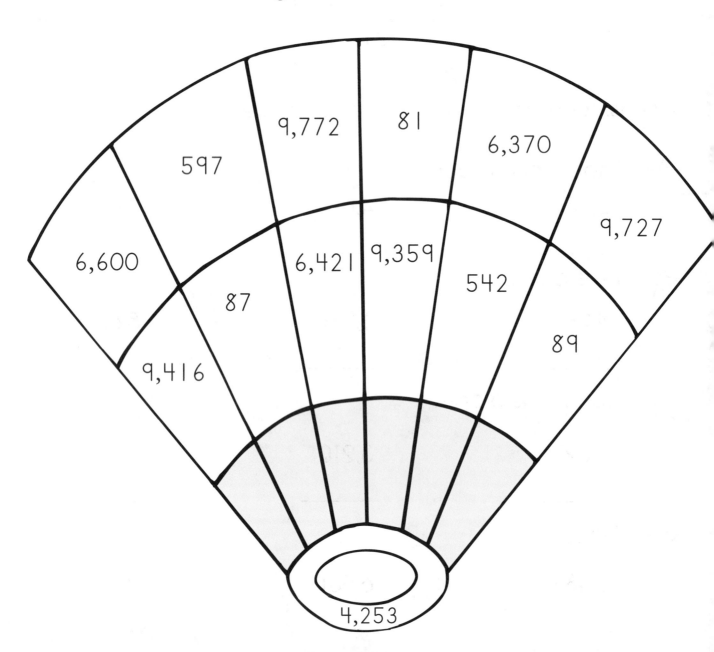

Name _____

Graphs

A graph is a drawing that shows information about numbers.

Directions: Count the apples in each row. Color the boxes to show how many apples have bites taken out of them.

Example:

1	2	3	4	5	6	7	8

Name _____

Graphs

Directions: Count the bananas in each row. Color the boxes to show how many have been eaten by the monkeys.

Graphs

Directions: Count the fish. Color the bowls to make a graph that shows the number of fish.

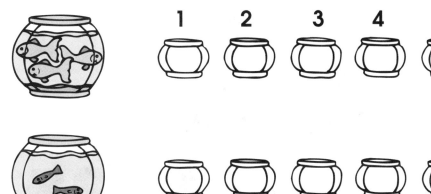

Directions: Use your fishbowl graphs to find the answers to the following questions. Draw a line to the correct bowl.

The most fish

The fewest fish

Name _____

Multiplication

Multiplication is a short way to find the sum of adding the same number a certain amount of times. For example, **4 x 7 = 28** instead of **7 + 7 + 7 + 7 = 28**.

Directions: Study the example. Solve the problems.

Example:

3 + 3 + 3 = 9
3 threes = 9
3 x 3 = 9

7 + 7 = __14__
2 sevens = __14__
2 x 7 = __14__

4 + 4 + 4 + 4 = ____
4 fours = ____
4 x ____ = ____

5 + 5 = ____
2 fives = ____
2 x ____ = ____

2 + 2 + 2 + 2 = ____
4 twos = ____
4 x ____ = ____

6 + 6 = ____
2 sixes = ____
2 x ____ = ____

Name _____

Multiplication

Multiplication is repeated addition.

Directions: Draw a picture for each problem. Then write the missing numbers.

Example:

Draw 2 groups of three apples.

$3 + 3 = 6$

or $2 \times 3 = 6$

Draw 3 groups of four hearts.	Draw 2 groups of five boxes.
 $4 + 4 + 4 =$ ____ or $3 \times$ ____ $=$ ____	$5 +$ ____ $=$ ____ or $2 \times$ ____ $=$ ____

Draw 6 groups of two circles.

$2 +$ ____ $+$ ____ $+$ ____ $+$ ____ $+$ ____ $=$ ____

or $6 \times$ ____ $=$ ____

Draw 7 groups of three triangles.

$3 +$ ____ $+$ ____ $+$ ____ $+$ ____ $+$ ____ $+$ ____ $=$ ____

or   ____ $\times$ ____ $=$ ____

Multiplication

Directions: Study the example. Draw the groups and write the total.

Example:

3×2

$2 + 2 + 2 = \rightarrow \underline{6}$

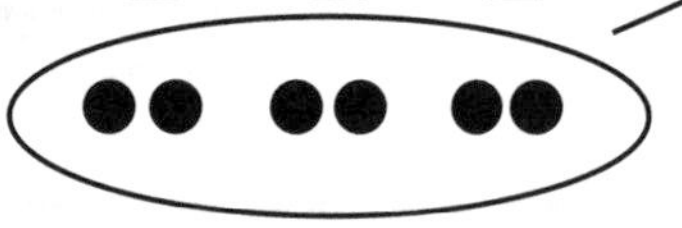

(●● ●● ●●)

3×4

___ + ___ + ___ = _____

2×5

____ + ____ = _____

5×3

___ + ___ + ___ + ___ + ___ = _____

Name _____

Multiplication

Directions: Solve the problems.

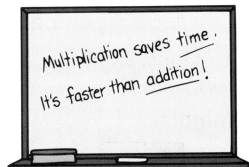

Multiplication saves time. It's faster than addition!

9 + 9 = __18__   7 + 7 = ____

2 nines = ____   2 sevens = ____

2 x 9 = ____   2 x __7__ = ____

4 + 4 + 4 + 4 = ____   8 + 8 + 8 + 8 + 8 = ____

__4__ fours = ____   ____ eights = ____

____ x 4 = ____   ____ x 8 = ____

5 + 5 + 5 = ____   9 + 9 = ____   6 + 6 + 6 = ____

____ fives = ____   ____ nines = ____   ____ sixes = ____

____ x 5 = ____   ____ x 9 = ____   ____ x 6 = ____

3 + 3 = ____   7 + 7 + 7 + 7 = ____   2 + 2 = ____

____ threes = ____   ____ sevens = ____   ____ twos = ____

____ x 3 = ____   ____ x 7 = ____   ____ x 2 = ____

Name _____

Fractions: Half, Third, Fourth

A fraction is a number that names part of a whole, such as $\frac{1}{2}$ or $\frac{1}{3}$.

Directions: Study the examples. Color the correct fraction of each shape.

Examples:

shaded part   1
equal parts   2
$\frac{1}{2}$ (one-half) shaded

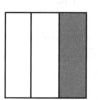

shaded part   1
equal parts   3
$\frac{1}{3}$ (one-third) shaded

shaded part   1
equal parts   4
$\frac{1}{4}$ (one-fourth) shaded

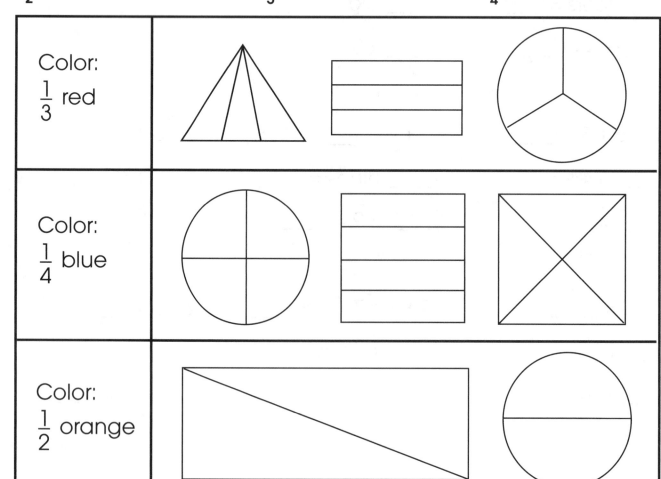

Color:
$\frac{1}{3}$ red

Color:
$\frac{1}{4}$ blue

Color:
$\frac{1}{2}$ orange

Name _____

Fractions: Half, Third, Fourth

Directions: Study the examples. Circle the fraction that shows the shaded part. Then circle the fraction that shows the white part.

Examples:

shaded $\frac{1}{4}$ $\frac{1}{3}$ ⓪$\frac{1}{2}$ white $\frac{1}{3}$ ⓪$\frac{1}{2}$ $\frac{1}{4}$

shaded $\frac{1}{2}$ ⓪$\frac{2}{3}$ $\frac{3}{4}$ white $\frac{2}{3}$ $\frac{1}{2}$ ⓪$\frac{1}{3}$

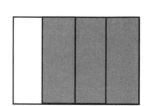

shaded $\frac{1}{4}$ $\frac{1}{2}$ ⓪$\frac{3}{4}$ white ⓪$\frac{1}{4}$ $\frac{2}{3}$ $\frac{1}{2}$

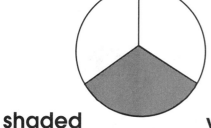

shaded $\frac{1}{4}$ $\frac{1}{3}$ $\frac{1}{2}$ white $\frac{2}{4}$ $\frac{2}{3}$ $\frac{2}{2}$

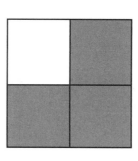

shaded $\frac{3}{4}$ $\frac{1}{3}$ $\frac{3}{2}$ white $\frac{1}{2}$ $\frac{1}{4}$ $\frac{1}{3}$

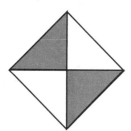

shaded $\frac{2}{3}$ $\frac{2}{4}$ $\frac{2}{2}$ white $\frac{1}{3}$ $\frac{2}{4}$ $\frac{2}{2}$

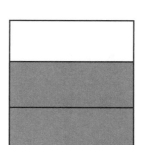

shaded $\frac{2}{4}$ $\frac{2}{3}$ $\frac{2}{2}$ white $\frac{1}{2}$ $\frac{1}{4}$ $\frac{1}{3}$

Fractions: Half, Third, Fourth

Directions: Draw a line from the fraction to the correct shape.

$\frac{1}{4}$ shaded

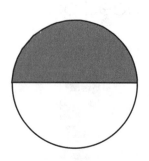

$\frac{2}{4}$ shaded

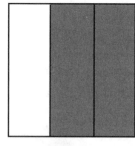

$\frac{1}{2}$ shaded

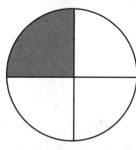

$\frac{1}{3}$ shaded

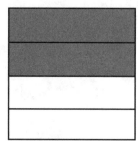

$\frac{2}{3}$ shaded

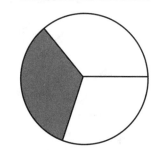

Geometry

Geometry is mathematics that has to do with lines and shapes.

Directions: Color the shapes.

Color the triangles blue.
Color the circles red.
Color the squares green.
Color the rectangles pink.

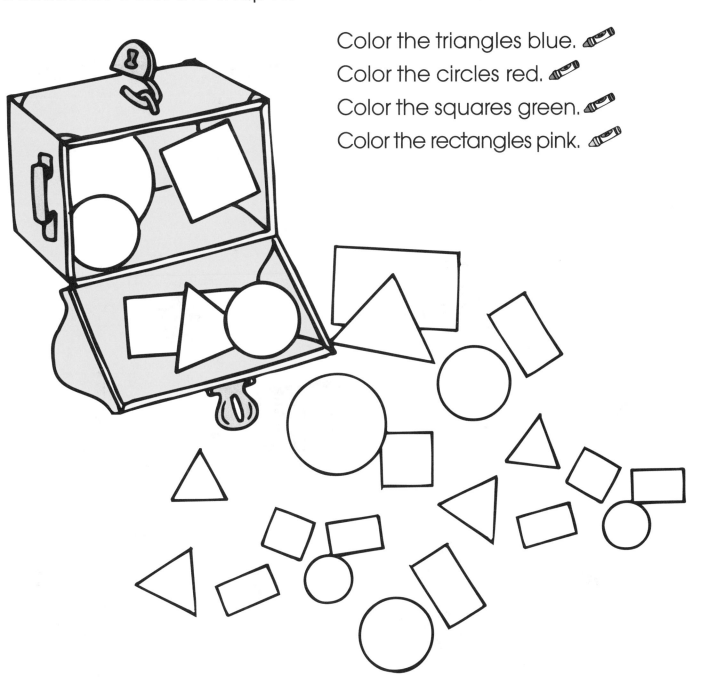

Name _____

Geometry

Directions: Draw a line from the word to the shape.

Use a red line for circles. Use a yellow line for rectangles.
Use a blue line for squares. Use a green line for triangles.

Circle   **Square**   **Triangle**   **Rectangle**

Name _____

Geometry

Directions: Cut out the tangram below. Mix up the pieces. Try to put it back together into a square.

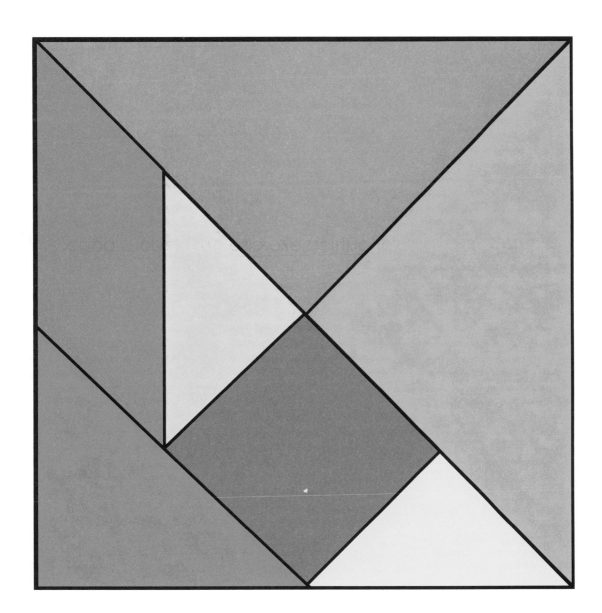

Page is blank for cutting exercise on previous page.

Measurement: Inches

Directions: Cut out the ruler. Measure each object to the nearest inch.

_____ inches

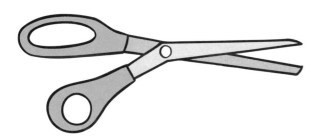

_____ inches

_____ inches

Measurement

Directions: Measure objects around your house. Write the measurement to the nearest inch.

can of soup   _____ inches

pen   _____ inches

toothbrush   _____ inches

paper clip   _____ inches

small toy   _____ inches

cut out

8
7
6
5
4
3
2
1

Page is blank for cutting exercise on previous page.

Measurement: Inches

An inch is a unit of length in the standard measurement system.

Directions: Use a ruler to measure each object to the nearest inch.

1 inch

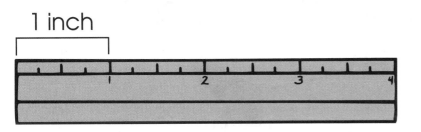

about __1__ inches

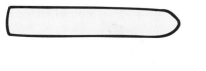

about _____ inches

about _____ inches

about _____ inches

about _____ inches

about _____ inches

about _____ inches

Name _____

Measurement: Inches

Directions: Use the ruler to measure the fish to the nearest inch.

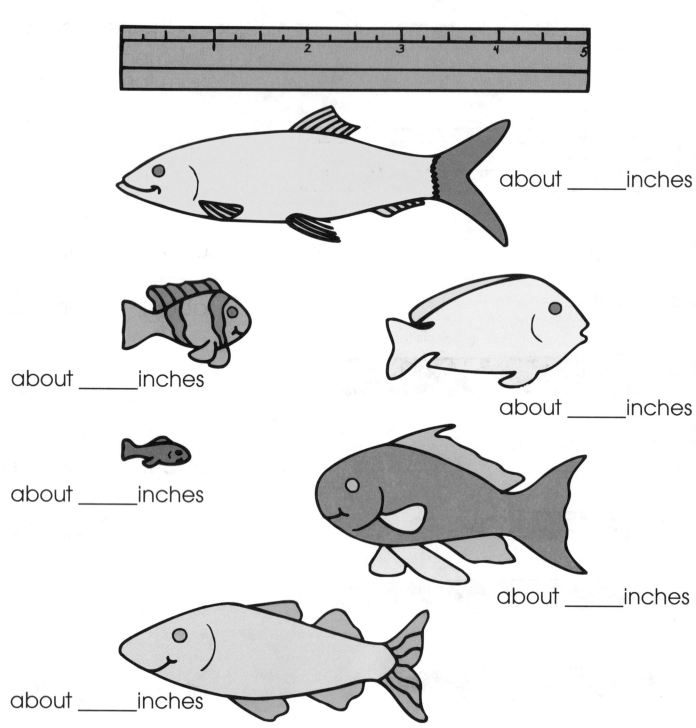

about _____ inches

about _____ inches

about _____ inches

about _____ inches

about _____ inches

about _____ inches

Measurement: Centimeters

A centimeter is a unit of length in the metric system. There are 2.54 centimeters in an inch.

Directions: Use a centimeter ruler to measure the crayons to the nearest centimeter.

Example: The first crayon is about 7 centimeters long.

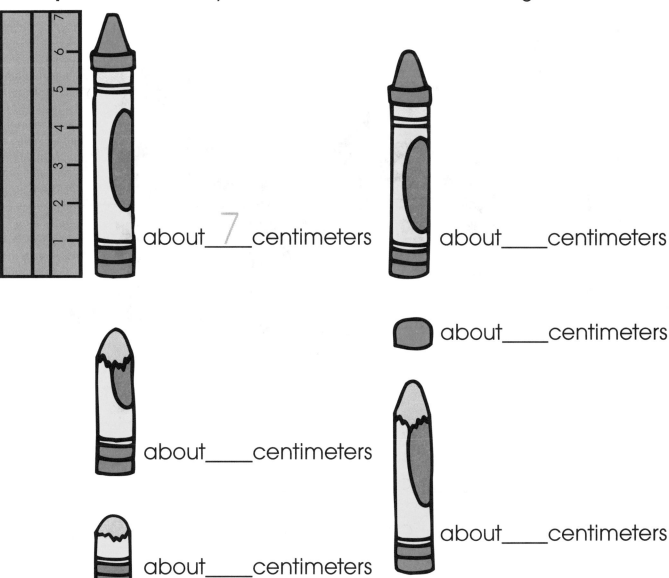

about__7__centimeters

about____centimeters

about____centimeters

about____centimeters

about____centimeters

about____centimeters

Name _____

Measurement: Centimeters

Directions: The giraffe is about 8 centimeters high. How many centimeters (cm) high are the trees? Write your answers in the blanks.

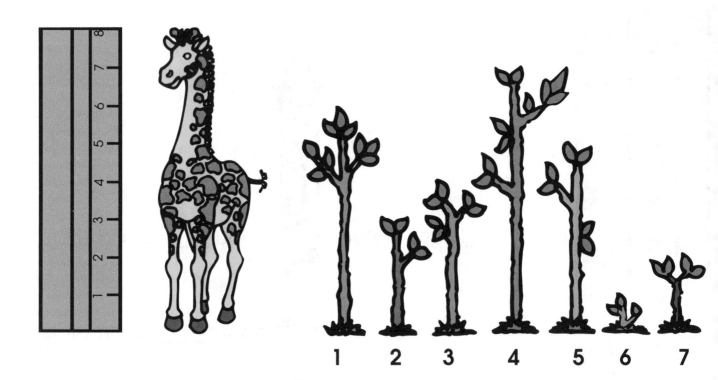

1   2   3   4   5   6   7

1)_____cm   2)_____cm   3)_____cm

4)_____cm   5)_____cm   6)_____cm   7)_____cm

Time: Hour, Half-Hour

An hour is sixty minutes. The short hand of a clock tells the hour. It is written **0:00**, such as **5:00**. A half-hour is thirty minutes. When the long hand of the clock is pointing to the six, the time is on the half-hour. It is written **:30**, such as **5:30**.

Directions: Study the examples. Tell what time it is on each clock.

Examples:

 9:00

The minute hand is on the 12.
The hour hand is on the 9.
It is 9 o'clock.

 4:30

The minute hand is on the 6.
The hour hand is *between* the 4 and 5.
It is 4:30.

_____ _____ _____ _____ _____

_____ _____ _____ _____ _____

Name _____

Time: Hour, Half-Hour

Directions: Draw lines between the clocks that show the same time.

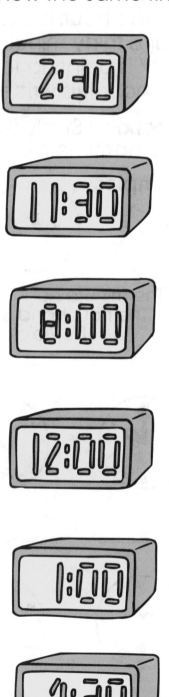

280

Math

Name _____

Time: Counting by 5's

The minute hand of a clock takes 5 minutes to move from one number to the next. Start at the 12 and count by fives to tell how many minutes it is past the hour.

Directions: Study the examples. Tell what time is on each clock.

Examples:

 9:10

 8:25

_____   _____   _____

_____   _____   _____

_____   _____   _____

Time: Quarter-Hours

Time can also be shown as fractions. 30 minutes = $\frac{1}{2}$ hour.

Directions: Shade the fraction of each clock and tell how many minutes you have shaded.

Example: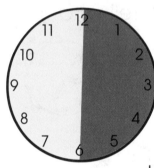

$\frac{1}{2}$ hour

__30__ minutes

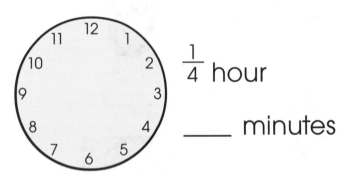

$\frac{1}{4}$ hour

___ minutes

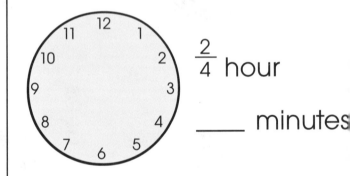

$\frac{2}{4}$ hour

___ minutes

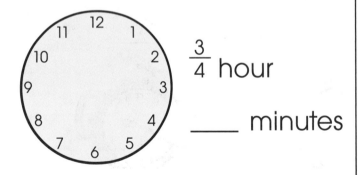

$\frac{3}{4}$ hour

___ minutes

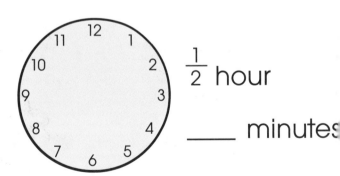

$\frac{1}{2}$ hour

___ minutes

Ma

Name _____

Review
Counting

Directions: Write the number that is:

next	one less	one greater
68, 69, ____	____ , 57	12, ____
786, 787, ____	____ , 650	843, ____

Place Value: Tens & Ones

Directions: Draw a line to the correct number.

4 tens + 7 ones   20

2 tens + 0 ones   51

7 tens + 3 ones   47

5 tens + 1 one   73

Addition and Subtraction

Directions: Add or subtract.

$$\begin{array}{cc} & 15 \\ + & 5 \\ \hline \end{array} \qquad \begin{array}{cc} & 14 \\ - & 4 \\ \hline \end{array} \qquad \begin{array}{cc} & 7 \\ + & 3 \\ \hline \end{array} \qquad \begin{array}{cc} & 8 \\ - & 6 \\ \hline \end{array} \qquad \begin{array}{cc} & 10 \\ + & 7 \\ \hline \end{array} \qquad \begin{array}{cc} & 14 \\ - & 5 \\ \hline \end{array}$$

Name _____

Review

2-Digit Addition and Subtraction

Directions: Add or subtract using regrouping, if needed.

66 - 37	38 + 18	87 - 69	52 - 15	40 + 17
84 + 17	65 + 14	99 - 48	61 - 36	56 + 46

Place Value: Hundreds and Thousands

Directions: Draw a line to the correct number.

4 hundreds + 3 tens + 2 ones   7,201

6 hundreds + 7 tens + 6 ones   290

5 thousands + 3 hundreds + 7 tens + 2 ones   432

2 hundreds + 9 tens + 0 ones   676

7 thousands + 2 hundreds + 0 tens + 1 one   5,372

3-Digit Addition and Subtraction

Directions: Add or subtract, remembering to regroup, if needed.

458 - 248	793 - 414	822 - 460	528 + 319	697 + 108	569 + 288

Name _____

Review

Multiplication

Directions: Solve the problems. Draw groups if necessary.

$$\begin{array}{r} 2 \\ \times\,8 \\ \hline \end{array} \qquad \begin{array}{r} 6 \\ \times\,4 \\ \hline \end{array} \qquad \begin{array}{r} 3 \\ \times\,2 \\ \hline \end{array} \qquad \begin{array}{r} 8 \\ \times\,4 \\ \hline \end{array} \qquad \begin{array}{r} 5 \\ \times\,3 \\ \hline \end{array} \qquad \begin{array}{r} 2 \\ \times\,2 \\ \hline \end{array}$$

Fractions

Directions: Circle the correct fraction of each shape's white part.

$\dfrac{1}{2}$ $\dfrac{1}{3}$ $\dfrac{1}{4}$

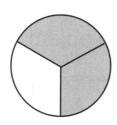

$\dfrac{1}{4}$ $\dfrac{1}{3}$ $\dfrac{1}{2}$

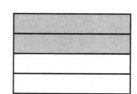

$\dfrac{2}{3}$ $\dfrac{2}{4}$ $\dfrac{1}{3}$

$\dfrac{1}{4}$ $\dfrac{1}{2}$ $\dfrac{3}{4}$

Graphs

Directions: Count the flowers. Color the pots to make a graph that shows the number of flowers.

1   2   3   4   5   6   7   8

Name _____

Review

Geometry

Directions: Match the shapes.

rectangle

square

circle

triangle

Measurement

Directions: Look at the ruler. Measure the objects to the nearest inch.

1   2   3   4   5

_____ inches

_____ inches

CRAYON

_____ inches

Time

Directions: Tell what time is on each clock.

_____   _____   _____   _____

Money: Penny, Nickel

Penny **1¢**   Nickel **5¢**

Directions: Count the coins and write the amount.

Example:

_____ 8 _____ ¢

5¢   1¢   1¢   1¢

_____ ¢

_____ ¢

_____ ¢

_____ ¢

Name _____

Money: Penny, Nickel, Dime

Penny **1¢**   Nickel **5¢**   Dime **10¢**

Directions: Count the coins and write the amount.

_____16_____ ¢

_____ ¢

_____ ¢

_____ ¢

_____ ¢

Name _____

Money: Penny, Nickel, Dime

Directions: Draw a line from the toy to the amount of money it costs.

Name _____

Money: Penny, Nickel, Dime

Directions: Draw a line to match the amounts of money.

Name _____

Money: Quarter

A quarter is worth 25¢.

Directions: Count the coins and write the amounts.

 _____ ¢

   _____ ¢

  _____ ¢

   _____ ¢

   _____ ¢

  _____ ¢

    _____ ¢

   _____ ¢

Name _____

Money: Decimal

A decimal is a number with one or more places to the right of a decimal point, such as 6.5 or 2.25. Money amounts are written with two places to the right of the decimal point.

| 25¢ | 10¢ | 5¢ | 1¢ |
| $.25 | $.10 | $.05 | $.01 |

Directions: Count the coins and circle the amount shown.

Example:

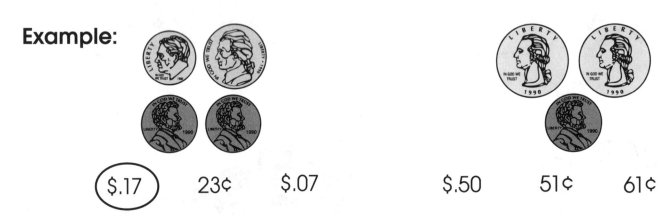

($.17)   23¢ $.07 $.50   51¢   61¢

$.28   36¢   42¢

37¢   43¢ $.47

Name _____

Money: Decimal

Directions: Draw a line from the coins to the correct amount in each column.

3¢ $.55

55¢ $.41

31¢ $.37

37¢ $.31

41¢ $.03

Name _____

Money: Dollar

One dollar equals 100 cents. It is written $1.00.

Directions: Count the money and write the amounts.

 $____.____

 $____.____

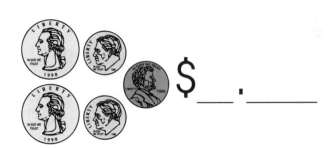 $____.____

 $____.____

 $____.____

 $____.____

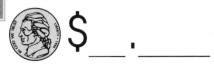 $____.____

 $____.____

Name _____

Adding Money

Directions: Write the amount of money using decimals. Then add to find the total amount.

Example:

$$
\begin{array}{r}
\$1.00 \\
.05 \\
+ \ \ .02 \\
\hline
\$1.07
\end{array}
$$

$ ___ . ___
$ ___ . ___
$ ___ . ___
+$ ___ . ___
_____
___ . ___

$ ___ . ___
$ ___ . ___
$ ___ . ___
+$ ___ . ___
_____
___ . ___

$ ___ . ___
$ ___ . ___
+$ ___ . ___
_____
___ . ___

$ ___ . ___
$ ___ . ___
$ ___ . ___
+$ ___ . ___
_____
___ . ___

Money: Practice

Directions: Draw a line from each food item to the correct amount of money.

$1.59

$.89

$1.27

$1.09

$.77

$1.95

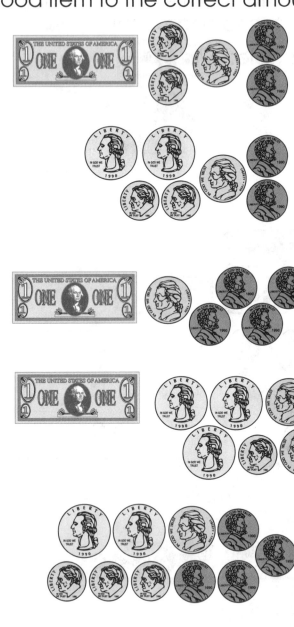

Name _____

Review

Directions: Add the money and write the total.

 _____ ¢

 _____ ¢

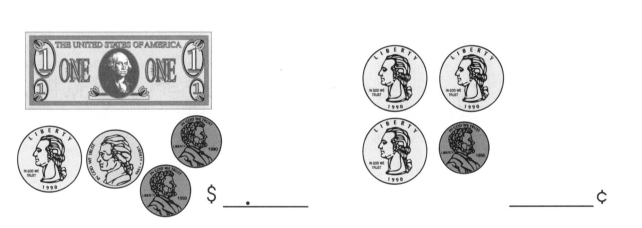

$ ___ . ___

_____ ¢

$ ___ . ___

Name _____

Problem-Solving

Directions: Tell whether you should add or subtract. "In all" is a clue to add. "Left" is a clue to subtract. Draw pictures to help you.

Example:

Jane's dog has 5 bones. He ate 3 bones. How many bones are left?

subtract

$$\begin{array}{r} 5 \\ \boxed{} - 3 \\ \hline 2 \end{array} \text{ bones}$$

Lucky the cat had 5 mice. She got 4 more for her birthday. How many mice did she have in all?

_____

$\boxed{}$

_____ mice

Sam bought 6 fish. She gave 2 fish to a friend. How many fish does she have left?

_____

$\boxed{}$

_____ fish

Name _____

Problem-Solving: Addition, Subtraction, Multiplication

Directions: Tell if you add, subtract or multiply. Then write the answer.

Example:
There were 12 frogs sitting on a log by a pond, but 3 frogs hopped away. How many frogs are left?

__Subtract__ ___9___ frogs

There are 9 flowers growing by the pond.
Each flower has 2 leaves.
How many leaves are there?

_____ _____ leaves

A tree had 7 squirrels playing in it.
Then 8 more came along.
How many squirrels are there in all?

_____ _____ squirrels

There were 27 birds living in the trees around the pond, but 9 flew away.
How many birds are left?

_____ _____ birds

Name _____

Problem-Solving: Fractions

A fraction is a number that names part of a whole, such as $\frac{1}{2}$ or $\frac{1}{3}$

Directions: Read each problem. Use the pictures to help you solve the problem. Write the fraction that answers the question.

Simon and Jessie shared a pizza.
Together they ate $\frac{3}{4}$ of the pizza.
How much of the pizza is left?   _____

Sylvia baked a cherry pie. She gave $\frac{1}{3}$
to her grandmother and $\frac{1}{3}$ to a friend.
How much of the pie did she keep?   _____

Timmy erased $\frac{1}{2}$ of the blackboard
before the bell rang for recess.
How much of the blackboard does
he have left to erase?   _____

Directions: Read the problem. Draw your own picture to help you solve the problem. Write the fraction that answers the question.

Sarah mowed $\frac{1}{4}$ of the yard before lunch.
How much does she have left to mow?   _____

Name _____

Problem-Solving: Time

Directions: Solve each problem.

Tracy wakes up at 7:00. She has 30 minutes before her bus comes. What time does her bus come?

_____ : _____

Vera walks her dog for 15 minutes after supper. She finishes supper at 6:30. When does she get home from walking her dog?

_____ : _____

Chip practices the piano for 30 minutes when he gets home from school. He gets home at 3:30. When does he stop practicing?

_____ : _____

Tanya starts mowing the grass at 4:30. She finishes at 5:00. For how many minutes does she mow the lawn?

_____ minutes

Don does his homework for 45 minutes. He starts his work at 7:15. When does he stop working?

_____ : _____

Name _____

Problem-Solving: Money

Directions: Read each problem. Use the pictures to help you solve the problems.

Ben bought a ball. He had 11¢ left.
How much money did he have at the start?

_____ ¢

Tara has 75¢. She buys a car.
How much money does she have left?

_____ ¢

Leah wants to buy a doll and a ball. She has 80¢.
How much more money does she need?

_____ ¢

Jacob has 95¢. He buys the car and the ball.
How much more money does he need to
buy a doll for his sister?

_____ ¢

Kim paid three quarters, one dime
and three pennies for a hat.
How much did it cost?

_____ ¢

Page 6

All About Me!

Directions: Fill in the blanks to tell all about you!

Name __Answers will vary.__
(First)   (Last)

Address _____

City _____ State _____

Phone number _____

Age _____

Places I have visited: __Answers will vary.__
_____
_____
_____

My favorite vacation: __Answers will vary.__
_____
_____
_____

Page 7

Review: Beginning Consonants: b, c, d, f, g, h, j
Directions: Fill in the beginning consonant for each word.

Example: __c__ at

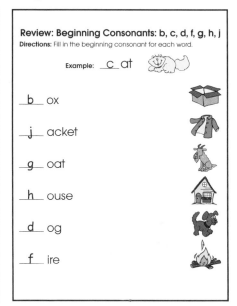

__b__ ox

__j__ acket

__g__ oat

__h__ ouse

__d__ og

__f__ ire

Page 8

Beginning Consonants: k, l, m, n, p, q, r
Directions: Write the letter that makes the beginning sound for each picture.

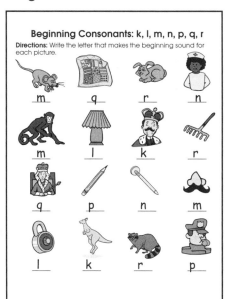

m	q	r	n
m	l	k	r
q	p	n	m
l	k	r	p

Page 9

Beginning Consonants: s, t, v, w, x, y, z
Directions: Write the letter under each picture that makes the beginning sound.

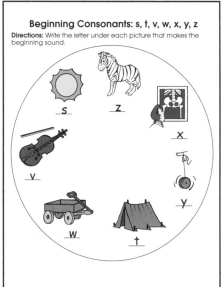

s   z

x

v   y

w   t

Page 10

Ending Consonants: b, d, f, g
Directions: Fill in the ending consonants for each word.

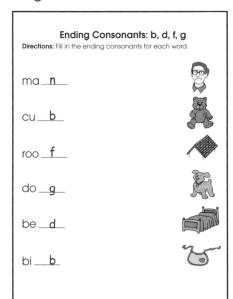

ma __n__

cu __b__

roo __f__

do __g__

be __d__

bi __b__

Page 11

Ending Consonants: k, l, m, n, p, r

Directions: Fill in the ending consonant for each word.

nai __l__

ca __n__

gu __m__

ca __r__

truc __k__

ca __p__

pai __l__

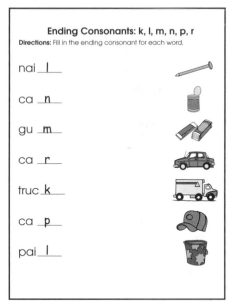

Page 12

Ending Consonants: s, t, x

Directions: Fill in the ending consonant for each word.

ca __t__

bo __x__

bu __s__

fo __x__

boa __t__

ma __t__

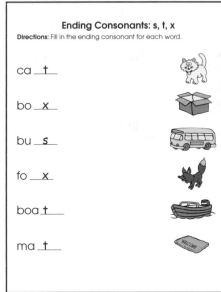

Page 13

Consonant Blends

Consonant blends are two or three consonant letters in a word whose sounds combine, or blend. **Examples:** br, fr, gr, pr, tr

Directions: Look at each picture. Say its name. Write the blend you hear at the beginning of each word.

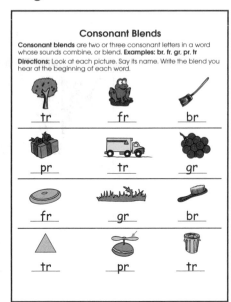

tr	fr	br
pr	tr	gr
fr	gr	br
tr	pr	tr

Page 14

Blends: fl, br, pl, sk, sn

Blends are two consonants put together to form a single sound.

Directions: Look at the pictures and say their names. Write the letters for the beginning sound in each word.

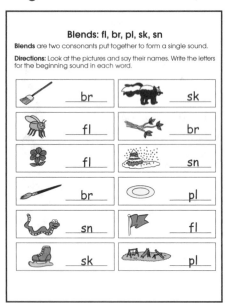

br		sk	
fl		br	
fl		sn	
br		pl	
sn		fl	
sk		pl	

Page 15

Blends: bl, sl, cr, cl

Directions: Look at the pictures and say their names. Write the letters for the beginning sound in each word.

__cl__ own   __bl__ anket   __cr__ ayon

__cl__ ock   __sl__ ide   __cl__ oud

__sl__ ed   __cr__ ab   __cr__ ocodile

Page 16

Consonant Teams

Consonant teams are two or three consonant letters that have a single sound. **Examples:** sh and tch

Directions: Write each word from the word box next to its picture. Underline the consonant team in each word. Circle the consonant team in each word in the box.

ben(ch)	ma(tch)	s(h)oe	(th)imble
s(h)ell	bru(sh)	pea(ch)	wa(tch)
w(h)ale	tee(th)	c(h)air	w(h)eel

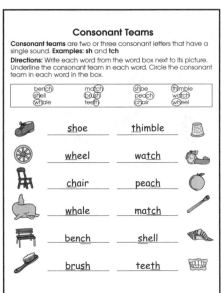

shoe	thimble
wheel	watch
chair	peach
whale	match
bench	shell
brush	teeth

Page 17

Consonant Teams

Directions: Read the words in the box. Write a word from the word box to finish each sentence. Circle the consonant team in each word. **Hint:** There are three letters in each team!

| splash | screen | spray | street | scream |
| screw | shrub | split | strong | string |

1. Another word for a bush is a __(shrub)__ .
2. I tied a __(string)__ to my tooth to help pull it out.
3. I have many friends who live on my __(street)__ .
4. We always __(scream)__ when we ride the roller coaster.
5. A __(screen)__ helps keep bugs out of the house.
6. It is fun to __(splash)__ in the water.
7. My father uses an ax to __(split)__ the firewood.
8. We will need a __(screw)__ to fix the chair.
9. You must be very __(strong)__ to lift this heavy box.
10. The firemen __(spray)__ the fire with water.

Page 18

Letter Teams: sh, ch, wh, th

Directions: Look at the first picture in each row. Circle the pictures that have the same sound.

whistle

shoe

chin

thumb

Page 19

Silent Letters

Some words have letters you can't hear at all, such as the **gh** in **night**, the **w** in **wrong**, the **l** in **walk**, the **k** in **knee**, the **b** in **climb** and the **t** in **listen**.

Directions: Look at the words in the word box. Write the word under its picture. Underline the silent letters.

| knife | light | calf | wrench | lamb | eight |
| wrist | whistle | comb | thumb | knob | knee |

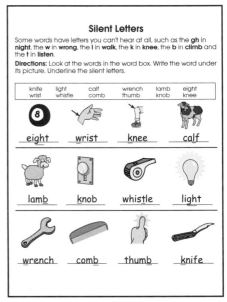

eight   wrist   knee   calf

lamb   knob   whistle   light

wrench   comb   thumb   knife

Page 20

Hard and Soft c

When **c** is followed by **e**, **i** or **y**, it usually has a **soft** sound. The **soft c** sounds like **s**. For example, **c**ircle and fen**c**e. When **c** is followed by **a** or **u**, it usually has a **hard** sound. The **hard c** sounds like **k**.

Example: **c**up and **c**art

Directions: Read the words in the word box. Write the words in the correct lists. Write a word from the word box to finish each sentence.

		pencil	cookie
		dance	cent
		popcorn	circus
		lucky	mice
		tractor	card

Words with soft c
pencil
dance
cent
mice
circus

Words with hard c
circus
popcorn
lucky
tractor
cookie
card

1. Another word for a penny is a __cent__ .
2. A cat likes to chase __mice__ .
3. You will see animals and clowns at the __circus__ .
4. Will you please sharpen my __pencil__ ?

Page 21

Hard and Soft g

When **g** is followed by **e**, **i** or **y**, it usually has a **soft** sound. The **soft g** sounds like **j**. **Example:** **g**entle and **g**entle. The **hard g** sounds like the **g** in **g**irl or **g**ate.

Directions: Read the words in the word box. Write the words in the correct lists. Write a word from the box to finish each sentence.

| engine | glove | cage | magic | frog |
| giant | flag | large | glass | goose |

Words with soft g
engine
giant
cage
large
magic

Words with hard g
glove
flag
glass
frog
goose

1. Our bird lives in a __cage__ .
2. Pulling a rabbit from a hat is a good __magic__ trick.
3. A car needs an __engine__ to run.
4. A __giant__ is a huge person.
5. An elephant is a very __large__ animal.

Page 22

Short Vowels

Vowels can make **short** or **long** sounds. The short **a** sounds like the **a** in **cat**. The short **e** is like the **e** in **leg**. The short **i** sounds like the **i** in **pig**. The short **o** sounds like the **o** in **box**. The short **u** sounds like the **u** in **cup**.

Directions: Look at each picture. Write the missing short vowel letter.

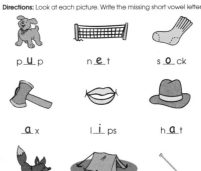

p_u_p   n_e_t   s_o_ck

_a_x   l_i_ps   h_a_t

f_o_x   t_e_nt   p_i_n

Page 23

Short Vowels

Vowels can make **short** or **long** sounds. The short **a** sounds like the **a** in **cat**. The short **e** is like the **e** in **leg**. The short **i** sounds like the **i** in **pig**. The short **o** sounds like the **o** in **box**. The short **u** is like the **u** in **cup**.

Directions: Look at the pictures. Their names all have short vowel sounds. But the vowels are missing! Fill in the missing vowels in each word.

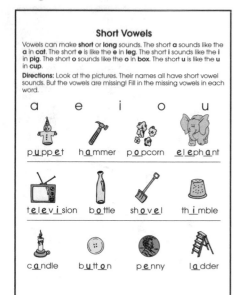

a   e   i   o   u

p_u_pp_e_t   h_a_mmer   p_o_pcorn   el_e_ph_a_nt

t_e_lev_i_sion   b_o_ttle   sh_o_vel   th_i_mble

c_a_ndle   b_u_tt_o_n   p_e_nny   l_a_dder

Page 24

Super Silent e

Long vowel sounds have the same sound as their names. When a **Super Silent e** appears at the end of a word, you can't hear it, but it makes the other vowel have a long sound. For example: **tub** has a **short** vowel sound, and **tube** has a **long** vowel sound.

Directions: Look at the following pictures. Decide if the word has a short or long vowel sound. Circle the correct word. Watch for the **Super Silent e**!

can (cane)   (tub) tube   rob (robe)   (rat) rate

(pin) pine   (cap) cape   not (note)   (pan) pane

slid (slide)   dim (dime)   tap (tape)   cub (cube)

Page 25

Long Vowels

Long vowel sounds have the same sound as their names. When a **Super Silent e** comes at the end of a word, you can't hear it, but it changes the short vowel sound to a long vowel sound.

Example: rope, skate, bee, pie, cute

Directions: Say the name of the pictures. Listen for the long vowel sounds. Write the missing long vowel sound under each picture.

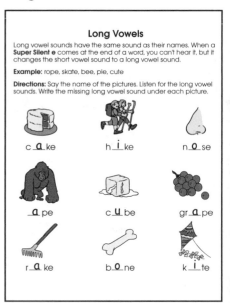

c_a_ke   h_i_ke   n_o_se

_a_pe   c_u_be   gr_a_pe

r_a_ke   b_o_ne   k_i_te

Page 26

R-Controlled Vowels

When a vowel is followed by the letter **r**, it has a different sound.

Example: he and her

Directions: Write a word from the word box to finish each sentence. Notice the sound of the vowel followed by an **r**.

park	chair	horse	bark	bird
hurt	girl	hair	store	ears

1. A dog likes to __bark__.
2. You buy food at a __store__.
3. Children like to play at the __park__.
4. An animal you can ride is a __horse__.
5. You hear with your __ears__.
6. A robin is a kind of __bird__.
7. If you fall down, you might get __hurt__.
8. The opposite of a boy is a __girl__.
9. You comb and brush your __hair__.
10. You sit down on a __chair__.

Page 27

R-Controlled Words

R-Controlled Words are words in which the **r** that comes after the vowel changes the sound of the vowel. **Examples:** bird, star, burn

Directions: Write the correct word in the sentences below.

horse	purple
jar	bird
dirt	turtle

1. Jelly comes in one of these. __jar__

2. This creature has feathers and can fly. __bird__

3. This animal lives in a shell. __turtle__

4. This animal can pull wagons. __horse__

5. If you mix water and this, you will have mud. __dirt__

6. This color starts with the letter **p**. __purple__

Page 28

Double Vowel Words

Usually when two vowels appear together, the first one says its name and the second one is silent.
Example: bean

Directions: Unscramble the double vowel words below. Write the correct word on the line.

 ocat __coat__   etar __tear__

mtea __meat__   eetf __feet__

teas __seat__   otab __boat__

ogat __goat__   spea __peas__

atli __tail__   apil __pail__

Page 29

Vowel Teams

The vowel teams **ou** and **ow** can have the same sound. You can hear it in the words **clown** and **cloud**. The vowel teams **au** and **aw** have the same sound. You hear it in the words **because** and **law**.

Directions: Look at the pictures. Write the correct vowel team to complete the words. The first one is done for you. You may need to use a dictionary to help you with the correct spelling.

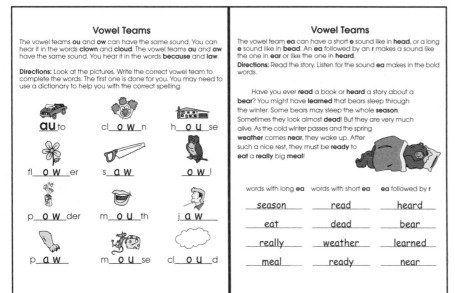

auto   cl**ow**n   h**ou**se

fl**ow**er   s**aw**   **ow**l

p**ow**der   m**ou**th   j**aw**

p**aw**   m**ou**se   cl**ou**d

Page 30

Vowel Teams

The vowel team **ea** can have a short **e** sound like in **head**, or a long **e** sound like in **bead**. An **ea** followed by an **r** makes a sound like the one in **ear** or like the one in **heard**.

Directions: Read the story. Listen for the sound **ea** makes in the bold words.

Have you ever **read** a book or **heard** a story about a **bear**? You might have **learned** that bears sleep through the winter. Some bears may sleep the whole **season**. Sometimes they look almost **dead**! But they are very much alive. As the cold winter passes and the spring **weather** comes **near**, they wake up. After such a nice rest, they must be **ready** to **eat** a **really** big **meal**!

words with long **ea**	words with short **ea**	**ea** followed by r
season	read	heard
eat	dead	bear
really	weather	learned
meal	ready	near

Page 31

Vowel Teams

The vowel team **ie** makes the long **e** sound like in **believe**. The team **ei** also makes the long **e** sound like in **either**. But **ei** can also make a long **a** sound like in **eight**.

Directions: Circle the **ei** words with the long **a** sound.

⬭neighbor⬭   ⬭veil⬭

receive   ⬭reindeer⬭

⬭reign⬭   ceiling

The teams **eigh** and **ey** also make the long **a** sound.

Directions: Finish the sentences with words from the word box.

chief	sleigh	obey	weigh	thief	field	ceiling

1. Eight reindeer pull Santa's _____ sleigh _____.
2. Rules are for us to _____ obey _____.
3. The bird got out of its cage and flew up to the _____ ceiling _____.
4. The leader of an Indian tribe is the _____ chief _____.
5. How much do you _____ weigh _____?
6. They caught the _____ thief _____ who took my bike.
7. Corn grows in a _____ field _____.

Page 32

Letter Teams: oi, oy, ou, ow

Directions: Look at the first picture in each row. Circle the pictures that have the same sound.

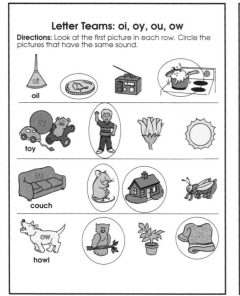

oil

toy

couch

howl

Page 33

Letter Teams: ai, ee

Directions: Write in the letter team **ai** or **ee** to complete each word.

r**ai**n   f**ee**d

s**ee**d   p**ai**l

s**ai**l   cr**ee**k

Page 34

Y as a Vowel

When **y** comes at the end of a word, it is a vowel. When **y** is the only vowel at the end of a one-syllable word, it has the sound of a long **i** (like in **my**). When **y** is the only vowel at the end of a word with more than one syllable, it has the sound of a long **e** (like in **baby**).

Directions: Look at the words in the word box. If the word has the sound of a long **i**, write it under the word **my**. If the word has the sound of a long **e**, write it under the word **baby**. Write the word from the word box that answers each riddle.

happy	penny	fry	try	sleepy	dry
bunny	why	windy	sky	party	fly

my	baby
why	happy
fry	bunny
try	penny
sky	windy
dry	sleepy
fly	party

1. It takes five of these to make a nickel.   penny
2. This is what you call a baby rabbit.   bunny
3. It is often blue and you can see it if you look up.   sky
4. You might have one of these on your birthday.   party
5. It is the opposite of wet.   dry
6. You might use this word to ask a question.   why

Page 35

Y as a Vowel

Directions: Read the rhyming story. Choose the words from the box to fill in the blanks.

Larry	Mary
money	funny
honey	bunny

_____Larry_____ and _____Mary_____ are friends. Larry is

selling _____honey_____. Mary needs _____money_____ to

buy the honey. "I want to feed it to my _____bunny_____," said

Mary. Larry laughed and said, "That is _____funny_____. Everyone

knows that bunnies do not eat honey."

Page 36

Y as a Vowel

Directions: Read the story. Choose the words from the box to fill in the blanks.

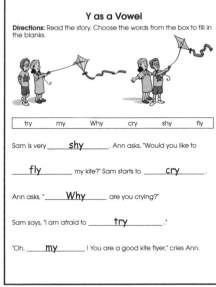

try	my	Why	cry	shy	fly

Sam is very _____shy_____. Ann asks, "Would you like to

_____fly_____ my kite?" Sam starts to _____cry_____.

Ann asks, "_____Why_____ are you crying?"

Sam says, "I am afraid to _____try_____."

"Oh, _____my_____! You are a good kite flyer," cries Ann.

Page 37

Days of the Week

Directions: Write the day of the week that answers each question.

Sunday	Monday	Tuesday
Wednesday	Thursday	Friday
	Saturday	

1. What is the first day of the week?
   _____Sunday_____

2. What is the last day of the week?
   _____Saturday_____

3. What day comes after Tuesday?
   _____Wednesday_____

4. What day comes between Wednesday and Friday?
   _____Thursday_____

5. What is the third day of the week?
   _____Tuesday_____

6. What day comes before Saturday?
   _____Friday_____

7. What day comes after Sunday?
   _____Monday_____

Page 38

Compound Words

Compound words are formed by putting together two smaller words.
Directions: Help the cook brew her stew. Mix words from the first column with words from the second column to make new words. Write your new words on the lines at the bottom.

grand	brows
snow	light
eye	stairs
down	string
rose	book
shoe	mother
note	ball
moon	bud

1. grandmother
2. snowball
3. eyebrows
4. downstairs
5. rosebud
6. shoestring
7. notebook
8. moonlight

Page 39

Compound Words

Compound words are two words that are put together to make one new word.

Directions: Read the sentences. Fill in the blank with a compound word from the box.

raincoat	bedroom	lunchbox	hallway	sandbox

1. A box with sand is a
   _____sandbox_____

2. The way through a hall is a
   _____hallway_____

3. A box for lunch is a
   _____lunchbox_____

4. A coat for the rain is a
   _____raincoat_____

5. A room with a bed is a
   _____bedroom_____

Page 40

Compound Words

Directions: Draw a line under the compound word in each sentence. On the line, write the two words that make up the compound word.

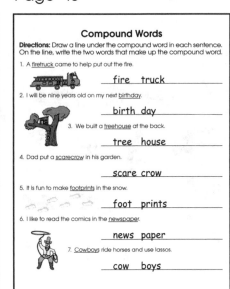

1. A firetruck came to help put out the fire.
   _____fire____truck_____

2. I will be nine years old on my next birthday.
   _____birth____day_____

3. We built a treehouse at the back.
   _____tree____house_____

4. Dad put a scarecrow in his garden.
   _____scare____crow_____

5. It is fun to make footprints in the snow.
   _____foot____prints_____

6. I like to read the comics in the newspaper.
   _____news____paper_____

7. Cowboys ride horses and use lassos.
   _____cow____boys_____

Page 41

Contractions

Contractions are a short way to write two words, such as **isn't, I've** and **weren't. Example: it is = it's**

Directions: Draw a line from each word pair to its contraction.

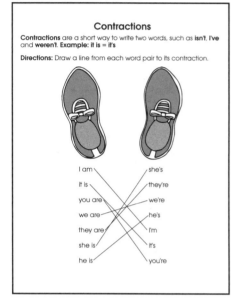

I am	she's
it is	they're
you are	we're
we are	he's
they are	I'm
she is	it's
he is	you're

Page 42

Contractions

Directions: Circle the contraction that would replace the underlined words.

Example: were not = weren't

1. The boy ___was not___ sad.
   (wasn't)   weren't

2. We ___were not___ working.
   wasn't   **(weren't)**

3. Jen and Caleb ___have not___ eaten lunch yet.
   (haven't)   hasn't

4. The mouse ___has not___ been here.
   haven't   **(hasn't)**

Page 43

Contractions

Directions: Match the words with their contractions.

would not	I've
was not	he'll
he will	wouldn't
could not	wasn't
I have	couldn't

Directions: Make the words at the end of each line into contractions to complete the sentences.

1. He ___didn't___ know the answer.   **did not**
2. ___It's___ a long way home.   **It is**
3. ___Here's___ my house.   **Here is**
4. ___We're___ not going to school today.   **We are**
5. ___They'll___ take the bus home tomorrow.   **They will**

Page 44

Syllables

Words are made up of parts called **syllables**. Each syllable has a vowel sound. One way to count syllables is to clap as you say the word.

Example: cat — 1 clap — 1 syllable
table — 2 claps — 2 syllables
butterfly — 3 claps — 3 syllables

Directions: "Clap out" the words below. Write how many syllables each word has.

movie	2	dog	1
piano	3	basket	2
tree	1	swimmer	2
bicycle	3	rainbow	2
sun	1	paper	2
cabinet	3	picture	2
football	2	run	1
television	4	enter	2

Page 45

Syllables

Dividing a word into syllables can help you read a new word. You also might divide syllables when you are writing if you run out of space on a line.
Many words contain two consonants that are next to each other. A word can usually be divided between the consonants.

Directions: Divide each word into two syllables. The first one is done for you.

kitten	kit	ten
lumber	lum	ber
batter	bat	ter
winter	win	ter
funny	fun	ny
harder	hard	er
dirty	dir	ty
sister	sis	ter
little	lit	tle
dinner	din	ner

Page 46

Syllables

One way to help you read a word you don't know is to divide it into parts called **syllables**. Every syllable has a vowel sound.

Directions: Say the words. Write the number of syllables. The first one is done for you.

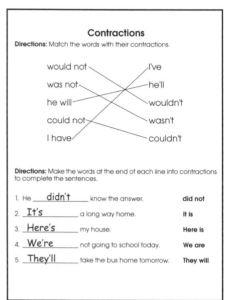

bird	1	rabbit	2
apple	2	elephant	3
balloon	2	family	3
basketball	3	fence	1
breakfast	2	ladder	2
block	1	open	2
candy	2	puddle	2
popcorn	2	Saturday	3
yellow	2	wind	1
understand	3	butterfly	3

Page 47

Syllables

When a double consonant is used in the middle of a word, the word can usually be divided between the consonants.

Directions: Look at the words in the word box. Divide each word into two syllables. Leave space between each syllable. One is done for you.

butter	puppy	kitten	yellow
dinner	chatter	ladder	happy
pillow	letter	mitten	summer

but ter	chat ter	mit ten
din ner	let ter	yel low
pil low	kit ten	hap py
pup py	lad der	sum mer

Many words are divided between two consonants that are not alike.

Directions: Look at the words in the word box. Divide each word into two syllables. One is done for you.

window	doctor	number	carpet
mister	winter	pencil	candle
barber	sister	picture	under

win dow	win ter	pic ture
mis ter	sis ter	car pet
bar ber	num ber	can dle
doc tor	pen cil	un der

Page 48

Syllables

Directions: Write 1 or 2 on the line to tell how many syllables are in each word. If the word has 2 syllables, draw a line between the syllables. **Example: sup|per**

dog	1	timber	2
bed|room	2	cat	1
slip|per	2	street	1
tree	1	chalk	1
bat|ter	2	blanket	2
chair	1	marker	2
fish	1	brush	1
mas|ter	2	rabbit	2

Page 49

Suffixes

A **suffix** is a syllable that is added at the end of a word to change its meaning.

Directions: Add the suffixes to the root words to make new words. Use your new words to complete the sentences.

help + ful =	helpful
care + less =	careless
build + er =	builder
talk + ed =	talked
love + ly =	lovely
loud + er =	louder

1. My mother __talked__ to my teacher about my homework.
2. The radio was __louder__ than the television.
3. Sally is always __helpful__ to her mother.
4. A __builder__ put a new garage on our house.
5. The flowers are __lovely__ .
6. It is __careless__ to cross the street without looking both ways.

Page 50

Suffixes

Adding **ing** to a word means that it is happening now. Adding **ed** to a word means it happened in the past.

Directions: Look at the words in the word box. Underline the root word in each one. Write a word to complete each sentence.

snowing	wished	played	looking	crying
talking	walked	eating	going	doing

1. We like to play. We __played__ yesterday.
2. Is that snow? Yes, it is __snowing__ .
3. Do you want to go with me? No, I am __going__ with my friend.
4. The baby will cry if we leave. The baby is __crying__ .
5. We will walk home from school. We __walked__ to school this morning.
6. Did you wish for a new bike? Yes, I __wished__ for one.
7. Who is going to do it while we are away? I am __doing__ it.
8. Did you talk to your friend? Yes, we are __talking__ now.
9. Will you look at my book? I am __looking__ at it now.
10. I like to eat pizza. We are __eating__ it today.

Page 51

Suffixes

Directions: Write a word from the word box next to its root word.

coming	running	sitting
lived	rained	swimming
visited	carried	racing
hurried		

run	running	come	coming
live	lived	carry	carried
hurry	hurried	race	racing
swim	swimming	rain	rained
visit	visited	sit	sitting

Directions: Write a word from the word box to finish each sentence.

1. I __visited__ my grandmother during vacation.
2. Mary went __swimming__ at the lake with her cousin.
3. Jim __carried__ the heavy package for his mother.
4. It __rained__ and stormed all weekend.
5. Cars go very fast when they are __racing__ .

Page 52

Suffixes

Directions: Read the story. Underline the words that end with **est**, **ed** or **ing**. On the lines below, write the root words for each word you underlined.

The <u>funni</u>est book I ever read was about a girl <u>named</u> Nan. Nan did everything backward. She even <u>spelled</u> her name backward. Nan slept in the day and <u>played</u> at night. She <u>dried</u> her hair before <u>washing</u> it. She <u>turned</u> on the light after she <u>finished</u> her book—which she read from the back to the front! When it <u>rained</u>, Nan <u>waited</u> until she was inside before <u>opening</u> her umbrella. She even <u>walked</u> backward. The <u>silli</u>est part: The only thing Nan did forward was back up!

1. __funny__ 6. __wash__ 11. __open__
2. __name__ 7. __turn__ 12. __walk__
3. __spell__ 8. __finish__ 13. __silly__
4. __play__ 9. __rain__
5. __dry__ 10. __wait__

Page 53

Prefixes: The Three R's

Prefixes are syllables added to the beginning of words that change their meaning. The prefix **re** means "again."

Directions: Read the story. Then follow the instructions.

Kim wants to find ways she can save the Earth. She studies the "three R's"—reduce, reuse and recycle. Reduce means to make less. Both reuse and recycle mean to use again.

Add **re** to the beginning of each word below. Use the new words to complete the sentences.

re	build	**re**	fill
re	read	**re**	tell
re	write	**re**	run

1. The race was a tie, so Dawn and Kathy had to _**rerun**_ it.
2. The block wall fell down, so Simon had to _**rebuild**_ it.
3. The water bottle was empty, so Luna had to _**refill**_ it.
4. Javier wrote a good story, but he wanted to _**rewrite**_ it to make it better.
5. The teacher told a story, and students had to _**retell**_ it.
6. Toni didn't understand the directions, so she had to _**reread**_ them.

Page 54

Prefixes

Directions: Read the story. Change Unlucky Sam to Lucky Sam by taking the **un** prefix off of the **bold** words.

Unlucky Sam

Sam was **unhappy** about a lot of things in his life. His parents were **uncaring**. His teacher was **unfair**. His big sister was **unkind**. His neighbors were **unfriendly**. He was **unhealthy**, too! How could one boy be as **unlucky** as Sam?

Lucky Sam

Sam was _**happy**_ about a lot of things in his life. His parents were _**caring**_. His teacher was _**fair**_. His big sister was _**kind**_. His neighbors were _**friendly**_. He was _**healthy**_, too! How could one boy be as _**lucky**_ as Sam?

Page 55

Prefixes

Directions: Change the meaning of the sentences by adding the prefixes to the **bold** words.

The boy was **lucky** because he guessed the answer **correctly**.

The boy was (un) _**unlucky**_ because he guessed the answer (in) _**incorrectly**_.

When Mary **behaved**, she felt **happy**.

When Mary (mis) _**misbehaved**_, she felt (un) _**unhappy**_.

Mike wore his jacket **buttoned** because the dance was **formal**.

Mike wore his jacket (un) _**unbuttoned**_ because the dance was (in) _**informal**_.

Tim **understood** because he was **familiar** with the book.

Tim (mis) _**misunderstood**_ because he was (un) _**unfamiliar**_ with the book.

Page 57

Parts of a Book

A book has many parts. The title is the name of the book. The author is the person who wrote the words. The illustrator is the person who drew the pictures. The table of contents is located at the beginning to list what is in the book. The glossary is a little dictionary in the back to help you with unfamiliar words. Books are often divided into smaller sections of information called chapters.

Directions: Look at one of your books. Write the parts you see below.

Answers will vary.

The title of my book is _____

The author is _____

The illustrator is _____

My book has a table of contents.   Yes or No

My book has a glossary.   Yes or No

My book is divided into chapters.   Yes or No

Page 58

Recalling Details: Nikki's Pets

Directions: Read about Nikki's pets. Then answer the questions.

Nikki has two cats, Tiger and Sniffer, and two dogs, Spot and Wiggles. Tiger is an orange striped cat who likes to sleep under a big tree and pretend she is a real tiger. Sniffer is a gray cat who likes to sniff the flowers in Nikki's garden. Spot is a Dalmatian with many black spots. Wiggles is a big furry brown dog who wiggles all over when he is happy.

1. Which dog is brown and furry? _**Wiggles**_
2. What color is Tiger? _**orange with stripes**_
3. What kind of dog is Spot? _**Dalmation**_
4. Which cat likes to sniff flowers? _**Sniffer**_
5. Where does Tiger like to sleep? _**under a big tree**_
6. Who wiggles all over when he is happy? _**Wiggles**_

Page 59

Reading for Details

Directions: Read the story about baby animals. Answer the questions with words from the story.

Baby cats are called kittens. They love to play and drink lots of milk. A baby dog is a puppy. Puppies chew on old shoes. They run and bark. A lamb is a baby sheep. Lambs eat grass. A baby duck is called a duckling. Ducklings swim with their wide, webbed feet. Foals are baby horses. A foal can walk the day it is born! A baby goat is a kid. Some people call children kids, too!

1. A baby cat is called a ___kitten___
2. A baby dog is a ___puppy___
3. A ___lamb___ is a baby sheep.
4. ___Ducklings___ swim with their webbed feet.
5. A ___foal___ can walk the day it is born.
6. A baby goat is a ___kid___

Page 60

Reading for Details

Directions: Read the story about bike safety. Answer the questions below the story.

Mike has a red bike. He likes his bike. Mike wears a helmet. Mike wears knee pads and elbow pads. They keep him safe. Mike stops at signs. Mike looks both ways. Mike is safe on his bike.

1. What color is Mike's bike? ___red___
2. Which sentence in the story tells why Mike wears pads and a helmet? Write it here.
   ___They keep him safe.___
3. What else does Mike do to keep safe?
   He ___stops___ at signs and ___looks___ both ways.

Page 61

Following Directions

Directions: Read the story. Answer the questions. Try the recipe.

Cows Give Us Milk

Cows live on a farm. The farmer milks the cow to get milk. Many things are made from milk. We make ice cream, sour cream, cottage cheese and butter from milk. Butter is fun to make! You can learn to make your own butter. First, you need cream. Put the cream in a jar and shake it. Then you need to pour off the liquid. Next, you put the butter in a bowl. Add a little salt and stir! Finally, spread it on crackers and eat!

1. What animal gives us milk? ___cow___
2. What 4 things are made from milk?
   ___ice cream___ ___sour cream___ ___cottage cheese___ ___butter___
3. What did the story teach you to make? ___butter___
4. Put the steps in order. Place 1, 2, 3, 4 by the sentence.
   __4__ Spread the butter on crackers and eat!
   __2__ Shake cream in a jar.
   __1__ Start with cream.
   __3__ Add salt to the butter.

Page 62

Following Directions: How to Treat a Ladybug

Directions: Read about how to treat ladybugs. Then follow the instructions.

Ladybugs are shy. If you see a ladybug, sit very still. Hold out your arm. Maybe the ladybug will fly to you. If it does, talk softly. Do not touch it. It will fly away when it is ready.

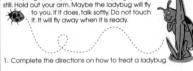

1. Complete the directions on how to treat a ladybug.
   a. Sit very still.
   b. ___Hold out your arm.___
   c. Talk softly.
   d. ___Do not touch it.___
2. Ladybugs are red. They have black spots. Color the ladybug.

Page 63

Sequencing: Packing Bags

Directions: Read about packing bags. Then number the objects in the order they should be packed.

Cans are heavy. Put them in first. Then put in boxes. Now, put in the apple. Put the bread in last.

3	1
2	4

Page 64

Sequencing: Story Events

Spencer likes to make new friends. Today, he made friends with the dog in the picture.

Directions: Number the sentences in order to find out what Spencer did today.

__3__ Spencer kissed his mother good-bye.
__5__ Spencer saw the new dog next door.
__4__ Spencer went outside.
__6__ Spencer said hello.
__2__ Spencer got dressed and ate breakfast.
__1__ Spencer woke up.

Page 65

Sequencing: Yo-Yo Trick

Directions: Read about the yo-yo trick.

Wind up the yo-yo string. Hold the yo-yo in your hand. Now, hold your palm up. Throw the yo-yo downward on the string. Hold your palm down. Now, swing the yo-yo forward. Make it "walk." This yo-yo trick is called "walk the dog."

Directions: Number the directions in order.

___3___ Swing the yo-yo forward and make it "walk."

___1___ Hold your palm up and drop the yo-yo.

___2___ Turn your palm down as the yo-yo reaches the ground.

Page 66

Following Directions

Here is a recipe for chocolate peanut butter cookies. When you use a recipe, you must follow the directions carefully. The sentences below are not in the correct order.

Directions: Write number 1 to show what you would do first. Then number each step to show the correct sequence.

___1___ Melt the chocolate almond bark in a microsafe bowl.

___6___ Eat!

___2___ While the chocolate is melting, spread peanut butter on a cracker and place another cracker on top.

___4___ Let the melted candy drip off the cracker into the bowl before you place it on wax paper.

___5___ Let it cool!

___3___ Carefully use a fork or spoon to dip the crackers into the melted chocolate.

Try the recipe with an adult.

Do you like to cook? __Answers will vary.__

Page 67

Sequencing: Story Events

Mari was sick yesterday.

Directions: Number the events in 1, 2, 3 order to tell the story about Mari.

_2_ She went to the doctor's office.

_9_ Mari felt much better.

_1_ Mari felt very hot and tired.

_6_ Mari's mother went to the drugstore.

_4_ The doctor wrote down something.

_3_ The doctor looked in Mari's ears.

_7_ Mari took a pill.

_5_ The doctor gave Mari's mother the piece of paper.

_8_ Mari drank some water with her pill.

Page 68

Sequencing: Making Clay

Directions: Read about making clay. Then follow the instructions.

It is fun to work with clay. Here is what you need to make it:

1 cup salt
2 cups flour
3/4 cup water

Mix the salt and flour. Then add the water. DO NOT eat the clay. It tastes bad. Use your hands to mix and mix. Now, roll it out. What can you make with your clay?

1. Circle the main idea:

   Do not eat clay.

   ⟨Mix salt, flour and water to make clay.⟩

2. Write the steps for making clay.

   a. __Mix the salt and flour.__

   b. __Add the water.__

   c. Mix the clay.

   d. __Roll it out.__

3. Write why you should not eat clay. __It tastes bad.__

Page 69

Sequencing: A Visit to the Zoo

Directions: Read the story. Then follow the instructions.

One Saturday morning in May, Gloria and Anna went to the zoo. First, they bought tickets to get into the zoo. Second, they visited the Gorilla Garden and had fun watching the gorillas stare at them. Then they went to Tiger Town and watched the tigers as they slept in the sunshine. Fourth, they went to Hippo Haven and laughed at the hippos cooling off in their pool. Next, they visited Snake Station and learned about poisonous and nonpoisonous snakes. It was noon, and they were hungry, so they ate lunch at the Parrot Patio.

Write **first**, **second**, **third**, **fourth**, **fifth** and **sixth** to put the events in order.

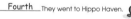

__Fourth__ They went to Hippo Haven.

__First__ Gloria and Anna bought zoo tickets.

__Third__ They watched the tigers sleep.

__Sixth__ They ate lunch at Parrot Patio.

__Second__ The gorillas stared at them.

__Fifth__ They learned about poisonous and nonpoisonous snakes.

Page 70

Same/Different: Stuffed Animals

Kate and Oralia like to collect and trade stuffed animals.

Directions: Draw two stuffed animals that are alike and two that are different.

Alike

Different

Answers will vary.

Page 71

Same/Different: Shell Homes

Directions: Read about shells. Then answer the questions.

Shells are the homes of some animals. Snails live in shells on the land. Clams live in shells in the water. Clam shells open. Snail shells stay closed. Both shells keep the animals safe.

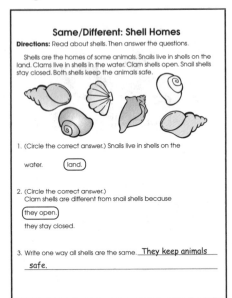

1. (Circle the correct answer.) Snails live in shells on the

   water.   (land.)

2. (Circle the correct answer.)
   Clam shells are different from snail shells because

   (they open.)

   they stay closed.

3. Write one way all shells are the same. __They keep animals__
   __safe.__

Page 72

Same/Different: Venn Diagram

A **Venn diagram** is a diagram that shows how two things are the same and different.

Directions: Choose two outdoor sports. Then follow the instructions to complete the Venn diagram.

1. Write the first sport name under the first circle. Write some words that describe the sport. Write them in the first circle.

2. Write the second sport name under the second circle. Write some words that describe the sport. Write them in the circle.

3. Where the 2 circles overlap, write some words that describe both sports.

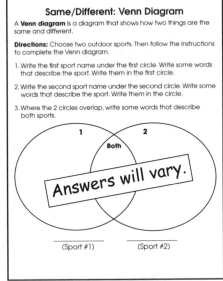

Answers will vary.

(Sport #1)   (Sport #2)

Page 73

Same/Different: Dina and Dina

Directions: Read the story. Then complete the Venn diagram, telling how Dina, the duck, is the same or different than Dina, the girl.

One day in the library, Dina found a story about a duck named Dina!

My name is Dina. I am a duck, and I like to swim. When I am not swimming, I walk on land or fly. I have two feet and two eyes. My feathers keep me warm. Ducks can be different colors. I am gray, brown and black. I really like being a duck. It is fun.

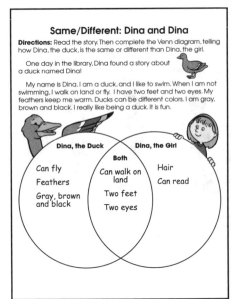

Dina, the Duck	Both	Dina, the Girl
Can fly	Can walk on land	Hair
Feathers	Two feet	Can read
Gray, brown and black	Two eyes	

Page 74

Same/Different: Cats and Tigers

Directions: Read about cats and tigers. Then complete the Venn diagram, telling how they are the same and different.

Tigers are a kind of cat. Pet cats and tigers both have fur. Pet cats are small and tame. Tigers are large and wild.

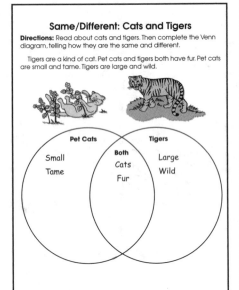

Pet Cats	Both	Tigers
Small	Cats	Large
Tame	Fur	Wild

Page 75

Same/Different: Bluebirds and Parrots

Directions: Read about parrots and bluebirds. Then complete the Venn diagram, telling how they are the same and different.

Bluebirds and parrots are both birds. Bluebirds and parrots can fly. They both have beaks. Parrots can live inside a cage. Bluebirds must live outdoors.

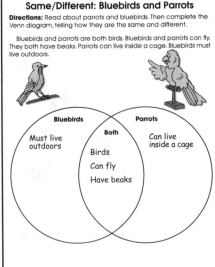

Bluebirds	Both	Parrots
Must live outdoors	Birds	Can live inside a cage
	Can fly	
	Have beaks	

Page 76

Similes

A **simile** is a figure of speech that compares two different things. The words **like** or **as** are used in similes.

Directions: Draw a line to the picture that goes with each set of words.

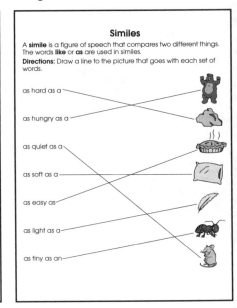

as hard as a

as hungry as a

as quiet as a

as soft as a

as easy as

as light as a

as tiny as an

Page 77

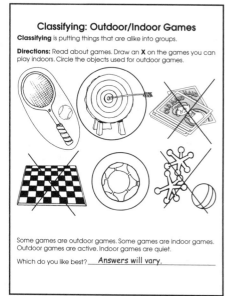

Classifying: Outdoor/Indoor Games

Classifying is putting things that are alike into groups.

Directions: Read about games. Draw an **X** on the games you can play indoors. Circle the objects used for outdoor games.

Some games are outdoor games. Some games are indoor games. Outdoor games are active. Indoor games are quiet.

Which do you like best? __Answers will vary.__

Page 78

Classifying

Classifying is putting similar things into groups.
Directions: Write each word from the word box on the correct line.

baby	donkey	whale	family	fox
uncle	goose	grandfather	kangaroo	policeman

people

baby

family

grandfather

policeman

uncle

animals

goose

whale

fox

kangaroo

donkey

Page 79

Classifying: Animals

Directions: Use a red crayon to circle the names of three animals that would make good pets. Use a blue crayon to circle the names of three wild animals. Use an orange crayon to circle the two animals that live on a farm.

BEAR CAT LION SHEEP BIRD DOG COW TIGER

```
A M E O W W N L I O N
B M D O G G X I I S O
A B E A R R V L M H R
R M R M O O U S E E K
K C A B B I R D S E M
I O T T I G E R M P Q
B W N O W W R Q N E N
D N C P H H I D U D N
F K C A T T R O A R M
```

Page 80

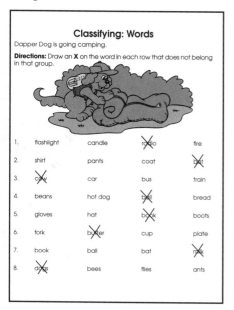

Classifying: Words

Dapper Dog is going camping.

Directions: Draw an **X** on the word in each row that does not belong in that group.

1.	flashlight	candle	~~radio~~	fire
2.	shirt	pants	coat	~~hat~~
3.	~~cow~~	car	bus	train
4.	beans	hot dog	~~ball~~	bread
5.	gloves	hat	~~book~~	boots
6.	fork	~~butter~~	cup	plate
7.	book	ball	bat	~~milk~~
8.	~~dogs~~	bees	flies	ants

Page 81

Classifying: Animal Habitats

Directions: Read the story. Then write each animal's name under **Water** or **Land** to tell where it lives.

Animals live in different habitats. A habitat is the place of an animal's natural home. Many animals live on land and others live in water. Most animals that live in water breathe with gills. Animals that live on land breathe with lungs.

fish	shrimp	giraffe	dog
cat	eel	whale	horse
bear	deer	shark	jellyfish

WATER
1. fish
2. shrimp
3. eel
4. whale
5. shark
6. jellyfish

LAND
1. cat
2. bear
3. deer
4. giraffe
5. dog
6. horse

Page 82

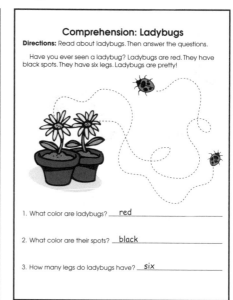

Comprehension: Ladybugs

Directions: Read about ladybugs. Then answer the questions.

Have you ever seen a ladybug? Ladybugs are red. They have black spots. They have six legs. Ladybugs are pretty!

1. What color are ladybugs? __red__

2. What color are their spots? __black__

3. How many legs do ladybugs have? __six__

Page 83

Comprehension: Types of Tops

The **main idea** is the most important point or idea in a story.

Directions: Read about tops. Then answer the questions.

Tops come in all sizes. Some tops are made of wood. Some tops are made of tin. All tops do the same thing. They spin! Do you have a top?

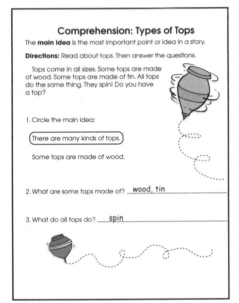

1. Circle the main idea:

   [There are many kinds of tops.]

   Some tops are made of wood.

2. What are some tops made of? __wood, tin__

3. What do all tops do? __spin__

Page 84

Comprehension: Singing Whales

Directions: Read about singing whales. Then follow the instructions.

Some whales can sing! We cannot understand the words. But we can hear the tune of the humpback whale. Each season, humpback whales sing a different song.

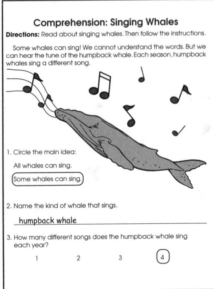

1. Circle the main idea:

   All whales can sing.

   [Some whales can sing.]

2. Name the kind of whale that sings.

   __humpback whale__

3. How many different songs does the humpback whale sing each year?

   1   2   3   (4)

Page 85

Comprehension: Sea Horses Look Strange!

Directions: Read about sea horses. Then answer the questions.

Sea horses are fish, not horses. A sea horse's head looks like a horse's head. It has a tail like a monkey's tail. A sea horse looks very strange!

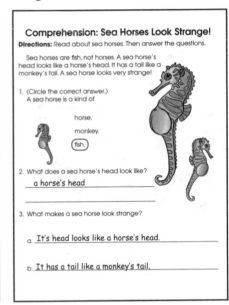

1. (Circle the correct answer.)
   A sea horse is a kind of

   horse.

   monkey.

   (fish.)

2. What does a sea horse's head look like?

   __a horse's head__

3. What makes a sea horse look strange?

   a. __It's head looks like a horse's head.__

   b. __It has a tail like a monkey's tail.__

Page 86

Comprehension: How to Stop a Dog Fight

Directions: Read about how to stop a dog fight. Then answer the questions.

Sometimes dogs fight. They bark loudly. They may bite. Do not try to pull apart fighting dogs. Turn on a hose and spray them with water. This will stop the fight.

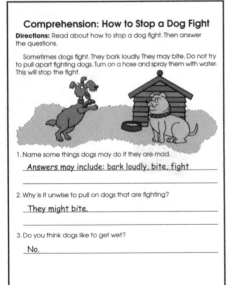

1. Name some things dogs may do if they are mad.

   __Answers may include: bark loudly, bite, fight__

2. Why is it unwise to pull on dogs that are fighting?

   __They might bite.__

3. Do you think dogs like to get wet?

   __No.__

Page 87

Comprehension: How to Meet a Dog

Directions: Read about how to meet a dog. Then follow the instructions.

Do not try to pet a dog right away. First, let the dog sniff your hand. Do not move quickly. Do not talk loudly. Just let the dog sniff.

1. Predict what the dog will let you do if it likes you.

   __Pet it.__

2. What should you let the dog do? __Sniff your hand.__

3. Name three things you should not do when you meet a dog.

   1) __try to pet it__

   2) __move quickly__

   3) __talk loudly__

Page 88

Comprehension: Pretty Parrots

Directions: Read about parrots. Then follow the instructions.

Big parrots are pretty. Their feet have four toes each. Two toes are in front. Two toes are in back. Parrots use their feet to climb. They use them to hold food.

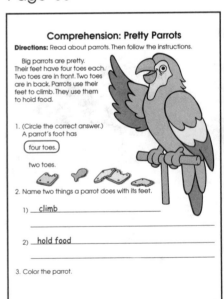

1. (Circle the correct answer.)
   A parrot's foot has

   (four toes.)

   two toes.

2. Name two things a parrot does with its feet.

   1) __climb__

   2) __hold food__

3. Color the parrot.

Page 89

Comprehension: The Puppet Play

Directions: Read the play out loud with a friend. Then answer the questions.

Pip: Hey, Pep. What kind of turkey eats very fast?

Pep: Uh, I don't know.

Pip: A gobbler!

Pep: I have a good joke for you, Pip. What kind of burger does a polar bear eat?

Pip: Uh, a cold burger?

Pep: No, an iceberg-er!

Pip: Hey, that was a great joke!

1. Who are the characters in the play? __Pip and Pep__

2. Who are the jokes about? __animals__

3. What are the characters in the play doing? __telling jokes__

Page 90

Comprehension: Snakes!

Directions: Read about snakes. Then answer the questions.

There are many facts about snakes that might surprise someone. A snake's skin is dry. Most snakes are shy. They will hide from people. Snakes eat mice and rats. They do not chew them up. Snakes' jaws drop open to swallow their food whole.

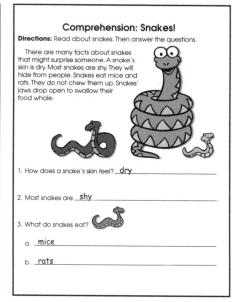

1. How does a snake's skin feel? __dry__

2. Most snakes are __shy__ .

3. What do snakes eat?

   a. __mice__

   b. __rats__

Page 91

Comprehension: Sean's Basketball Game

Directions: Read about Sean's basketball game. Then answer the questions.

Sean really likes to play basketball. One sunny day, he decided to ask his friends to play basketball at the park, but there were six people—Sean, Aki, Lance, Kate, Zac and Oralia. A basketball team only allows five to play at a time. So, Sean decided to be the coach. Sean and his friends had fun.

1. How many kids wanted to play basketball? __six__

2. Write their names in ABC order:

   __Aki__   __Lance__   __Sean__

   __Kate__   __Oralia__   __Zac__

3. How many players can play on a basketball team

   at a time? __five__

4. Where did they play basketball? __at the park__

5. Who decided to be the coach? __Sean__

Page 92

Comprehension: Amazing Ants

Directions: Read about ants. Then answer the questions.

Ants are insects. Ants live in many parts of the world and make their homes in soil, sand, wood and leaves. Most ants live for about 6 to 10 weeks. But the queen ant, who lays the eggs, can live for up to 15 years.

The largest ant is the bulldog ant. This ant can grow to be 5 inches long, and it eats meat! The bulldog ant can be found in Australia.

1. Where do ants make their homes? __in soil, sand, wood__
   __and leaves__

2. How long can a queen ant live? __up to 15 years__

3. What is the largest ant? __bulldog ant__

4. What does it eat? __meat__

Page 93

Comprehension: Fish

Directions: Read about fish. Then follow the instructions.

Some fish live in warm water. Some live in cold water. Some fish live in lakes. Some fish live in oceans. There are 20,000 kinds of fish!

1. Name two types of water in which fish live.

   a. __warm water__

   b. __cold water__

2. Name another place fish live __Answers may include: fish__
   __tank, ponds__
   Some fish live in lakes and some live in __oceans__

3. There are __20,000__ kinds of fish.

Page 94

Predicting: A Rainy Game

Predicting is telling what is likely to happen based on the facts.

Directions: Read the story. Then check each sentence below that tells how the story could end.

One cloudy day, Juan and his baseball team, the Bears, played the Crocodiles. It was the last half of the fifth inning, and it started to rain. The coaches and umpires had to decide what to do.

__✓__ They kept playing until nine innings were finished.

__✓__ They ran for cover and waited until the rain stopped.

_____ Each player grabbed an umbrella and returned to the field to finish the game.

__✓__ They canceled the game and played it another day.

_____ They acted like crocodiles and slid around the wet bases.

_____ The coaches played the game while the players sat in the dugout.

Page 95

Predicting: Dog Derby

Directions: Read the story. Then answer the questions.

Marcy had a great idea for a game to play with her dogs, Marvin and Mugsy. The game was called "Dog Derby." Marcy would stand at one end of the driveway and hold on to the dogs by their collars. Her friend Mitch would stand at the other end of the driveway. When he said, "Go!" Marcy would let go of the dogs and they would race to Mitch. The first one there would get a dog biscuit. If there was a tie, both dogs would get a biscuit.

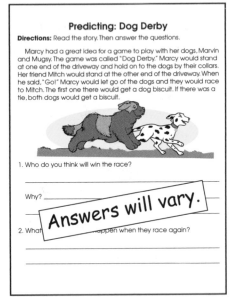

1. Who do you think will win the race?

Why? _____

Answers will vary.

2. What _____ happen when they race again?
_____

Page 96

Predicting: Dog-Gone!

Directions: Read the story. Then follow the instructions.

Scotty and Simone were washing their dog, Willis. His fur was wet. Their hands were wet. Willis did NOT like to be wet. Scotty dropped the soap. Simone picked it up and let go of Willis. Uh-oh!

1. Write what happened next.
_____
_____

2. Draw ...

Answers and drawings will vary.

Page 97

Predicting Outcome

Directions: Read the story. Complete the story in the last box.

1. "Look at that elephant! He sure is big!"

3. "Stop, Amy! Look at that sign!"

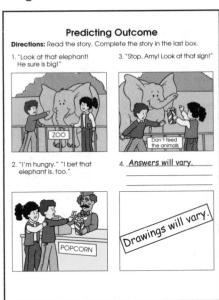

2. "I'm hungry." "I bet that elephant is, too."

4. **Answers will vary.**
_____

Drawings will vary.

Page 98

Predicting Outcomes

Directions: Complete the story. Then draw pictures to match the four parts.

1. Sylvia and Marge are flying a kite.

3. **Answers will vary.**

Drawings will vary.

Middle

2. T... 4. **Answers will vary.**

Middle   End

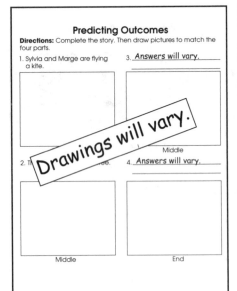

Page 99

Predicting Outcome

Kelly and Gina always have fun at the fair.

Directions: Read the sentences. Write what you think will happen next.

1. Kelly and Gina are riding the Ferris wheel. It stops when they are at the top.
_____

2. As they walk into the anim... ...rds them.

Answers will vary.

3. Snow c... ...their favorite way to cool off. The ones they bought are made from real snow.
_____

4. They play a "toss the ring over the bottle" game, but when the ring goes around the bottle, it disappears.
_____

Page 100

Fact and Opinion: Games!

A **fact** is something that can be proven. An **opinion** is a feeling or belief about something and cannot be proven.

Directions: Read these sentences about different games. Then write **F** next to each fact and **O** next to each opinion.

O 1. Tennis is cool!

F 2. There are red and black markers in a Checkers game.

F 3. In football, a touchdown is worth six points.

O 4. Being a goalie in soccer is easy.

F 5. A yo-yo moves on a string.

O 6. June's sister looks like the queen on the card.

F 7. The six kids need three more players for a baseball team.

O 8. Table tennis is more fun than court tennis.

F 9. Hide-and-Seek is a game that can be played outdoors or indoors.

F 10. Play money is used in many board games.

Page 101

Fact and Opinion: Recycling

Directions: Read about recycling. Then follow the instructions.

What do you throw away every day? What could you do with these things? You could change an old greeting card into a new card. You could make a puppet with an old paper bag. Old buttons make great refrigerator magnets. You can plant seeds in plastic cups. Cardboard tubes make perfect rockets. So, use your imagination!

1. Write **F** next to each fact and **O** next to each opinion.

O Cardboard tubes are ugly.

F Buttons can be made into refrigerator magnets.

F An old greeting card can be changed into a new card.

O Paper-bag puppets are cute.

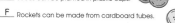

F Seeds can be planted in plastic cups.

F Rockets can be made from cardboard tubes.

2. What could you do with a cardboard tube? __Make a rocket.__

Page 102

Fact and Opinion: An Owl Story

Directions: Read the story. Then follow the instructions.

My name is Owen Owl, and I am a bird. I go to Nocturnal School. Our teacher is Mr. Screech Owl. In his class I learned that owls are birds and can sleep all day and hunt at night. Some of us live in nests in trees. In North America, it is against the law to harm owls. I like being an owl!

Write **F** next to each fact and **O** next to each opinion.

F 1. No one can harm owls in North America.

O 2. It would be great if owls could talk.

F 3. Owls sleep all day.

F 4. Some owls sleep in nests.

O 5. Mr. Screech Owl is a good teacher.

F 6. Owls are birds.

O 7. Owen Owl would be a good friend.

F 8. Owls hunt at night.

O 9. Nocturnal School is a good school for smart owls.

O 10. This story is for the birds.

Page 103

Fact and Opinion: Henrietta the Humpback

Directions: Read the story. Then follow the instructions.

My name is Henrietta, and I am a humpback whale. I live in cold seas in the summer and warm seas in the winter. My long flippers are used to move forward and backward. I like to eat fish. Sometimes, I show off by leaping out of the water. Would you like to be a humpback whale?

Write **F** next to each fact and **O** next to each opinion.

O 1. Being a humpback whale is fun.

F 2. Humpback whales live in cold seas during the summer.

O 3. Whales are fun to watch.

F 4. Humpback whales use their flippers to move forward and backward.

O 5. Henrietta is a great name for a whale.

O 6. Leaping out of water would be hard.

F 7. Humpback whales like to eat fish.

F 8. Humpback whales show off by leaping out of the water.

Page 104

Making Inferences: Ryan's Top

Directions: Read about Ryan's top. Then follow the instructions.

Ryan got a new top. He wanted to place it where it would be safe. He asked his dad to put it up high. Where can his dad put the top?

1. Write where Ryan's dad can put the top. __Answers may include:__

__on top of the refrigerator, on a closet shelf__

Draw a place Ryan's dad can put the top.

Drawings will vary.

Page 105

Making Inferences: Down on the Ant Farm

Directions: Read about ant farms. Then answer the questions.

Ants are busy on the farm. They dig in the sand. They make roads in the sand. They look for food in the sand. When an ant dies, other ants bury it.

1. Where do you think ants are buried? __in the sand__

2. Is it fair to say ants are lazy? __no__

3. Write a word that tells about ants. __Answers may include: busy, hard-working__

Page 106

Making Inferences

Directions: Read the story. Then answer the questions.

Jeff is baking cookies. He wears special clothes when he bakes. He puts flour, sugar, eggs and butter into a bowl. He mixes everything together. He puts the cookies in the oven at 11:15 A.M. It takes 15 minutes for the cookies to bake. Jeff wants something cold and white to drink when he eats his cookies.

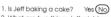

1. Is Jeff baking a cake?   Yes (No)

2. What are two things Jeff might wear when he bakes?
(hat)   boots   (apron)   tie   raincoat   roller skates

3. What didn't Jeff put in the cookies?
flour   eggs   (milk)   butter   sugar

4. What do you think Jeff does after he mixes the cookies but before he bakes them? __Answers may include: rolling dough into small balls or dropping dough from a teaspoon onto a cookie sheet.__

5. What time will the cookies be done? __11:30 a.m.__

6. What will Jeff drink with his cookies? __milk__

7. Why do you think Jeff wanted to bake cookies? _____
__Answers will vary.__

Page 107

Making Inferences

Directions: Read the story. Then answer the questions.

Mrs. Sweet looked forward to a visit from her niece, Candy. In the morning, she cleaned her house. She also baked a cherry pie. An hour before Candy was to arrive, the phone rang. Mrs. Sweet said, "I understand." When she hung up the phone, she looked very sad.

Answers may include:

1. Who do you think called Mrs. Sweet?

   Candy called Mrs. Sweet.

2. How do you know that?

   Mrs. Sweet probably said, "I understand," when Candy said she wouldn't visit today.

3. Why is Mrs. Sweet sad?

   Her niece, Candy, probably can't come visit today.

Page 108

Making Inferences: Using Pictures

Directions: Draw a picture for each idea. Then write two sentences that tell about it.

You and a friend are playing your favorite game.

Answers will vary.

You and a friend are sharing your favorite food.

Answers will vary.

Drawings will vary.

Page 109

Making Inferences: Visualizing

Directions: Read the story about Melinda. Then draw pictures that describe each part of the story.

Beginning: It was Halloween. Melinda's costume was a black cat with super-duper, polka-dot sunglasses.

Middle: Her little brown dog, Marco, yelped and ran under a big red chair when he saw her come into the room.

End: Melinda took off her black cat mask and sunglasses. Then she held out a dog biscuit. She picked Marco up and hugged him. Then he was happy.

Drawings will vary.

Page 110

Making Inferences: Point of View

Juniper has three problems to solve. She needs your help.

Directions: Read each problem. Write what you think she should do.

1. Juniper is watching her favorite TV show when the power goes out.

2. Juniper is riding her bike to school when she gets a flat.

3. Juniper loses her father while shopping in the supermarket.

Answers will vary.

Page 111

Making Inferences: Sequencing

Directions: Draw three pictures to tell a story about each topic.

1. Feeding a pet

   | Beginning | Middle | End |

2. Playing a game

   | Beginning | Middle | End |

Drawings will vary.

Page 112

Making Deductions: Find the Books

Directions: Use the clues to help the children find their books. Draw a line from each child's name to the correct book.

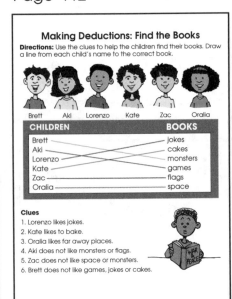

Brett   Aki   Lorenzo   Kate   Zac   Oralia

CHILDREN	BOOKS
Brett	jokes
Aki	cakes
Lorenzo	monsters
Kate	games
Zac	flags
Oralia	space

Clues
1. Lorenzo likes jokes.
2. Kate likes to bake.
3. Oralia likes far away places.
4. Aki does not like monsters or flags.
5. Zac does not like space or monsters.
6. Brett does not like games, jokes or cakes.

Page 113

Making Deductions: Sports

Children all over the world like to play sports. They like many different kinds of sports: football, soccer, basketball, softball, in-line skating, swimming and more.

Directions: Read the clues. Draw dots and **X**'s on the chart to match the children with their sports.

	swimming	football	soccer	basketball	baseball	in-line skating
J.J.	X	●	X	X	X	X
Zoe	X	X	X	X	X	●
Andy	X	X	X	●	X	X
Amber	X	X	●	X	X	X
Raul	X	X	X	X	●	X
Sierra	●	X	X	X	X	X

Clues
1. Zoe hates football.
2. Andy likes basketball.
3. Raul likes to pitch in his favorite sport.
4. J.J. likes to play what Zoe hates.
5. Amber is good at kicking the ball to her teammates.
6. Sierra needs a pool for her favorite sport.

Page 114

Fiction/Nonfiction: Heavy Hitters

Fiction is a make-believe story. **Nonfiction** is a true story.

Directions: Read the stories about two famous baseball players. Then write **fiction** or **nonfiction** in the baseball bats.

In 1998, Mark McGwire played for the St. Louis Cardinals. He liked to hit home runs. On September 27, 1998, he hit home run number 70, to set a new record for the most home runs hit in one season. The old record was set in 1961 by Roger Maris, who later played for the St. Louis Cardinals (1967 to 1968), when he hit 61 home runs.

nonfiction

The Mighty Casey played baseball for the Mudville Nine and was the greatest of all baseball players. He could hit the cover off the ball with the power of a hurricane. But, when the Mudville Nine was behind 4 to 2 in the championship game, Mighty Casey struck out with the bases loaded. There was no joy in Mudville that day, because the Mudville Nine had lost the game.

fiction

Page 115

Nonfiction: Tornado Tips

Directions: Read about tornadoes. Then follow the instructions.

A tornado begins over land with strong winds and thunderstorms. The spinning air becomes a funnel. It can cause damage. If you are inside, go to the lowest floor of the building. A basement is a safe place. A bathroom or closet in the middle of a building can be a safe place, too. If you are outside, lie in a ditch. Remember, tornadoes are dangerous.

Answers may include:

Write five facts about tornadoes.

1. A tornado begins over land.

2. Spinning air becomes a funnel.

3. Tornadoes can cause damage.

4. A basement is a safe place to be in a tornado.

5. If you are outside during a tornado, you should lie in a ditch.

Page 116

Fiction: Hercules

The setting is where a story takes place. The characters are the people in a story or play.

Directions: Read about Hercules. Then answer the questions.

Hercules was born in the warm Atlantic Ocean. He was a very small and weak baby. He wanted to be the strongest hurricane in the world. But he had one problem. He couldn't blow 75-mile-per-hour winds. Hercules blew and blew in the ocean, until one day, his sister, Hola, told him it would be more fun to be a breeze than a hurricane. Hercules agreed. It was a breeze to be a breeze!

1. What is the setting of the story? Atlantic Ocean

2. Who are the characters? Hercules, Hola

3. What is the problem? Hercules couldn't blow 75 mile-per-hour winds.

4. How does Hercules solve his problem? He decides that it is more fun to be a breeze than a hurricane.

Page 117

Fiction/Nonfiction: The Fourth of July

Directions: Read each story. Then write whether it is fiction or nonfiction.

One sunny day in July, a dog named Stan ran away from home. He went up one street and down the other looking for fun, but all the yards were empty. Where was everybody? Stan kept walking until he heard the sound of band music and happy people. Stan walked faster until he got to Central Street. There he saw men, women, children and dogs getting ready to walk in a parade. It was the Fourth of July!

Fiction or Nonfiction? Fiction

Americans celebrate the Fourth of July every year, because it is the birthday of the United States of America. On July 4, 1776, the United States got its independence from Great Britain. Today, Americans celebrate this holiday with parades, picnics and fireworks as they proudly wave the red, white and blue American flag.

Fiction or Nonfiction? Nonfiction

Page 118

Fiction and Nonfiction: Which Is It?

Directions: Read about fiction and nonfiction books. Then follow the instructions.

There are many kinds of books. Some books have make-believe stories about princesses and dragons. Some books contain poetry and rhymes, like Mother Goose. These are fiction.

Some books contain facts about space and plants. And still other books have stories about famous people in history like Abraham Lincoln. These are nonfiction.

Write **F** for fiction and **NF** for nonfiction.

F 1. nursery rhyme

F 2. fairy tale

NF 3. true life story of a famous athlete

F 4. Aesop's fables

NF 5. dictionary entry about foxes

NF 6. weather report

F 7. story about a talking tree

NF 8. story about how a tadpole becomes a frog

NF 9. story about animal habitats

F 10. riddles and jokes

Page 120

ABC Order

Directions: Put the words in ABC order on the bags.

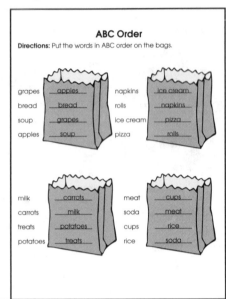

grapes	apples	napkins	ice cream
bread	bread	rolls	napkins
soup	grapes	ice cream	pizza
apples	soup	pizza	rolls

milk	carrots	meat	cups
carrots	milk	soda	meat
treats	potatoes	cups	rice
potatoes	treats	rice	soda

Page 121

ABC Order

Directions: Write these words in order. If two words start with the same letter, look at the second letter in each word.

Example: lamb   Lamb comes first because **a** comes before **i**
          light   in the alphabet.

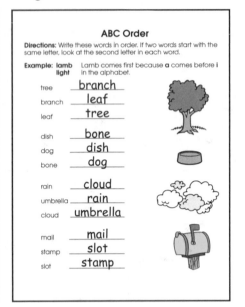

tree	branch
branch	leaf
leaf	tree
dish	bone
dog	dish
bone	dog
rain	cloud
umbrella	rain
cloud	umbrella
mail	mail
stamp	slot
slot	stamp

Page 122

Sequencing: ABC Order

If the first letters of two words are the same, look at the second letters in both words. If the second letters are the same, look at the third letters.

Directions: Write 1, 2, 3 or 4 on the lines in each row to put the words in ABC order.

Example:

1. **1** candy **2** carrot **4** duck **3** dance

2. **2** cold **4** hot **1** carry **3** hit

3. **2** flash **1** fan **3** fun **4** garden

4. **2** seat **4** sun **1** saw **3** sit

5. **3** row **1** ring **2** rock **4** run

6. **2** truck **3** turn **4** twin **1** talk

7. **1** seven **2** shoe **4** soup **3** smell

Page 123

Sequencing: ABC Order

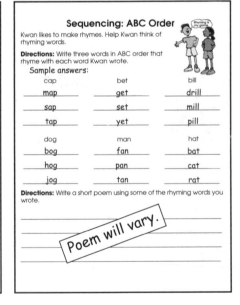

Kwan likes to make rhymes. Help Kwan think of rhyming words.

Directions: Write three words in ABC order that rhyme with each word Kwan wrote.

Sample answers:

cap	bet	bill
map	get	drill
sap	set	mill
tap	yet	pill
dog	man	hat
bog	fan	bat
hog	pan	cat
jog	tan	rat

Directions: Write a short poem using some of the rhyming words you wrote.

Poem will vary.

Page 124

Synonyms

Words that mean the same or nearly the same are called **synonyms**.
Directions: Read the sentence that tells about the picture. Draw a circle around the word that means the same as the **bold** word.

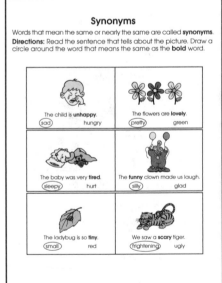

The child is **unhappy**.
(sad)   hungry

The flowers are **lovely**.
(pretty)   green

The baby was very **tired**.
(sleepy)   hurt

The **funny** clown made us laugh.
(silly)   glad

The ladybug is so **tiny**.
(small)   red

We saw a **scary** tiger.
(frightening)   ugly

Page 125

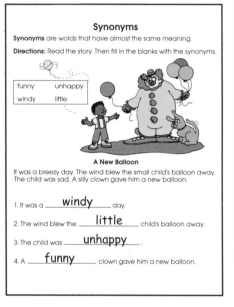

Synonyms

Synonyms are words that have almost the same meaning.

Directions: Read the story. Then fill in the blanks with the synonyms.

| funny | unhappy |
| windy | little |

A New Balloon

It was a breezy day. The wind blew the small child's balloon away. The child was sad. A silly clown gave him a new balloon.

1. It was a **windy** day.

2. The wind blew the **little** child's balloon away.

3. The child was **unhappy**.

4. A **funny** clown gave him a new balloon.

Page 126

Synonyms

Directions: Read each sentence. Fill in the blanks with the synonyms.

| friend | tired | story |
| presents | little | |

I want to go to bed because I am very <u>sleepy</u>.   **tired**

On my birthday I like to open my <u>gifts</u>.   **presents**

My <u>pal</u> and I like to play together.   **friend**

My favorite <u>tale</u> is Cinderella.   **story**

The mouse was so <u>tiny</u> that it was hard to catch him.   **little**

Page 127

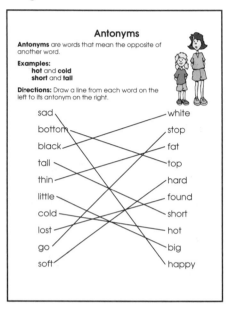

Antonyms

Antonyms are words that mean the opposite of another word.

Examples:
hot and **cold**
short and **tall**

Directions: Draw a line from each word on the left to its antonym on the right.

sad	white
bottom	stop
black	fat
tall	top
thin	hard
little	found
cold	short
lost	hot
go	big
soft	happy

Page 128

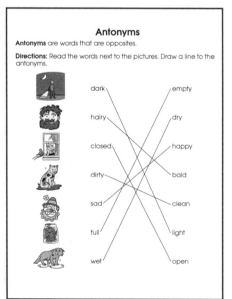

Antonyms

Antonyms are words that are opposites.

Directions: Read the words next to the pictures. Draw a line to the antonyms.

dark	empty
hairy	dry
closed	happy
dirty	bald
sad	clean
full	light
wet	open

Page 129

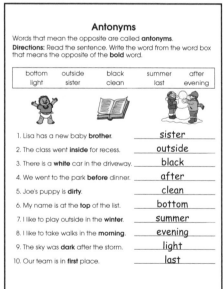

Antonyms

Words that mean the opposite are called **antonyms**.

Directions: Read the sentence. Write the word from the word box that means the opposite of the **bold** word.

| bottom | outside | black | summer | after |
| light | sister | clean | last | evening |

1. Lisa has a new baby **brother**.   **sister**
2. The class went **inside** for recess.   **outside**
3. There is a **white** car in the driveway.   **black**
4. We went to the park **before** dinner.   **after**
5. Joe's puppy is **dirty**.   **clean**
6. My name is at the **top** of the list.   **bottom**
7. I like to play outside in the **winter**.   **summer**
8. I like to take walks in the **morning**.   **evening**
9. The sky was **dark** after the storm.   **light**
10. Our team is in **first** place.   **last**

Page 130

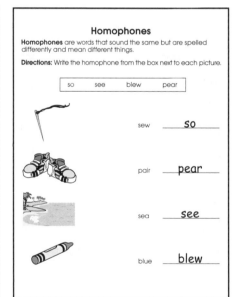

Homophones

Homophones are words that sound the same but are spelled differently and mean different things.

Directions: Write the homophone from the box next to each picture.

| so | see | blew | pear |

sew   **so**

pair   **pear**

sea   **see**

blue   **blew**

GRADE 2

Page 131

Homophones

Directions: Look at each picture. Circle the correct homophone.

(deer) dear

blue (blew)

2 (two) to

hi (high)

by (bye)

(new) knew

8 ate (eight)

(red) read

Page 132

Homophones

Directions: Match each word with its homophone.

eight — ate
buy — by
pail — pale
red — read
hole — whole
blue — blew
our — hour

Directions: Choose 3 homophone pairs and write sentences using them.

1. _____ **Answers will vary.** _____

2. _____

3. _____

Page 133

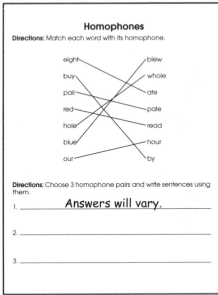

Nouns

A **noun** is the name of a person, place or thing.

Directions: Read the story and circle all the nouns. Then write the nouns next to the pictures below.

Our (family) likes to go to the (park)   **family**   **park**

We play on the (swings)   **swings**

We eat (cake)   **cake**

We drink (lemonade)   **lemonade**

We throw the (ball) to our (dog)   **ball**   **dog**

Then we go (home)   **home**

Page 134

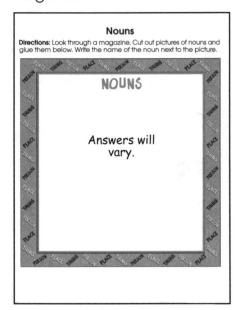

Nouns

Directions: Look through a magazine. Cut out pictures of nouns and glue them below. Write the name of the noun next to the picture.

NOUNS

Answers will vary.

Page 135

Proper Nouns

Proper nouns are the names of specific people, places and pets. Proper nouns begin with a capital letter.

Directions: Write the proper nouns on the lines below. Use capital letters at the beginning of each word.

logan, utah — **Logan, Utah**

mike smith — **Mike Smith**

lynn cramer — **Lynn Cramer**

buster — **Buster**

fluffy — **Fluffy**

chicago, illinois — **Chicago, Illinois**

Page 136

Proper Nouns

The days of the week and the months of the year are always capitalized.

Directions: Circle the words that are written correctly. Write the words that need capital letters on the lines below.

sunday	(July)	(Wednesday)	may	december
friday	tuesday	june	august	(Monday)
january	(February)	(March)	(Thursday)	(April)
(September)	saturday	(October)		

Days of the Week

1. Sunday
2. Friday
3. Tuesday
4. Saturday

Months of the Year

1. January
2. June
3. May
4. August
5. December

Page 137

Capitalization

The first word and all of the important words in a title begin with a capital letter.

Directions: Write the book titles on the lines below. Use capital letters.

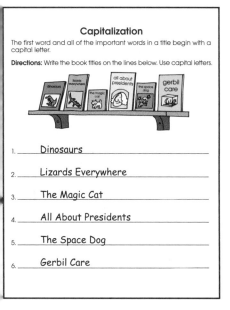

1. Dinosaurs
2. Lizards Everywhere
3. The Magic Cat
4. All About Presidents
5. The Space Dog
6. Gerbil Care

Page 138

Plural Nouns

Plural nouns name more than one person, place or thing.

Directions: Read the words in the box. Write the words in the correct column.

hats	girl	cows	kittens	cake
spoons	glass	book	horse	trees

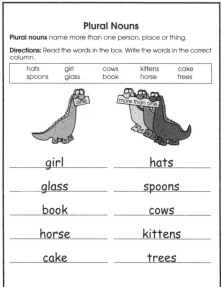

one	more than one
girl	hats
glass	spoons
book	cows
horse	kittens
cake	trees

Page 139

Plurals

Plurals are words that mean more than one. You usually add an **s** or **es** to the word. In some words ending in **y**, the **y** changes to an **i** before adding **es**. For example, **baby** changes to **babies**.

Directions: Look at the following lists of plural words. Write the word that means one next to it. The first one has been done for you.

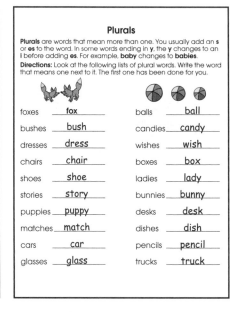

foxes	fox	balls	ball
bushes	bush	candies	candy
dresses	dress	wishes	wish
chairs	chair	boxes	box
shoes	shoe	ladies	lady
stories	story	bunnies	bunny
puppies	puppy	desks	desk
matches	match	dishes	dish
cars	car	pencils	pencil
glasses	glass	trucks	truck

Page 140

Pronouns

Pronouns are words that can be used instead of nouns. **She, he, it** and **they** are pronouns.

Directions: Read the sentence. Then write the sentence again, using **she, he, it** or **they** in the blank.

1. Dan likes funny jokes. He likes funny jokes.

2. Peg and Sam went to the zoo. They went to the zoo.

3. My dog likes to dig in the yard. It likes to dig in the yard.

4. Sara is a very good dancer. She is a very good dancer.

5. Fred and Ted are twins. They are twins.

Page 141

Subjects

The **subject** of a sentence is the person, place or thing the sentence is about.

Directions: Underline the subject in each sentence.

Example: Mom read a book.
(Think: Who is the sentence about? Mom)

1. The bird flew away.

2. The kite was high in the air.

3. The children played a game.

4. The books fell down.

5. The monkey climbed a tree.

Page 142

Compound Subjects

Two similar sentences can be joined into one sentence if the predicate is the same. A **compound subject** is made up of two subjects joined together by the word **and**.

Example: Jamie can sing.
Sandy can sing.
Jamie **and** Sandy can sing.

Directions: Combine the sentences. Write the new sentence on the line.

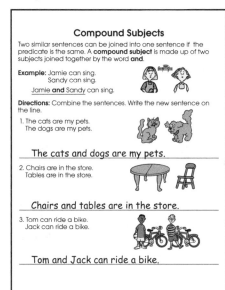

1. The cats are my pets.
The dogs are my pets.

The cats and dogs are my pets.

2. Chairs are in the store.
Tables are in the store.

Chairs and tables are in the store.

3. Tom can ride a bike.
Jack can ride a bike.

Tom and Jack can ride a bike.

325

Total Basic Skills Grade 2

Page 143

Verbs

A **verb** is the action word in a sentence. Verbs tell what something does or that something exists.

Example: Run, sleep and **jump** are verbs.

Directions: Circle the verbs in the sentences below.

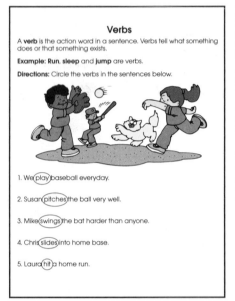

1. We (play) baseball everyday.

2. Susan (pitches) the ball very well.

3. Mike (swings) the bat harder than anyone.

4. Chris (slides) into home base.

5. Laura (hit) a home run.

Page 144

Verbs

We use verbs to tell when something happens. Sometimes we add an **ed** to verbs that tell us if something has already happened.

Example: Today, we will **play**. Yesterday, we **played**.

Directions: Write the correct verb in the blank.

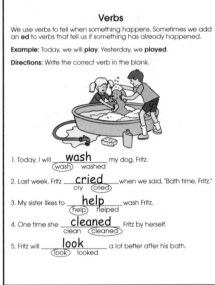

1. Today, I will **wash** my dog, Fritz.
   (wash)   washed

2. Last week, Fritz **cried** when we said, "Bath time, Fritz."
   cry   (cried)

3. My sister likes to **help** wash Fritz.
   (help)   helped

4. One time she **cleaned** Fritz by herself.
   clean   (cleaned)

5. Fritz will **look** a lot better after his bath.
   (look)   looked

Page 145

Predicates

The **predicate** is the part of the sentence that tells about the action.

Directions: Circle the predicate in each sentence.

Example: The boys ran on the playground.
           (Think: The boys did what? (Ran))

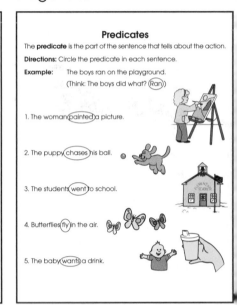

1. The woman (painted) a picture.

2. The puppy (chases) his ball.

3. The students (went) to school.

4. Butterflies (fly) in the air.

5. The baby (wants) a drink.

Page 146

Subjects and Predicates

The **subject** part of the sentence is the person, place or thing the sentence is about. The **predicate** is the part of the sentence that tells what the subject does.

Directions: Draw a line between the subject and the predicate. Underline the noun in the subject and circle the verb.

Example: The furry <u>cat</u> | (ate) food.

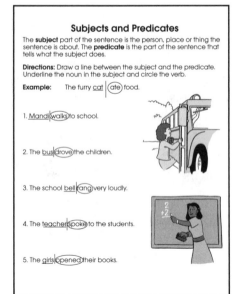

1. <u>Mandi</u> (walks) to school.

2. The <u>bus</u> (drove) the children.

3. The school <u>bell</u> (rang) very loudly.

4. The <u>teacher</u> (spoke) to the students.

5. The <u>girls</u> (opened) their books.

Page 147

Parts of a Sentence

Directions: Draw a circle around the noun, the naming part of the sentence. Draw a line under the verb, the action part of the sentence.

Example: (John) <u>drinks</u> juice every morning. ♫

1. Our (class) <u>skates</u> at the roller-skating rink.

2. (Mike) and (Jan) <u>go</u> very fast.

3. (Fred) <u>eats</u> hot dogs.

4. (Sue) <u>dances</u> to the music.

5. (Everyone) <u>likes</u> the skating rink.

Page 148

Parts of a Sentence

Directions: Look at the pictures. Draw a line from the naming part of the sentence to the action part to complete the sentence.

The boy — delivered the mail.

A small dog — threw a football.

The mailman — fell down.

The goalie — chased the ball.

Page 149

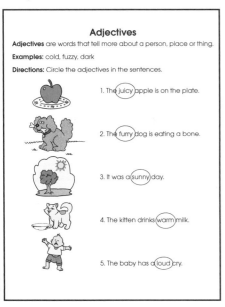

Adjectives

Adjectives are words that tell more about a person, place or thing.

Examples: cold, fuzzy, dark

Directions: Circle the adjectives in the sentences.

1. The (juicy) apple is on the plate.

2. The (furry) dog is eating a bone.

3. It was a (sunny) day.

4. The kitten drinks (warm) milk.

5. The baby has a (loud) cry.

Page 150

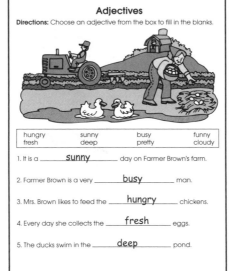

Adjectives

Directions: Choose an adjective from the box to fill in the blanks.

hungry	sunny	busy	funny
fresh	deep	pretty	cloudy

1. It is a **sunny** day on Farmer Brown's farm.

2. Farmer Brown is a very **busy** man.

3. Mrs. Brown likes to feed the **hungry** chickens.

4. Every day she collects the **fresh** eggs.

5. The ducks swim in the **deep** pond.

Page 151

Adjectives

Directions: Think of your own adjectives. Write a story about Fluffy the cat.

Answers will vary.

1. Fluffy is a _____ cat.

2. The color of his fur is _____ .

3. He likes to chew on my _____ shoes.

4. He likes to eat _____ cat food.

5. I like Fluffy because he is so _____ .

Page 152

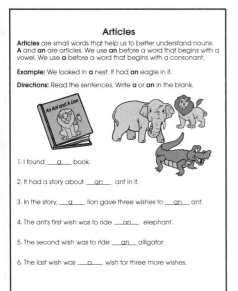

Articles

Articles are small words that help us to better understand nouns. **A** and **an** are articles. We use **an** before a word that begins with a vowel. We use **a** before a word that begins with a consonant.

Example: We looked in **a** nest. It had **an** eagle in it.

Directions: Read the sentences. Write **a** or **an** in the blank.

1. I found __a__ book.

2. It had a story about __an__ ant in it.

3. In the story, __a__ lion gave three wishes to __an__ ant.

4. The ant's first wish was to ride __an__ elephant.

5. The second wish was to ride __an__ alligator.

6. The last wish was __a__ wish for three more wishes.

Page 153

Sentences and Non-Sentences

A **sentence** tells a complete idea. It has a noun and a verb. It begins with a capital letter and has punctuation at the end.

Directions: Circle the group of words if it is a sentence.

1. (Grass is a green plant.)

2. Mowing the lawn.

3. (Grass grows in fields and lawns.)

4. Tickle the feet.

5. (Sheep, cows and horses eat grass.)

6. We like to play in.

7. (My sister likes to mow the lawn.)

8. A picnic on the grass.

9. (My dog likes to roll in the grass.)

10. Plant flowers around.

Page 154

Sentences and Non-Sentences

Directions: Circle the group of words if it tells a complete idea.

1. (A secret is something you know.)

2. (My mom's birthday gift is a secret.)

3. No one else.

4. If you promise not to.

5. (I'll tell you a secret.)

6. Something nobody knows.

Page 155

Statements

Statements are sentences that tell us something. They begin with a capital letter and end with a period.

Directions: Write the sentences on the lines below. Begin each sentence with a capital letter and end it with a period.

1. we like to ride our bikes

   We like to ride our bikes.

2. we go down the hill very fast

   We go down the hill very fast.

3. we keep our bikes shiny and clean

   We keep our bikes shiny and clean.

4. we know how to change the tires

   We know how to change the tires.

Page 156

Surprising Sentences

Surprising sentences tell a strong feeling and end with an exclamation point. A surprising sentence may be only one or two words showing fear, surprise or pain. **Example: Oh, no!**

Directions: Put a period at the end of the sentences that tell something. Put an exclamation point at the end of the sentences that tell a strong feeling. Put a question mark at the end of the sentences that ask a question.

1. The cheetah can run very fast .

2. Wow !

3. Look at that cheetah go !

4. Can you run fast ?

5. Oh, my !

6. You're faster than I am .

7. Let's run together .

8. We can run as fast as a cheetah .

9. What fun !

10. Do you think cheetahs get tired ?

Page 157

Commands

Commands tell someone to do something. **Example: "Be careful."** It can also be written as "Be careful!" if it tells a strong feeling.

Directions: Put a period at the end of the command sentences. Use an exclamation point if the sentence tells a strong feeling. Write your own commands on the lines below.

1. Clean your room .

2. Now !

3. Be careful with your goldfish .

4. Watch out !

5. Be a little more careful .

Answers will vary.

Page 158

Questions

Questions are sentences that ask something. They begin with a capital letter and end with a question mark.

Directions: Write the questions on the lines below. Begin each sentence with a capital letter and end with a question mark.

1. will you be my friend

   Will you be my friend?

2. what is your name

   What is your name?

3. are you eight years old

   Are you eight years old?

4. do you like rainbows

   Do you like rainbows?

Page 159

Making Inferences: Writing Questions

Tommy likes to answer questions. He knows the answers, but you need to write the questions.

Directions: Write two questions for each answer.

Answer: It has four legs.

1. _____ ?
   _____ ?

Answer: It lives on a farm.

2. _____ ?
   _____ ?

Answer: ___ soft.

3. _____ ?
   _____ ?

Questions will vary.

Page 160

Making Inferences: Writing Questions

Toban and Sean use many colors when they paint.

Directions: Write two questions for each answer.

Answer: It is red.

1. _____ ?
   _____ ?

Answer: It is purple.

2. _____ ?
   _____ ?

Answer: ___

3. _____ ?
   _____ ?

Questions will vary.

Page 161

Making Inferences: Point of View

Chelsea likes to pretend she will meet famous people someday. She would like to ask them many questions.

Directions: Write a question you think Chelsea would ask if she met these people.

1. an actor in a popular, new film _____
_____?

2. an Olympic gold medal _____?

3. an alien ___ space _____?
_____?

Questions will vary.

Directions: Now, write the answers these people might have given to Chelsea's questions.

4. an actor in a popular, new film _____

5. an Olympic Gold _____

Answers will vary.

6. an alien from outer space _____
_____

Page 162

Making Inferences: Point of View

Ellen likes animals. Someday she might want to be an animal doctor.

Directions: Write one question you think Ellen would ask each of these animals if she could speak their language.

1. a giraffe _____?
2. a mouse _____?
3. a shark _____?
4. a hippopotamus _____?
5. a penguin _____?
6. a gorilla _____?
7. an eagle _____?

Questions will vary.

Directions: Now, write the answers you think these animals might have given Ellen.

9. a giraffe _____
10. a mouse _____
11. a shark _____
12. a hippopotamus _____
13. a penguin _____
14. a gorilla _____
15. an eagle _____

Answers will vary.

Page 163

Creative Writing

Directions: Look at the picture below. Write a story about the picture.

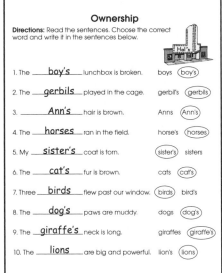

_____
_____ Results will vary. _____
_____
_____
_____
_____
_____

Page 164

Ownership

We add **'s** to nouns (people, places or things) to tell who or what owns something.

Directions: Read the sentences. Fill in the blanks to show ownership.

Example: The doll belongs to **Sara**.
It is **Sara's** doll.

1. Sparky has a red collar.

__**Sparky's**__ collar is red.

2. Jimmy has a blue coat.

__**Jimmy's**__ coat is blue.

3. The tail of the cat is short.

The __**cat's**__ tail is short.

4. The name of my mother is Karen.

My __**mother's**__ name is Karen.

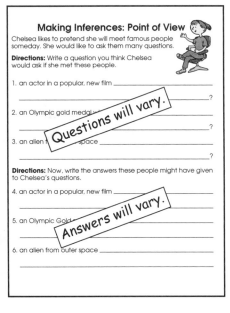

Page 165

Ownership

Directions: Read the sentences. Choose the correct word and write it in the sentences below.

1. The __**boy's**__ lunchbox is broken.   boys   (boy's)

2. The __**gerbils**__ played in the cage.   gerbil's   (gerbils)

3. __**Ann's**__ hair is brown.   Anns   (Ann's)

4. The __**horses**__ ran in the field.   horse's   (horses)

5. My __**sister's**__ coat is torn.   (sister's)   sisters

6. The __**cat's**__ fur is brown.   cats   (cat's)

7. Three __**birds**__ flew past our window.   (birds)   bird's

8. The __**dog's**__ paws are muddy.   dogs   (dog's)

9. The __**giraffe's**__ neck is long.   giraffes   (giraffe's)

10. The __**lions**__ are big and powerful.   lion's   (lions)

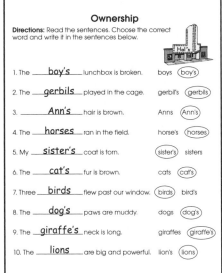

Page 166

Is, Are and Am

Is, are and **am** are special action words that tell us something is happening now.
Use **am** with **I**. **Example: I am.**
Use **is** to tell about one person or thing. **Example: He is.**
Use **are** to tell about more than one. **Example: We are.**
Use **are** with **you**. **Example: You are.**

Directions: Write **is**, **are** or **am** in the sentences below.

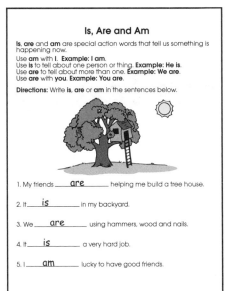

1. My friends __**are**__ helping me build a tree house.

2. It __**is**__ in my backyard.

3. We __**are**__ using hammers, wood and nails.

4. It __**is**__ a very hard job.

5. I __**am**__ lucky to have good friends.

Page 167

Was and Were

Was and **were** tell us about something that already happened.
Use **was** to tell about one person or thing. **Example: I was, he was.**
Use **were** to tell about more than one person or thing or when using the word you. **Example: We were, you were.**

Directions: Write **was** or **were** in each sentence.

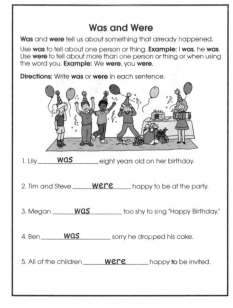

1. Lily _____ **was** _____ eight years old on her birthday.

2. Tim and Steve _____ **were** _____ happy to be at the party.

3. Megan _____ **was** _____ too shy to sing "Happy Birthday."

4. Ben _____ **was** _____ sorry he dropped his cake.

5. All of the children _____ **were** _____ happy **to** be invited.

Page 168

Go, Going and Went

We use **go** or **going** to tell about now or later. Sometimes we use **going** with the words **am** or **are**. We use **went** to tell about something that already happened.

Directions: Write **go**, **going** or **went** in the sentences below.

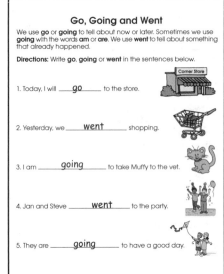

1. Today, I will _____ **go** _____ to the store.

2. Yesterday, we _____ **went** _____ shopping.

3. I am _____ **going** _____ to take Muffy to the vet.

4. Jan and Steve _____ **went** _____ to the party.

5. They are _____ **going** _____ to have a good day.

Page 169

Have, Has and Had

We use **have** and **has** to tell about now. We use **had** to tell about something that already happened.

Directions: Write **has**, **have** or **had** in the sentences below.

1. We _____ **have** _____ three cats at home.

2. Ginger _____ **has** _____ brown fur.

3. Bucky and Charlie _____ **have** _____ gray fur.

4. My friend Tom _____ **had** _____ one cat, but he died.

5. Tom _____ **has** _____ a new cat now.

Page 170

See, Saw and Sees

We use **see** or **sees** to tell about now. We use **saw** to tell about something that already happened.

Directions: Write **see**, **sees** or **saw** in the sentences below.

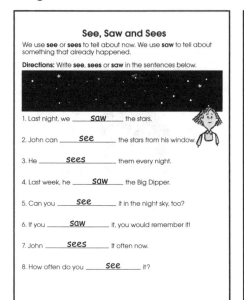

1. Last night, we _____ **saw** _____ the stars.

2. John can _____ **see** _____ the stars from his window.

3. He _____ **sees** _____ them every night.

4. Last week, he _____ **saw** _____ the Big Dipper.

5. Can you _____ **see** _____ it in the night sky, too?

6. If you _____ **saw** _____ it, you would remember it!

7. John _____ **sees** _____ It often now.

8. How often do you _____ **see** _____ it?

Page 171

Eat, Eats and Ate

We use **eat** or **eats** to tell about now. We use **ate** to tell about what already happened.

Directions: Write **eat**, **eats** or **ate** in the sentences below.

1. We like to _____ **eat** _____ in the lunchroom.

2. Today, my teacher will _____ **eat** _____ in a different room.

3. She _____ **eats** _____ with the other teachers.

4. Yesterday, we _____ **ate** _____ pizza, pears and peas.

5. Today, we will _____ **eat** _____ turkey and potatoes.

Page 172

Leave, Leaves and Left

We use **leave** and **leaves** to tell about now. We use **left** to tell about what already happened.

Directions: Write **leave**, **leaves** or **left** in the sentences below.

1. Last winter, we _____ **left** _____ seeds in the bird feeder everyday.

2. My mother likes to _____ **leave** _____ food out for the squirrels.

3. When it rains, she _____ **leaves** _____ bread for the birds.

4. Yesterday, she _____ **left** _____ popcorn for the birds.

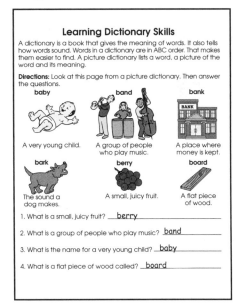

Page 173

Learning Dictionary Skills

A dictionary is a book that gives the meaning of words. It also tells how words sound. Words in a dictionary are in ABC order. That makes them easier to find. A picture dictionary lists a word, a picture of the word and its meaning.

Directions: Look at this page from a picture dictionary. Then answer the questions.

baby — A very young child.
band — A group of people who play music.
bank — A place where money is kept.
bark — The sound a dog makes.
berry — A small, juicy fruit.
board — A flat piece of wood.

1. What is a small, juicy fruit? __berry__
2. What is a group of people who play music? __band__
3. What is the name for a very young child? __baby__
4. What is a flat piece of wood called? __board__

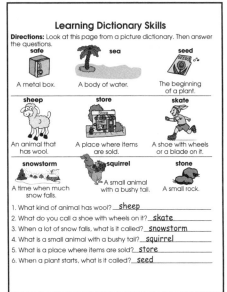

Page 174

Learning Dictionary Skills

Directions: Look at this page from a picture dictionary. Then answer the questions.

safe — A metal box.
sea — A body of water.
seed — The beginning of a plant.
sheep — An animal that has wool.
store — A place where items are sold.
skate — A shoe with wheels or a blade on it.
snowstorm — A time when much snow falls.
squirrel — A small animal with a bushy tail.
stone — A small rock.

1. What kind of animal has wool? __sheep__
2. What do you call a shoe with wheels on it? __skate__
3. When a lot of snow falls, what is it called? __snowstorm__
4. What is a small animal with a bushy tail? __squirrel__
5. What is a place where items are sold? __store__
6. When a plant starts, what is it called? __seed__

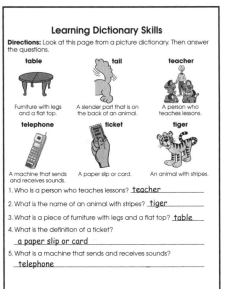

Page 175

Learning Dictionary Skills

Directions: Look at this page from a picture dictionary. Then answer the questions.

table — Furniture with legs and a flat top.
tail — A slender part that is on the back of an animal.
teacher — A person who teaches lessons.
telephone — A machine that sends and receives sounds.
ticket — A paper slip or card.
tiger — An animal with stripes.

1. Who is a person who teaches lessons? __teacher__
2. What is the name of an animal with stripes? __tiger__
3. What is a piece of furniture with legs and a flat top? __table__
4. What is the definition of a ticket?
   __a paper slip or card__
5. What is a machine that sends and receives sounds?
   __telephone__

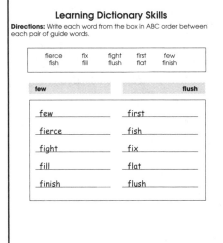

Page 176

Learning Dictionary Skills

Directions: Write each word from the box in ABC order between each pair of guide words.

| fierce | fix | fight | first | few |
| fish | fill | flush | flat | finish |

few		flush
few		first
fierce		fish
fight		fix
fill		flat
finish		flush

Page 178

Number Words

Directions: Write the correct number words in the blanks.

| one two three four five six seven eight nine ten |

Add a letter to each of these words to make a number word.

Example:

even — __seven__
on — __one__
tree — __three__

Change a letter to make these words into number words.

Example:

live — __five__
fix — __six__
line — __nine__

Write the number words that sound the same as these:

Example:

ate — __eight__
to — __two__
for — __four__

Write the number word you did not use: __ten__

Page 179

Number Words: Sentences

Directions: Change the telling sentences into asking sentences. Change the asking sentences into telling sentences. Begin each one with a capital letter and end it with a period or a question mark.

Examples:

Is she eating three cookies?

She is eating three cookies.

He is bringing one truck.

Is he bringing one truck?

1. Is he painting two blue birds?

He is painting two bluebirds.

2. Did she find four apples?

She did find four apples.

3. She will be six on her birthday.

Will she be six on her birthday?

Page 180

Short a Words: Rhyming Words

Short a is the sound you hear in the word **math**.

Directions: Use the **short a** words in the box to write rhyming words.

lamp	fat	bat	van
path	can	cat	Dan
math	stamp	fan	sat

1. Write four words that rhyme with **mat**.

fat   bat

cat   sat

2. Write two words that rhyme with **bath**.

path   math

3. Write two words that rhyme with **damp**.

lamp   stamp

4. Write four words that rhyme with **pan**.

can   fan

van   Dan

Page 181

Short a Words: Sentences

Directions: Use a word from the box to complete each sentence.

fat	path	lamp	can
van	stamp	Dan	math
sat	cat	fan	bat

Example:

1. The __lamp__ had a pink shade.
2. The bike __path__ led us to the park.
3. I like to add in __math__ class.
4. The cat is very __fat__.
5. The __can__ of beans was hard to open.
6. The envelope needed a __stamp__.
7. He swung the __bat__ and hit the ball.
8. The __fan__ blew air around.
9. My mom drives a blue __van__.
10. I __sat__ in the backseat.

Page 182

Long a Words

Long a is the vowel sound which says its own name. **Long a** can be spelled **ai** as in the word **mail**, **ay** as in the word **say** and **a** with a **silent e** at the end of a word as in the word **same**.

Directions: Say each word and listen for the **long a** sound. Then write each word and underline the letters that make the **long a** vowel sound.

mail	bake	train
game	day	sale
paint	play	name
made	gray	tray

1. mail
2. paint
3. game
4. made
5. bake
6. play
7. day
8. gray
9. train
10. name
11. sale
12. tray

Page 183

Long a Words: Sentence Order

Directions: Write the words in order so that each sentence tells a complete idea. Begin each Sentence with a capital letter and end it with a period or a question mark.

1. plate was on the cake a

The cake was on a plate.

2. like you would to play a game

You would like to play a game.

3. gray around the a corner train came

A gray train came around the corner.

4. was on mail Bob's name the

Bob's name was on the mail.

5. sail for on day we went a nice a

We went for a sail on a nice day.

Page 184

Short o Words

Short o is the vowel sound you hear in the word **pot**.

Directions: Say each word and listen for the **short o** sound. Then write each word and underline the letter that makes the **short o** sound.

hot	box	sock	mop
stop	not	fox	cot
Bob	rock	clock	lock

1. hot
2. stop
3. Bob
4. box
5. not
6. rock
7. sock
8. fox
9. clock
10. mop
11. cot
12. lock

Page 185

Short o Words: Rhyming Words

Short o is the vowel sound you hear in the word **got**.

Directions: Use the **short o** words in the box to write rhyming words.

hot	rock	lock	cot
stop	sock	fox	mop
box	mob	clock	Bob

1. Write the words that rhyme with **dot**.
hot   cot

2. Write the words that rhyme with **socks**.
box   fox

3. Write the words that rhyme with **hop**.
stop   mop

4. Write the words that rhyme with **dock**.
rock   sock
lock   clock

5. Write the words that rhyme with **cob**.
mob   Bob

Page 186

Long o Words

Long o is the vowel sound which says its own name. **Long o** can be spelled **oa** as in the word **float** or **o** with a **silent e** at the end as in **cone**.

Directions: Say each word and listen for the **long o** sound. Then write each word and underline the letters that make the **long o** sound.

rope	coat	soap	wrote
note	hope	boat	cone
bone	pole	phone	hole

1. rope   7. soap
2. note   8. boat
3. bone   9. phone
4. coat   10. wrote
5. hope   11. cone
6. pole   12. hole

Page 187

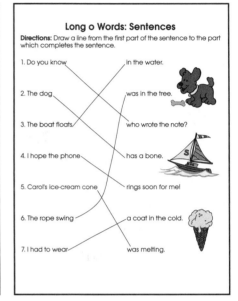

Long o Words: Sentences

Directions: Draw a line from the first part of the sentence to the part which completes the sentence.

1. Do you know   in the water.

2. The dog   was in the tree.

3. The boat floats   who wrote the note?

4. I hope the phone   has a bone.

5. Carol's ice-cream cone   rings soon for me!

6. The rope swing   a coat in the cold.

7. I had to wear   was melting.

Page 188

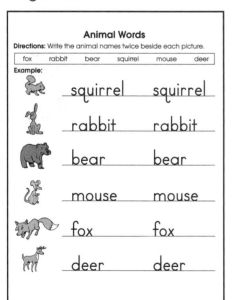

Animal Words

Directions: Write the animal names twice beside each picture.

| fox | rabbit | bear | squirrel | mouse | deer |

Example:

squirrel   squirrel

rabbit   rabbit

bear   bear

mouse   mouse

fox   fox

deer   deer

Page 189

Animal Words: More Than One

To show more than one of something, we add **s** to most words.

Example: one dog – **two dogs**   one book – **two books**
But some words are different. For words that end with **x**, use **es** to show two.

Example: one fox – **two foxes**   one box – **two boxes**
The spelling of some words changes a lot when there are two.

Example: one mouse – **two mice**
Some words stay the same, even when you mean two of something.

Example: one deer – **two deer**   one fish – **two fish**

Directions: Complete the sentences below with the correct word.

1. The ____ run fast.   rabbits

2. The ____ are eating.   deer

3. Have you seen any ____ today?   bears

4. Where do the ____ live?   foxes

5. Did you ever have ____ for pets?   mice

Page 190

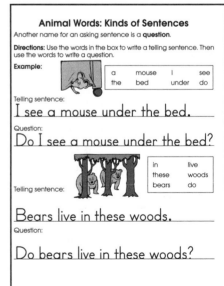

Animal Words: Kinds of Sentences

Another name for an asking sentence is a **question**.

Directions: Use the words in the box to write a telling sentence. Then use the words to write a question.

Example:

| a | mouse | I | see |
| the | bed | under | do |

Telling sentence:
I see a mouse under the bed.

Question:
Do I see a mouse under the bed?

in	live
these	woods
bears	do

Telling sentence:
Bears live in these woods.

Question:
Do bears live in these woods?

Page 191

Animal Words: Sentences

Directions: Read the sentences on each line and draw a line between them. Then write each sentence again on the lines below. Begin each one with a capital letter and put a period or question mark at the end.

Example:

why do squirrels hide nuts | they eat them in the winter

Why do squirrels hide nuts?
They eat them in the winter.

1. bears sleep in the winter | they don't need food then

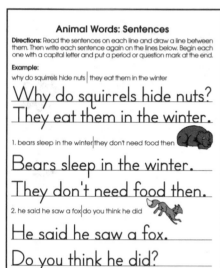

Bears sleep in the winter.
They don't need food then.

2. he said he saw a fox | do you think he did

He said he saw a fox.
Do you think he did?

Page 192

Family Words

Directions: This is Andy's **family tree**. It shows all the people in his family. Use the words in the box to finish writing the names in Andy's family tree.

grandmother	mother
grandfather	father
aunt	uncle
brother	sister

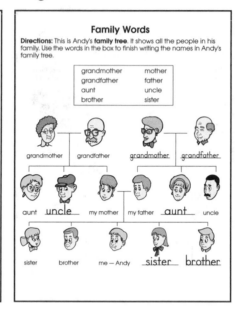

grandmother grandfather   grandmother   grandfather

aunt uncle   my mother   my father   aunt   uncle

sister   brother   me — Andy   sister   brother

Page 193

Family Words

Some words tell how a person looks or feels. These are called **describing** words or **adjectives**.

Directions: Help Andy write about the people in his family. Cross out the **describing** word that does not tell about each picture. Write a sentence that uses the other two describing words.

Example:

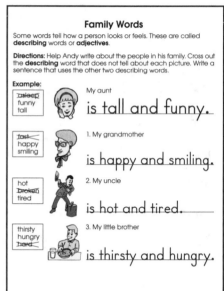

~~asleep~~
funny
tall

My aunt
is tall and funny.

~~fast~~
happy
smiling

1. My grandmother
is happy and smiling.

hot
~~broken~~
tired

2. My uncle
is hot and tired.

thirsty
hungry
~~hard~~

3. My little brother
is thirsty and hungry.

Page 194

Family Words: Joining Words

Joining words join two ideas to make one long sentence. Three words help do this:

and — if both sentences are much the same.
Example: I took my dog for a walk, **and** I played with my cat.
but — if the second sentence says something different than the first sentence. Sometimes the second sentence tells why you can't do the first sentence.
Example: I want to play outside, **but** it is raining.
or — if each sentence names a different thing you could do.
Example: You could eat your cookie, **or** you could give it to me.

Directions: Use the word given to join the two short sentences into one longer sentence.

(but)
My aunt lives far away. She calls me often.

My aunt lives far away, but she calls me often.

1. **(and)**
My sister had a birthday. She got a new bike.

My sister had a birthday, and she got a new bike.

2. **(or)**
We can play outside. We can play inside.

We can play outside, or we can play inside.

Page 195

Family Words: Joining Words

Directions: Read each pair of sentences. Then join them with **and**, **but** or **or**.

1. My uncle likes popcorn.
He does not like peanuts.

My uncle likes popcorn, but he does not like peanuts.

2. He could read a book.
He could tell me his own story.

He could read a book, and he could tell me his own story.

3. My little brother is sleepy.
He wants to go to bed.

My little brother is sleepy, and he wants to go to bed.

Page 196

Short e Words

Short e is the vowel sound you hear in the word **pet**.

Directions: Say each word and listen for the **short e** sound. Then write each word and underline the letter that makes the **short e** sound.

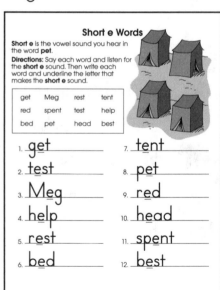

get	Meg	rest	tent
red	spent	test	help
bed	pet	head	best

1. g<u>e</u>t
2. t<u>e</u>st
3. M<u>e</u>g
4. h<u>e</u>lp
5. r<u>e</u>st
6. b<u>e</u>d
7. t<u>e</u>nt
8. p<u>e</u>t
9. r<u>e</u>d
10. h<u>e</u>ad
11. sp<u>e</u>nt
12. b<u>e</u>st

Page 197

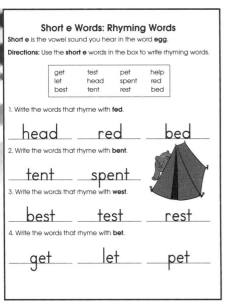

Short e Words: Rhyming Words

Short e is the vowel sound you hear in the word **egg**.

Directions: Use the **short e** words in the box to write rhyming words.

get	test	pet	help
let	head	spent	red
best	tent	rest	bed

1. Write the words that rhyme with **fed**.

head   red   bed

2. Write the words that rhyme with **bent**.

tent   spent

3. Write the words that rhyme with **west**.

best   test   rest

4. Write the words that rhyme with **bet**.

get   let   pet

Page 198

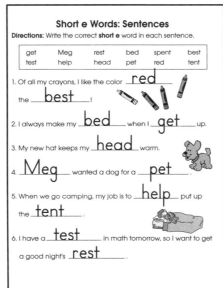

Short e Words: Sentences

Directions: Write the correct **short e** word in each sentence.

| get | Meg | rest | bed | spent | best |
| test | help | head | pet | red | tent |

1. Of all my crayons, I like the color red the best !

2. I always make my bed when I get up.

3. My new hat keeps my head warm.

4. Meg wanted a dog for a pet .

5. When we go camping, my job is to help put up the tent .

6. I have a test in math tomorrow, so I want to get a good night's rest .

Page 199

Long e Words

Long e is the vowel sound which says its own name. Long e can be spelled **ee** as in the word **teeth**, **ea** as in the word **meat** or **e** as in the word **me**.

Directions: Say each word and listen for the **long e** sound. Then write the words and underline the letters that make the **long e** sound.

street	neat	treat	feet
sleep	keep	deal	meal
mean	clean	beast	feast

1. street
2. sleep
3. mean
4. neat
5. keep
6. clean
7. treat
8. deal
9. beast
10. feet
11. meal
12. feast

Page 200

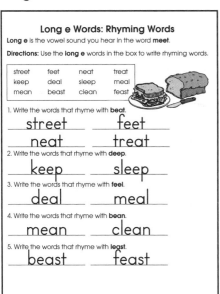

Long e Words: Rhyming Words

Long e is the vowel sound you hear in the word **meet**.

Directions: Use the **long e** words in the box to write rhyming words.

street	feet	neat	treat
keep	deal	sleep	meal
mean	beast	clean	feast

1. Write the words that rhyme with **beat**.

street   feet
neat   treat

2. Write the words that rhyme with **deep**.

keep   sleep

3. Write the words that rhyme with **feel**.

deal   meal

4. Write the words that rhyme with **bean**.

mean   clean

5. Write the words that rhyme with **least**.

beast   feast

Page 201

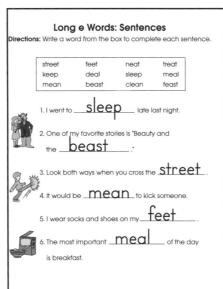

Long e Words: Sentences

Directions: Write a word from the box to complete each sentence.

street	feet	neat	treat
keep	deal	sleep	meal
mean	beast	clean	feast

1. I went to sleep late last night.

2. One of my favorite stories is "Beauty and the beast ."

3. Look both ways when you cross the street .

4. It would be mean to kick someone.

5. I wear socks and shoes on my feet .

6. The most important meal of the day is breakfast.

Page 202

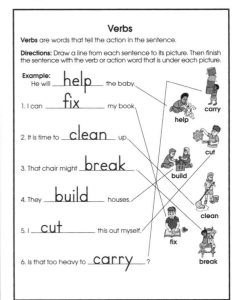

Verbs

Verbs are words that tell the action in the sentence.

Directions: Draw a line from each sentence to its picture. Then finish the sentence with the verb or action word that is under each picture.

Example:
He will help the baby.

1. I can fix my book.

2. It is time to clean up.

3. That chair might break .

4. They build houses.

5. I cut this out myself.

6. Is that too heavy to carry ?

carry
help
cut
build
clean
fix
break

Page 203

Verbs: Sentences

Directions: Read the two sentences in each story below. Then write one more sentence to tell what happened next. Use the verbs from the box.

| break | build | fix | clean | cut | carry |

Today is Mike's birthday.

Mike asked four friends to come.

He cut each person a piece of cake.

Edith's dog walked in the mud.

He got mud in the house.

Edith had to clean up the mess.

Page 204

Verbs: Sentences

Directions: Join each pair of sentences to make one longer sentence. Use one of the **joining** words: **and**, **but** or **or**. In the second part of the sentence, use **he**, **she** or **they** in place of the person's name.

Example: I asked Tim to help me. Tim wanted to play.

I asked Tim to help me, but he wanted to play.

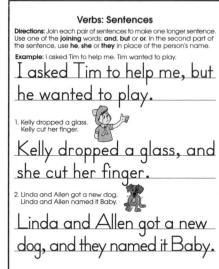

1. Kelly dropped a glass. Kelly cut her finger.

Kelly dropped a glass, and she cut her finger.

2. Linda and Allen got a new dog. Linda and Allen named it Baby.

Linda and Allen got a new dog, and they named it Baby.

Page 205

Verbs: Word Endings

Most **verbs** end with **s** when the sentence tells about one thing. The **s** is taken away when the sentence tells about more than one thing.
Example:
One dog walks.   One boy runs.
Two **dogs** walk.   Three **boys** run.
The spelling of some **verbs** changes when the sentence tells about only one thing.
Example:
One girl carries her lunch.   The boy fixes his car.
Two girls **carry** their lunches.   Two boys **fix** their cars.

Directions: Write the missing verbs in the sentences.
Example:
Pam works hard. She and Peter ___work___ all day.

1. The father bird builds a nest.
The mother and father ___build___ it together.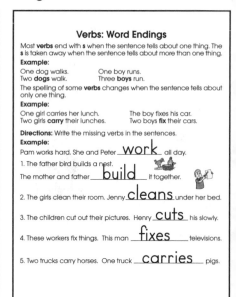

2. The girls clean their room. Jenny ___cleans___ under her bed.

3. The children cut out their pictures. Henry ___cuts___ his slowly.

4. These workers fix things. This man ___fixes___ televisions.

5. Two trucks carry horses. One truck ___carries___ pigs.

Page 206

Short i Words

Short i is the vowel sound you hear in the word **pig**.

Directions: Say each word and listen for the **short i** sound. Then write each word and underline the letter that makes the **short i** sound.

pin	fin	dip	dish
kick	rich	ship	wish
win	fish	sick	pitch

1. pin
2. ship
3. fin
4. wish
5. dip
6. win
7. dish
8. fish
9. kick
10. sick
11. rich
12. pitch

Page 207

Short i Words: Sentences

Directions: Complete the sentences by matching the words to the correct sentence.

1. I made a _wish_ on a star.
2. All we could see was the shark's _fin_ above the water.
3. I like to eat vegetables with _dip_.
4. We saw lots of _fish_ in the water.
5. The soccer player will _kick_ the ball and score a goal.
6. If you feel _sick_, see a doctor.
7. Did Bob _win_ the race?
8. The _dish_ was full of candy.

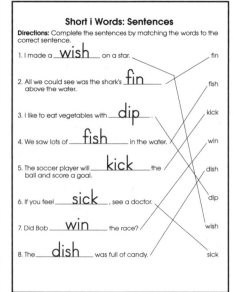

fin
fish
kick
win
dish
dip
wish
sick

Page 208

Long i Words

Long i is the vowel sound which says its own name. **Long i** can be spelled **igh** as in **sight**, **i** with a **silent e** at the end as in **mine** and **y** at the end as in **fly**.

Directions: Say each word and listen for the **long i** sound. Then write each word and underline the letters that make the **long i** sound.

bike	hike	ride	line
glide	ripe	nine	pipe
fight	high	light	sigh

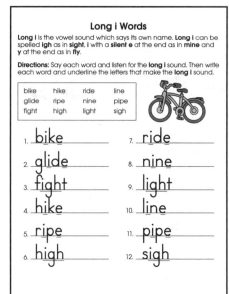

1. bike
2. glide
3. fight
4. hike
5. ripe
6. high
7. ride
8. nine
9. light
10. line
11. pipe
12. sigh

Page 209

Long i Words: Rhyming Words

Long i is the sound you hear in the word **fight**.

Directions: Use the **long i** words in the box to write rhyming words.

bike	hide	ride	line
side	my	by	nine
high	light	sight	fly

1. Write the words that rhyme with **sigh**.

high   my   by   fly

2. Write the words that rhyme with **side**.

hide   ride

3. Write the words that rhyme with **fine**.

line   nine

4. Write the words that rhyme with **fight**.

light   sight

Page 210

Location Words

Directions: Use one of the location words from the box to complete each sentence.

| between | around | inside | outside | beside | across |

Example:
She will hide **under** the basket.

1. In the summer, we like to play **outside**

2. She can swim **across** the lake.

3. Put the bird **inside** its cage so it won't fly away.

4. Sit **between** Bill and me so we can all work together.

5. Your picture is right **beside** mine on the wall.

6. The fence goes **around** the house.

Page 211

Location Words

Directions: Draw a line from each sentence to its picture. Then complete each sentence with the word under the picture.

Example:
He is walking **behind** the tree.

1. We stay **inside** when it rains.

2. She drew a dog **beside** his house.

3. She stands **between** her friends.

4. They walked **across** the bridge.

5. Let the cat go **outside**

6. Draw a circle **around** the fish.

outside

behind

between

across

around

beside

inside

Page 212

Short u Words

Short u is the sound you hear in the word **bug**.

Directions: Say each word and listen for the **short u** sound. Then write each word and underline the letter that makes the **short u** sound.

dust	must	nut	bug
bump	pump	tub	jump
cut	hug	rug	cub

1. dust
2. bump
3. cut
4. must
5. pump
6. hug
7. nut
8. tub
9. rug
10. bug
11. jump
12. cub

Page 213

Short u Words: Sentences

Directions: Circle the words in each sentence which are not correct. Then write the correct **short u** words from the box on the lines.

tub	cub	bump	pump
bug	dust	cut	must
nut	jump	rug	hug

1. The crust made me sneeze.   dust

2. I need to take a bath in the cub.   tub

3. The mug bite left a big pump on my arm.   bug   bump

4. It is time to get my hair hut.   cut

5. The mother bear took care of her shrub.   cub

6. We need to jump more gas into the car.   pump

Page 214

Long u Words

Long u is the vowel sound which says its own name. **Long u** is spelled **u** with a silent **e** at the end as in **cute**. The letters **oo** make a sound very much like long **u**. They make the sound you hear in the word **zoo**. The letters **ew** also make the **oo** sound as in the word **grew**.

Directions: Say the words and listen for the **u** and **oo** sounds. Then write each word and underline the letters that make the **long u** and **oo** sounds.

choose	blew	moon	fuse
cube	Ruth	tooth	use
flew	loose	goose	noon

1. choose
2. cube
3. flew
4. blew
5. Ruth
6. loose
7. moon
8. tooth
9. goose
10. fuse
11. use
12. noon

Page 215

Long u Words: Sentences

Directions: Write the words in the sentences below in the correct order. Begin each sentence with a capital letter and end it with a period or a question mark.

1. the pulled dentist tooth my loose

The dentist pulled my loose tooth.

2. ice cubes I choose in my drink to put

I choose to put ice cubes in my drink.

3. a Ruth fuse blew yesterday

Ruth blew a fuse yesterday.

4. loose the got in garden goose the

The goose got loose in the garden.

5. flew the goose winter for the south

The goose flew south for the winter.

6. is full there a moon tonight

Answer may vary.

Page 216

Opposite Words

Directions: Opposites are words which are different in every way. Use the opposite word from the box to complete these sentences.

| hard | hot | bottom | quickly | happy |
| sad | slowly | cold | soft | top |

Example:

My new coat is blue on ___top___ and

red on the ___bottom___ .

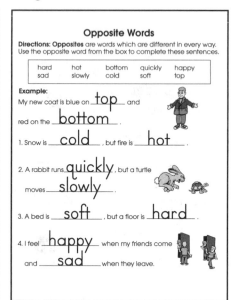

1. Snow is ___cold___ , but fire is ___hot___ .

2. A rabbit runs ___quickly___ , but a turtle

moves ___slowly___

3. A bed is ___soft___ , but a floor is ___hard___

4. I feel ___happy___ when my friends come

and ___sad___ when they leave.

Page 217

Opposite Words

Directions: Draw a line from each sentence to its picture. Then complete each sentence with the word under the picture.

Example:

She bought a ___new___ bat.

1. I like my ___soft___ pillow.

2. Birthdays make me ___happy___

3. Put that book on ___top___

4. Jenny runs ___quickly___

5. A rock makes a ___hard___ seat.

6. I feel ___sad___ when it rains.

7. He eats ___slowly___ .

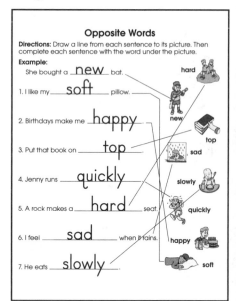

hard

new

top

sad

slowly

quickly

happy

soft

Page 218

Opposite Words: Sentences

Directions: Cross out the word in each box that does not tell about the picture. Write a sentence about the picture using the other two words.

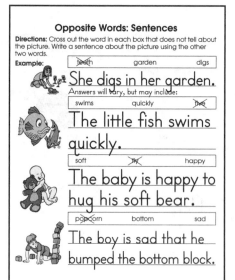

Example:

| ~~teeth~~ | garden | digs |

She digs in her garden.

Answers will vary, but may include:

| swims | quickly | ~~live~~ |

The little fish swims quickly.

| soft | ~~fly~~ | happy |

The baby is happy to hug his soft bear.

| ~~popcorn~~ | bottom | sad |

The boy is sad that he bumped the bottom block.

Page 219

Opposite Words: Sentences

Directions: Look at each picture. Then write a sentence that uses the word under the picture and tells how something is the same as the picture.

Example:

cold — My hands are as cold as ice.

Answers will vary, but may include:

hard — This cookie is as hard as a rock.

slow — When he walked to school, he was as slow as a turtle.

soft — The chair was as soft as a pillow.

happy — The girl was as happy as a lark.

Page 220

Opposite Words: Completing a Story

Directions: Write opposite words in the blanks to complete the story.

| hot | hard | top | cold | bottom |
| soft | quickly | happy | slowly | sad |

One day, Grandma came for a visit. She gave my sister Jenny and me a box of chocolate candy. We said, "Thank you!" Then Jenny ___quickly___ took the ___top___ off the box. The pieces all looked the same! I couldn't tell which pieces were ___soft___ inside and which were ___hard___ ! I only liked the ___soft___ ones. Jenny didn't care. She was ___happy___ to get any kind of candy! I ___slowly___ looked at all the pieces. I didn't know which one to pick. Just then Dad called us. Grandma was going home. He wanted us to say good-bye to her. I hurried to the front door where they were standing. Jenny came a minute later.

I told Grandma I hoped I would see her soon. I always feel ___sad___ when she leaves. Jenny stood behind me and didn't say anything. After Grandma went home, I found out why. Jenny had most of our candy in her mouth! Only a few pieces were left in the ___bottom___ of the box! Then I was ___sad___ ! That Jenny!

Page 221

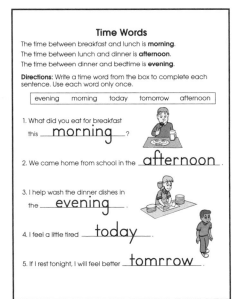

Time Words

The time between breakfast and lunch is **morning**.
The time between lunch and dinner is **afternoon**.
The time between dinner and bedtime is **evening**.

Directions: Write a time word from the box to complete each sentence. Use each word only once.

| evening | morning | today | tomorrow | afternoon |

1. What did you eat for breakfast this **morning**?

2. We came home from school in the **afternoon**.

3. I help wash the dinner dishes in the **evening**.

4. I feel a little tired **today**.

5. If I rest tonight, I will feel better **tomrrow**.

Page 222

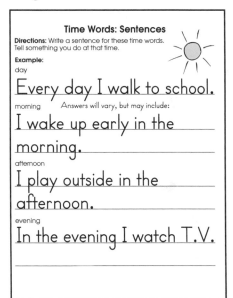

Time Words: Sentences

Directions: Write a sentence for these time words. Tell something you do at that time.

Example:

day

Every day I walk to school.

morning   Answers will vary, but may include:

I wake up early in the morning.

afternoon

I play outside in the afternoon.

evening

In the evening I watch T.V.

Page 224

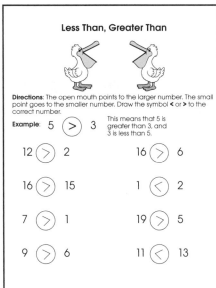

Less Than, Greater Than

Directions: The open mouth points to the larger number. The small point goes to the smaller number. Draw the symbol < or > to the correct number.

Example: 5 > 3   This means that 5 is greater than 3, and 3 is less than 5.

12 > 2   16 > 6

16 > 15   1 < 2

7 > 1   19 > 5

9 > 6   11 < 13

Page 225

Counting

Directions: Write the numbers that are:

next in order	one less	one greater
22, 23, **24**, **25**	**15**, 16	6, **7**
674, **675**, **676**	**246**, 247	125, **126**
227, **228**, **229**	**549**, 550	499, **500**
199, **200**, **201**	**332**, 333	750, **751**
329, **330**, **331**	**861**, 862	933, **934**

Directions: Write the missing numbers.

13 14 15 16 17 18

163 164 165 166 167 168

821 822 823 824 825 826

Page 226

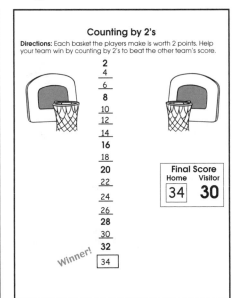

Counting by 2's

Directions: Each basket the players make is worth 2 points. Help your team win by counting by 2's to beat the other team's score.

2
4
6
8
10
12
14
16
18
20
22
24
26
28
30
32
34

Winner!

Final Score	
Home	Visitor
34	30

Page 227

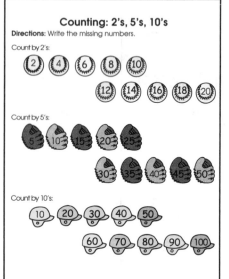

Counting: 2's, 5's, 10's

Directions: Write the missing numbers.

Count by 2's:

2, 4, 6, 8, 10
12, 14, 16, 18, 20

Count by 5's:

5, 10, 15, 20, 25
30, 35, 40, 45, 50

Count by 10's:

10, 20, 30, 40, 50
60, 70, 80, 90, 100

Page 228

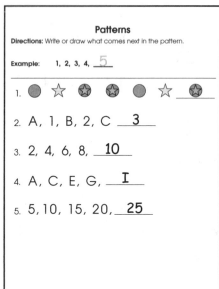

Patterns

Directions: Write or draw what comes next in the pattern.

Example: 1, 2, 3, 4, __5__

1. ● ☆ ⊕ ⊕ ● ☆ ⊛

2. A, 1, B, 2, C __3__

3. 2, 4, 6, 8, __10__

4. A, C, E, G, __I__

5. 5, 10, 15, 20, __25__

Page 229

Finding Patterns: Numbers

Mia likes to count by twos, threes, fours, fives, tens and hundreds.

Directions: Complete the number patterns.

1. 5, _10_ , _15_ , 20, _25_ , _30_ , 35, _40_ , _45_ , 50

2. 100, _200_, _300_, 400, _500_, _600_, _700_, 800, _900_

3. _2_ , 4, 6, _8_ , _10_ , 12, _14_ , 16, _18_ , _20_

4. 10, _20_ , _30_ , 40, _50_ , _60_ , 70, _80_ , 90

5. 4, _8_ , 12, _16_ , _20_ , 24, _28_ , 32, _36_ , 40

6. _3_ , 6, 9, _12_ , _15_ , 18, _21_ , 24, _27_ , 30

Directions: Make up two of your own number patterns.

___, ___, ___, ___, ___, ___
___, ___, ___, ___, ___, ___

Answers will vary.

Page 230

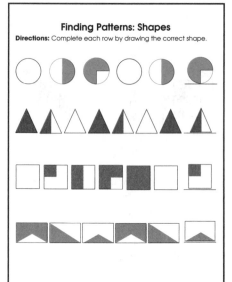

Finding Patterns: Shapes

Directions: Complete each row by drawing the correct shape.

Page 231

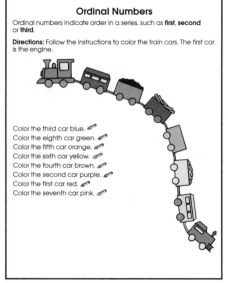

Ordinal Numbers

Ordinal numbers indicate order in a series, such as **first**, **second** or **third**.

Directions: Follow the instructions to color the train cars. The first car is the engine.

Color the third car blue.
Color the eighth car green.
Color the fifth car orange.
Color the sixth car yellow.
Color the fourth car brown.
Color the second car purple.
Color the first car red.
Color the seventh car pink.

Page 232

Ordinal Numbers

Directions: Follow the instructions.

Draw glasses on the second one.
Put a hat on the fourth one.
Color blonde hair on the third one.
Draw a tie on the first one.
Draw ears on the fifth one.
Draw black hair on the seventh one.
Put a bow on the head of the sixth one.

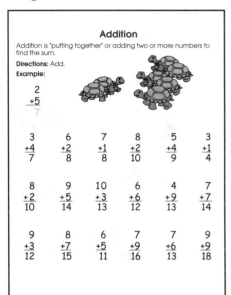

Addition

Addition is "putting together" or adding two or more numbers to find the sum.

Directions: Add.

Example:

$\begin{array}{r} 2 \\ +5 \\ \hline 7 \end{array}$

| $\begin{array}{r}3\\+4\\\hline 7\end{array}$ | $\begin{array}{r}6\\+2\\\hline 8\end{array}$ | $\begin{array}{r}7\\+1\\\hline 8\end{array}$ | $\begin{array}{r}8\\+2\\\hline 10\end{array}$ | $\begin{array}{r}5\\+4\\\hline 9\end{array}$ | $\begin{array}{r}3\\+1\\\hline 4\end{array}$ |

| $\begin{array}{r}8\\+2\\\hline 10\end{array}$ | $\begin{array}{r}9\\+5\\\hline 14\end{array}$ | $\begin{array}{r}10\\+3\\\hline 13\end{array}$ | $\begin{array}{r}6\\+6\\\hline 12\end{array}$ | $\begin{array}{r}4\\+9\\\hline 13\end{array}$ | $\begin{array}{r}7\\+7\\\hline 14\end{array}$ |

| $\begin{array}{r}9\\+3\\\hline 12\end{array}$ | $\begin{array}{r}8\\+7\\\hline 15\end{array}$ | $\begin{array}{r}6\\+5\\\hline 11\end{array}$ | $\begin{array}{r}7\\+9\\\hline 16\end{array}$ | $\begin{array}{r}7\\+6\\\hline 13\end{array}$ | $\begin{array}{r}9\\+9\\\hline 18\end{array}$ |

Addition: Commutative Property

The commutative property of addition states that even if the order of the numbers is changed in an addition sentence, the sum will stay the same.

Example: 2 + 3 = 5
3 + 2 = 5

Directions: Look at the addition sentences below. Complete the addition sentences by writing the missing numerals.

5 + 4 = 9   3 + 1 = 4   2 + 6 = 8
4 + 5 = 9   1 + 3 = 4   6 + 2 = 8

6 + 1 = 7   4 + 3 = 7   1 + 9 = 10
1 + 6 = 7   3 + 4 = 7   9 + 1 = 10

Now try these:

6 + 3 = 9   10 + 2 = 12   8 + 3 = 11
3 + 6 = 9   2 + 10 = 12   3 + 8 = 11

Look at these sums. Can you think of two number sentences that would show the commutative property of addition?

__ + __ = 7   __ + __ = 11   __ + __ = 9

__ + __ = 7   __ + __ = 11   __ + __ = 9

Answers will vary.

Adding 3 or More Numbers

Directions: Add all the numbers to find the sum. Draw pictures to help or break up the problem into two smaller problems.

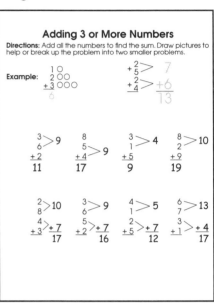

Example:

| $\begin{array}{r}3\\6\\+2\\\hline 11\end{array}$ 9 | $\begin{array}{r}8\\5\\+4\\\hline 17\end{array}$ 9 | $\begin{array}{r}3\\1\\+5\\\hline 9\end{array}$ 4 | $\begin{array}{r}8\\2\\+9\\\hline 19\end{array}$ 10 |

| $\begin{array}{r}2\\8\\+3\\\hline 17\end{array}$ 10 | $\begin{array}{r}3\\6\\+2\\\hline 16\end{array}$ 9 | $\begin{array}{r}4\\6\\+5\\\hline 12\end{array}$ 5 | $\begin{array}{r}6\\7\\+1\\\hline 17\end{array}$ 13 |

Subtraction

Subtraction is "taking away" or subtracting one number from another to find the difference.

Directions: Subtract.

Example:

$\begin{array}{r} 4 \\ -3 \\ \hline 1 \end{array}$

| $\begin{array}{r}5\\-3\\\hline 2\end{array}$ | $\begin{array}{r}6\\-1\\\hline 5\end{array}$ | $\begin{array}{r}4\\-3\\\hline 1\end{array}$ | $\begin{array}{r}3\\-1\\\hline 2\end{array}$ | $\begin{array}{r}2\\-0\\\hline 2\end{array}$ | $\begin{array}{r}1\\-1\\\hline 0\end{array}$ |

| $\begin{array}{r}9\\-2\\\hline 7\end{array}$ | $\begin{array}{r}7\\-4\\\hline 3\end{array}$ | $\begin{array}{r}10\\-5\\\hline 5\end{array}$ | $\begin{array}{r}14\\-6\\\hline 8\end{array}$ | $\begin{array}{r}15\\-9\\\hline 6\end{array}$ | $\begin{array}{r}12\\-3\\\hline 9\end{array}$ |

| $\begin{array}{r}18\\-8\\\hline 10\end{array}$ | $\begin{array}{r}13\\-5\\\hline 8\end{array}$ | $\begin{array}{r}14\\-7\\\hline 7\end{array}$ | $\begin{array}{r}11\\-4\\\hline 7\end{array}$ | $\begin{array}{r}17\\-9\\\hline 8\end{array}$ | $\begin{array}{r}16\\-8\\\hline 8\end{array}$ |

Addition and Subtraction

Addition is "putting together" or adding two or more numbers to find the sum. Subtraction is "taking away" or subtracting one number from another to find the difference.

Directions: Add or subtract. Circle the answers that are less than 10.

Examples:

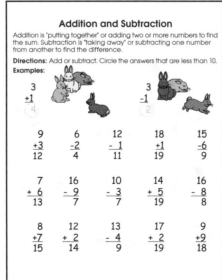

$\begin{array}{r}3\\+1\\\hline 4\end{array}$ $\begin{array}{r}3\\-1\\\hline 2\end{array}$

| $\begin{array}{r}9\\+3\\\hline 12\end{array}$ | $\begin{array}{r}6\\-2\\\hline 4\end{array}$ | $\begin{array}{r}12\\-1\\\hline 11\end{array}$ | $\begin{array}{r}18\\+1\\\hline 19\end{array}$ | $\begin{array}{r}15\\-6\\\hline 9\end{array}$ |

| $\begin{array}{r}7\\+6\\\hline 13\end{array}$ | $\begin{array}{r}16\\-9\\\hline 7\end{array}$ | $\begin{array}{r}10\\-3\\\hline 7\end{array}$ | $\begin{array}{r}14\\+5\\\hline 19\end{array}$ | $\begin{array}{r}16\\-8\\\hline 8\end{array}$ |

| $\begin{array}{r}8\\+7\\\hline 15\end{array}$ | $\begin{array}{r}12\\+2\\\hline 14\end{array}$ | $\begin{array}{r}13\\-4\\\hline 9\end{array}$ | $\begin{array}{r}17\\+2\\\hline 19\end{array}$ | $\begin{array}{r}9\\+9\\\hline 18\end{array}$ |

Place Value: Ones, Tens

The place value of a digit or numeral is shown by where it is in the number. For example, in the number **23**, **2** has the place value of **tens**, and **3** is **ones**.

Directions: Add the tens and ones and write your answers in the blanks.

Example:

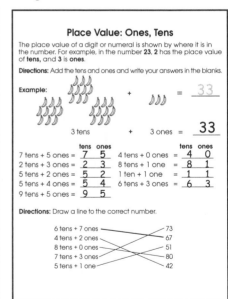

= 33

3 tens   +   3 ones =   **33**

	tens ones		tens ones
7 tens + 5 ones =	**7 5**	4 tens + 0 ones =	**4 0**
2 tens + 3 ones =	**2 3**	8 tens + 1 one =	**8 1**
5 tens + 2 ones =	**5 2**	1 ten + 1 one =	**1 1**
5 tens + 4 ones =	**5 4**	6 tens + 3 ones =	**6 3**
9 tens + 5 ones =	**9 5**		

Directions: Draw a line to the correct number.

6 tens + 7 ones —— 73
4 tens + 2 ones —— 67
8 tens + 0 ones —— 51
7 tens + 3 ones —— 80
5 tens + 1 one —— 42

Page 239

Place Value: Ones, Tens

Directions: Write the numbers for the tens and ones. Then add.

Example:

2 tens + 7 ones
20 + 7
27

6 tens + 2 ones
60 + 2
62

3 tens + 4 ones
30 + 4
34

8 tens + 3 ones
80 + 3
83

5 tens + 0 ones
50 + 0
50

Page 240

2-Digit Addition

Directions: Study the example. Follow the steps to add.

Example: 33
              +41

Step 1: Add the ones.

tens	ones
3	3
+4	1
	4

Step 2: Add the tens.

tens	ones
3	3
+4	1
7	4

tens	ones
4	2
+2	4
6	6

tens	ones
5	0
+4	7
9	7

24	15	38	11	37	72	33	10
+62	+23	+61	+26	+42	+11	+51	+30
86	38	99	37	79	83	84	40

25	62	32	25	82	91	16	55
+42	+14	+44	+13	+6	+5	+71	+3
67	76	76	38	88	96	87	58

Page 241

2-Digit Addition

Directions: Add the total points scored in each game. Remember to add **ones** first and **tens** second.

Example:

HOME 22
VISITOR 17   Total 39

HOME 28
VISITOR 30   Total 58

HOME 55
VISITOR 21   Total 76

HOME 14
VISITOR 33   Total 47

HOME 24
VISITOR 13   Total 37

HOME 46
VISITOR 32   Total 78

HOME 83
VISITOR 06   Total 89

HOME 30
VISITOR 20   Total 50

HOME 17
VISITOR 42   Total 59

HOME 24
VISITOR 45   Total 69

Page 242

2-Digit Addition: Regrouping

Addition is "putting together" or adding two or more numbers to find the sum. Regrouping is using **ten ones** to form **one ten, ten tens** to form **one 100, fifteen ones** to form **one ten** and **five ones** and so on.

Directions: Study the examples. Follow the steps to add.

Example: 14
              + 8

Step 1: Add the ones.

tens	ones
1	4
+	8
	12

Step 2: Regroup the tens.

tens	ones
1	4
+	8

Step 3: Add the tens.

tens	ones
1	4
+	8
2	2

tens	ones
1	6
+3	7
5	3

tens	ones
3	8
+5	3
9	1

tens	ones
2	4
+4	7
7	1

28	32	54	19	44	25	29	79
+17	+38	+25	+55	+48	+64	+33	+15
45	70	79	74	92	89	62	94

Page 243

2-Digit Addition: Regrouping

Directions: Add the total points scored in the game. Remember to add the ones, regroup, and then add the tens.

Example:

HOME 47
VISITOR 38   Total 85

HOME 33
VISITOR 57   Total 90

HOME 43
VISITOR 49   Total 92

HOME 57
VISITOR 34   Total 91

HOME 29
VISITOR 22   Total 51

HOME 36
VISITOR 58   Total 94

HOME 45
VISITOR 39   Total 84

HOME 66
VISITOR 26   Total 92

HOME 72
VISITOR 19   Total 91

HOME 54
VISITOR 26   Total 80

Page 244

2-Digit Subtraction

Directions: Study the example. Follow the steps to subtract.

Example: 28
              -14

Step 1: Subtract the ones.

tens	ones
2	8
-1	4
	4

Step 2: Subtract the tens.

tens	ones
2	8
-1	4
1	4

tens	ones
2	4
-1	2
1	2

tens	ones
3	8
-1	5
2	3

24	61	77	85	57	87	59	96
-12	-30	-44	-24	-23	-33	-34	-16
12	31	33	61	34	54	25	80

29	74	46	69	95	33	78	22
-15	-51	-32	-35	-32	-33	-26	-11
14	23	14	34	63	0	52	11

2-Digit Subtraction: Regrouping

Subtraction is "taking away" or subtracting one number from another to find the difference. Regrouping is using **one ten to form ten ones, one 100 to form ten tens** and so on.

Directions: Study the examples. Follow the steps to subtract.

Example: 37
−19

Step 1: Regroup.   **Step 2:** Subtract the ones.   **Step 3:** Subtract the tens.

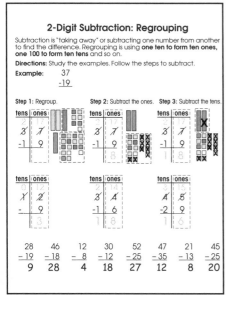

28	46	12	30	52	47	21	45
−19	−18	−8	−12	−25	−35	−13	−25
9	28	4	18	27	12	8	20

2-Digit Subtraction: Regrouping

Directions: Study the steps for subtracting. Solve the problems using the steps.

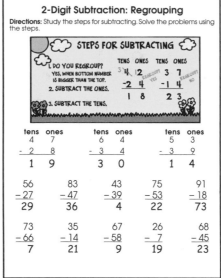

STEPS FOR SUBTRACTING

1. DO YOU REGROUP? YES, WHEN BOTTOM NUMBER IS BIGGER THAN THE TOP.
2. SUBTRACT THE ONES.
3. SUBTRACT THE TENS.

tens ones	tens ones	tens ones
4 7	6 4	5 3
− 2 8	− 3 4	− 3 9
1 9	3 0	1 4

56	83	43	75	91
− 27	− 47	− 39	− 53	− 18
29	36	4	22	73

73	35	67	26	68
− 66	− 14	− 58	− 7	− 45
7	21	9	19	23

Review

Directions: Add or subtract. Use regrouping when needed. Always do ones first and tens last.

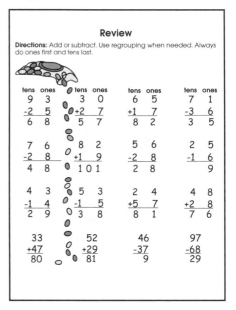

tens ones	tens ones	tens ones	tens ones
9 3	3 0	6 5	7 1
−2 5	+2 7	+1 7	−3 6
6 8	5 7	8 2	3 5

7 6	8 2	5 6	2 5
−2 8	+1 9	−2 8	−1 6
4 8	101	2 8	9

4 3	5 3	2 4	4 8
−1 4	−1 5	+5 7	+2 8
2 9	3 8	8 1	7 6

33	52	46	97
+47	+29	−37	−68
80	81	9	29

2-Digit Addition and Subtraction

Addition is "putting together" or adding two or more numbers to find the sum. Subtraction is "taking away" or subtracting one number from another to find the difference. Regrouping is using **one ten** to form **ten ones, one 100** to form **ten tens**, and so on.

Directions: Add or subtract using regrouping.

Example:

tens ones
2 15
3   5
−2   7
8

56	40	35	42	53	97	44	93
− 27	− 16	+ 27	− 14	+38	− 48	+ 27	− 39
29	24	62	28	91	49	71	54

56	44	68	73	33	49	77	27
− 17	+ 28	− 49	− 24	+ 18	+ 32	− 68	+ 19
39	72	19	49	51	81	9	46

2-Digit Addition and Subtraction

Directions: Add or subtract using regrouping.

23	84	69	41
+48	−56	+29	−17
71	28	98	24

52	73	84	57
−28	+18	−27	−39
24	91	57	18

33	64	37	36
−15	+17	+58	−19
18	81	95	17

65	48	33	25
−28	−30	+18	+35
37	18	51	60

Place Value: Hundreds

The place value of a digit or numeral is shown by where it is in the number. For example, in the number **123**, **1** has the place value of **hundreds**, **2** is **tens** and **3** is **ones**.

Directions: Study the examples. Then write the missing numbers in the blanks.

Examples:

2 hundreds + 3 tens + 6 ones =

hundreds	tens	ones
2	3	6	= 236

1 hundred + 4 tens + 9 ones =

hundreds	tens	ones
1	4	9	= 149

	hundreds	tens	ones	total
3 hundreds + 4 tens + 8 ones =	3	4	8	= 348
2 hundreds + 1 tens + 7 ones =	2	1	7	= 217
6 hundreds + 3 tens + 5 ones =	6	3	5	= 635
4 hundreds + 7 tens + 9 ones =	4	7	9	= 479
2 hundreds + 9 tens + 4 ones =	2	9	4	= 294
4 hundreds + 5 tens + 6 ones =	4	5	6	= 456
3 hundreds + 1 tens + 3 ones =	3	1	3	= 313
3 hundreds + 5 tens + 7 ones =	3	5	7	= 357
6 hundreds + 2 tens + 8 ones =	6	2	8	= 628

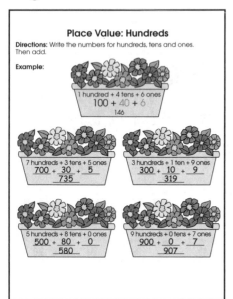

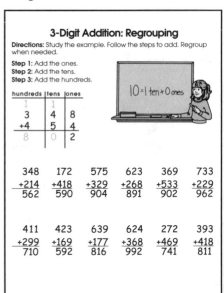

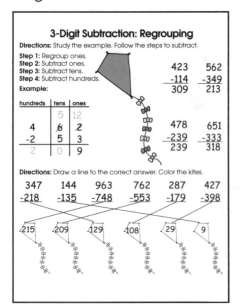

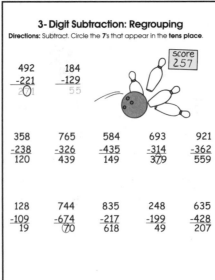

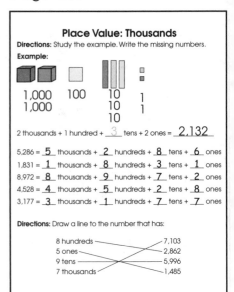

Page 251

Place Value: Hundreds

Directions: Write the numbers for hundreds, tens and ones. Then add.

Example:

1 hundred + 4 tens + 6 ones
100 + 40 + 6
146

7 hundreds + 3 tens + 5 ones
700 + 30 + 5
735

3 hundreds + 1 ten + 9 ones
300 + 10 + 9
319

5 hundreds + 8 tens + 0 ones
500 + 80 + 0
580

9 hundreds + 0 tens + 7 ones
900 + 0 + 7
907

Page 252

3-Digit Addition: Regrouping

Directions: Study the examples. Follow the steps to add.

Example:

Step 1: Add the ones.
Step 2: Add the tens.
Step 3: Add the hundreds.

Do you regroup? Do you regroup?

hundreds	tens	ones
	1	
3	4	8
+4	4	4
		2

hundreds	tens	ones
	1	
3	4	8
+4	4	4
	9	2

hundreds	tens	ones
	1	
3	4	8
+4	4	4
7	9	2

hundreds	tens	ones
2	1	4
+2	3	8
4	5	2

hundreds	tens	ones
3	6	8
+2	1	3
5	8	1

hundreds	tens	ones
1	1	9
+5	6	5
6	8	4

418   471   334   659   736   426   567   327
+323 +319 +528 +127 +145 +165 +228 +354
741   790   862   786   881   591   795   681

Page 253

3-Digit Addition: Regrouping

Directions: Study the example. Follow the steps to add. Regroup when needed.

Step 1: Add the ones.
Step 2: Add the tens.
Step 3: Add the hundreds.

10 = 1 ten + 0 ones

hundreds	tens	ones
1	1	
3	4	8
+4	5	4
8	0	2

348   172   575   623   369   733
+214 +418 +329 +268 +533 +229
562   590   904   891   902   962

411   423   639   624   272   393
+299 +169 +177 +368 +469 +418
710   592   816   992   741   811

Page 254

3-Digit Subtraction: Regrouping

Directions: Study the example. Follow the steps to subtract.

Step 1: Regroup ones.
Step 2: Subtract ones.
Step 3: Subtract tens.
Step 4: Subtract hundreds.

Example:

hundreds	tens	ones
	5	12
4	6	2
-2	5	3
2	0	9

423   562
-114 -349
309   213

478   651
-239 -333
239   318

Directions: Draw a line to the correct answer. Color the kites.

347   144   963   762   287   427
-218 -135 -748 -553 -179 -398

215   209   129   108   29   9

Page 255

3-Digit Subtraction: Regrouping

Directions: Subtract. Circle the 7's that appear in the **tens place**.

score
257

492   184
-221 -129
201   55

358   765   584   693   921
-238 -326 -435 -314 -362
120   439   149   379   559

128   744   835   248   635
-109 -674 -217 -199 -428
19   70   618   49   207

Page 256

Place Value: Thousands

Directions: Study the example. Write the missing numbers.

Example:

1,000   100   10   1
1,000   10   1
              10

2 thousands + 1 hundred + __3__ tens + 2 ones = __2,132__

5,286 = __5__ thousands + __2__ hundreds + __8__ tens + __6__ ones
1,831 = __1__ thousands + __8__ hundreds + __3__ tens + __1__ ones
8,972 = __8__ thousands + __9__ hundreds + __7__ tens + __2__ ones
4,528 = __4__ thousands + __5__ hundreds + __2__ tens + __8__ ones
3,177 = __3__ thousands + __1__ hundreds + __7__ tens + __7__ ones

Directions: Draw a line to the number that has:

8 hundreds   7,103
5 ones   2,862
9 tens   5,996
7 thousands   1,485

Page 257

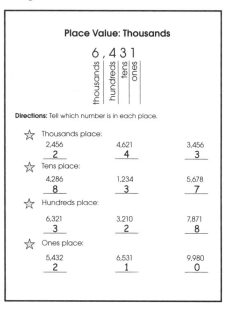

Place Value: Thousands

6,431
thousands hundreds tens ones

Directions: Tell which number is in each place.

☆ Thousands place:

2,456	4,621	3,456
2	4	3

☆ Tens place:

4,286	1,234	5,678
8	3	7

☆ Hundreds place:

6,321	3,210	7,871
3	2	8

☆ Ones place:

5,432	6,531	9,980
2	1	0

Page 258

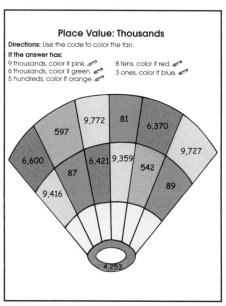

Place Value: Thousands
Directions: Use the code to color the fan.
If the answer has:
9 thousands, color it pink.
6 thousands, color it green.
5 hundreds, color it orange.
8 tens, color it red.
3 ones, color it blue.

Page 259

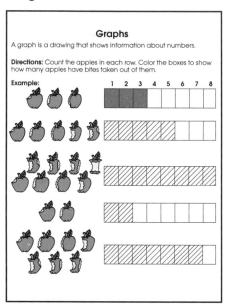

Graphs
A graph is a drawing that shows information about numbers.

Directions: Count the apples in each row. Color the boxes to show how many apples have bites taken out of them.

Example:

Page 260

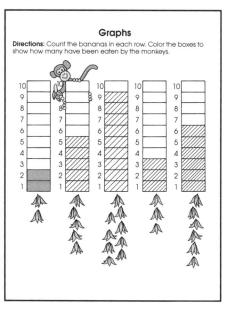

Graphs
Directions: Count the bananas in each row. Color the boxes to show how many have been eaten by the monkeys.

Page 261

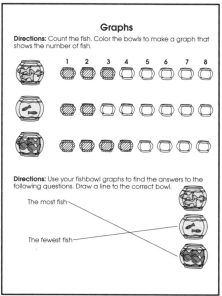

Graphs
Directions: Count the fish. Color the bowls to make a graph that shows the number of fish.

Directions: Use your fishbowl graphs to find the answers to the following questions. Draw a line to the correct bowl.

The most fish

The fewest fish

Page 262

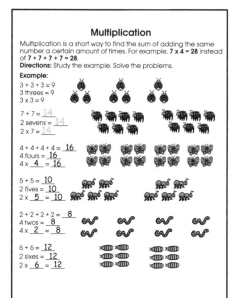

Multiplication
Multiplication is a short way to find the sum of adding the same number a certain amount of times. For example, **7 x 4 = 28** instead of **7 + 7 + 7 + 7 = 28**.
Directions: Study the example. Solve the problems.
Example:

3 + 3 + 3 = 9
3 threes = 9
3 x 3 = 9

7 + 7 = 14
2 sevens = 14
2 x 7 = 14

4 + 4 + 4 + 4 = 16
4 fours = 16
4 x 4 = 16

5 + 5 = 10
2 fives = 10
2 x 5 = 10

2 + 2 + 2 + 2 = 8
4 twos = 8
4 x 2 = 8

6 + 6 = 12
2 sixes = 12
2 x 6 = 12

Page 263

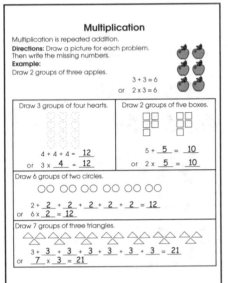

Multiplication

Multiplication is repeated addition.

Directions: Draw a picture for each problem. Then write the missing numbers.

Example:
Draw 2 groups of three apples.

$3 + 3 = 6$
or $2 \times 3 = 6$

Draw 3 groups of four hearts.	Draw 2 groups of five boxes.
$4 + 4 + 4 = \underline{12}$ or $3 \times \underline{4} = \underline{12}$	$5 + \underline{5} = \underline{10}$ or $2 \times \underline{5} = \underline{10}$

Draw 6 groups of two circles.

$2 + \underline{2} + \underline{2} + \underline{2} + \underline{2} + \underline{2} = \underline{12}$
or $6 \times \underline{2} = \underline{12}$

Draw 7 groups of three triangles.

$3 + \underline{3} + \underline{3} + \underline{3} + \underline{3} + \underline{3} + \underline{3} = \underline{21}$
or $\underline{7} \times \underline{3} = \underline{21}$

Page 264

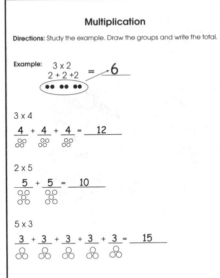

Multiplication

Directions: Study the example. Draw the groups and write the total.

Example:
3×2
$2 + 2 + 2 = 6$

3×4

$\underline{4} + \underline{4} + \underline{4} = \underline{12}$

2×5

$\underline{5} + \underline{5} = \underline{10}$

5×3

$\underline{3} + \underline{3} + \underline{3} + \underline{3} + \underline{3} = \underline{15}$

Page 265

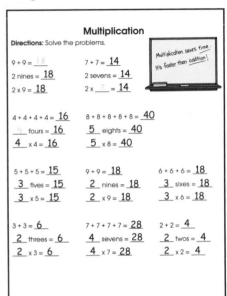

Multiplication

Directions: Solve the problems.

Multiplication saves time. It's faster than addition!

$9 + 9 = \underline{18}$ $7 + 7 = \underline{14}$
2 nines = $\underline{18}$ 2 sevens = $\underline{14}$
$2 \times 9 = \underline{18}$ $2 \times \underline{7} = \underline{14}$

$4 + 4 + 4 + 4 = \underline{16}$ $8 + 8 + 8 + 8 + 8 = \underline{40}$
$\underline{4}$ fours = $\underline{16}$ $\underline{5}$ eights = $\underline{40}$
$\underline{4} \times 4 = \underline{16}$ $\underline{5} \times 8 = \underline{40}$

$5 + 5 + 5 = \underline{15}$ $9 + 9 = \underline{18}$ $6 + 6 + 6 = \underline{18}$
$\underline{3}$ fives = $\underline{15}$ $\underline{2}$ nines = $\underline{18}$ $\underline{3}$ sixes = $\underline{18}$
$\underline{3} \times 5 = \underline{15}$ $\underline{2} \times 9 = \underline{18}$ $\underline{3} \times 6 = \underline{18}$

$3 + 3 = \underline{6}$ $7 + 7 + 7 + 7 = \underline{28}$ $2 + 2 = \underline{4}$
$\underline{2}$ threes = $\underline{6}$ $\underline{4}$ sevens = $\underline{28}$ $\underline{2}$ twos = $\underline{4}$
$\underline{2} \times 3 = \underline{6}$ $\underline{4} \times 7 = \underline{28}$ $\underline{2} \times 2 = \underline{4}$

Page 266

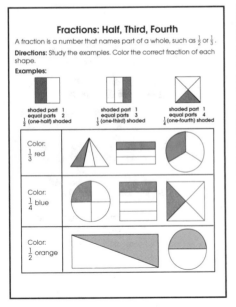

Fractions: Half, Third, Fourth

A fraction is a number that names part of a whole, such as $\frac{1}{2}$ or $\frac{1}{3}$.

Directions: Study the examples. Color the correct fraction of each shape.

Examples:

shaded part 1
equal parts 2
$\frac{1}{2}$ (one-half) shaded

shaded part 1
equal parts 3
$\frac{1}{3}$ (one-third) shaded

shaded part 1
equal parts 4
$\frac{1}{4}$ (one-fourth) shaded

Color: $\frac{1}{3}$ red	
Color: $\frac{1}{4}$ blue	
Color: $\frac{1}{2}$ orange	

Page 267

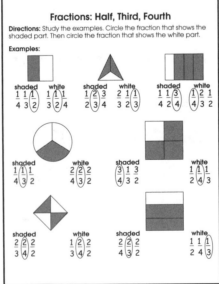

Fractions: Half, Third, Fourth

Directions: Study the examples. Circle the fraction that shows the shaded part. Then circle the fraction that shows the white part.

Examples:

Page 268

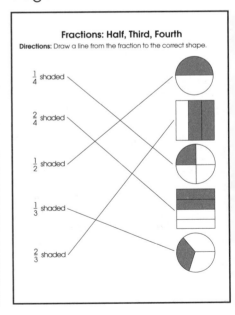

Fractions: Half, Third, Fourth

Directions: Draw a line from the fraction to the correct shape.

$\frac{1}{4}$ shaded

$\frac{2}{4}$ shaded

$\frac{1}{2}$ shaded

$\frac{1}{3}$ shaded

$\frac{2}{3}$ shaded

Page 269

Geometry

Geometry is mathematics that has to do with lines and shapes.

Directions: Color the shapes.

Color the triangles blue. ✏
Color the circles red. ✏
Color the squares green. ✏
Color the rectangles pink. ✏

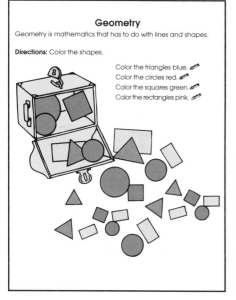

Page 270

Geometry

Directions: Draw a line from the word to the shape.
Use a red line for circles. ✏ Use a yellow line for rectangles. ✏
Use a blue line for squares. ✏ Use a green line for triangles. ✏

Circle   Square   Triangle   Rectangle

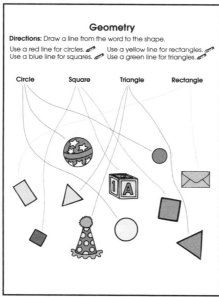

Page 271

Geometry

Directions: Cut out the tangram below. Mix up the pieces. Try to put it back together into a square.

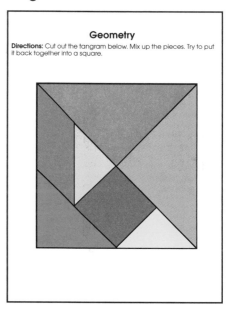

Page 273

Measurement: Inches

Directions: Cut out the ruler. Measure each object to the nearest inch.

_2_ inches

_3_ inches

_1_ inches

Measurement

Directions: Measure objects around your house. Write the measurement to the nearest inch.

Answers will vary.

can of soup _____ inches
pen _____ inches
toothbrush _____ inches
paper clip _____ inches
small toy _____ inches

cut out

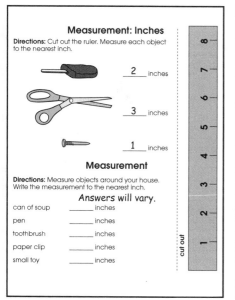

Page 275

Measurement: Inches

An inch is a unit of length in the standard measurement system.
Directions: Use a ruler to measure each object to the nearest inch.

1 inch

about _1_ inches

about _1_ inches

about _4_ inches

about _2_ inches

about _2_ inches

about _4_ inches

about _3_ inches

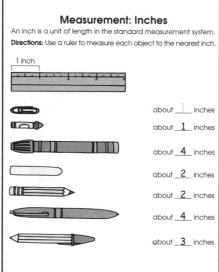

Page 276

Measurement: Inches

Directions: Use the ruler to measure the fish to the nearest inch.

about _4_ inches

about _1_ inches

about _2_ inches

about _1_ inches

about _3_ inches

about _3_ inches

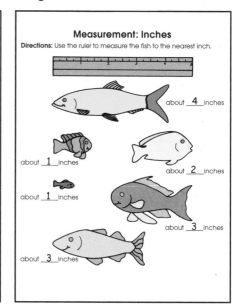

Page 277

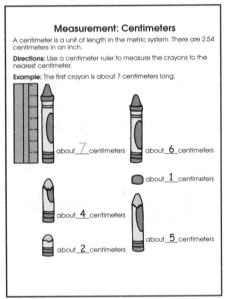

Measurement: Centimeters

A centimeter is a unit of length in the metric system. There are 2.54 centimeters in an inch.

Directions: Use a centimeter ruler to measure the crayons to the nearest centimeter.

Example: The first crayon is about 7 centimeters long.

about __7__ centimeters   about __6__ centimeters

about __1__ centimeters

about __4__ centimeters

about __2__ centimeters   about __5__ centimeters

Page 278

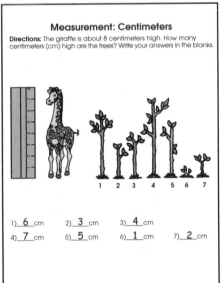

Measurement: Centimeters

Directions: The giraffe is about 8 centimeters high. How many centimeters (cm) high are the trees? Write your answers in the blanks.

1 2 3 4 5 6 7

1) __6__ cm   2) __3__ cm   3) __4__ cm

4) __7__ cm   5) __5__ cm   6) __1__ cm   7) __2__ cm

Page 279

Time: Hour, Half-Hour

An hour is sixty minutes. The short hand of a clock tells the hour. It is written **0:00**, such as **5:00**. A half-hour is thirty minutes. When the long hand of the clock is pointing to the six, the time is on the half-hour. It is written **:30**, such as **5:30**.

Directions: Study the examples. Tell what time it is on each clock.

Examples:

__9:00__   __4:30__

The minute hand is on the 12. The hour hand is on the 9. It is 9 o'clock.

The minute hand is on the 6. The hour hand is *between* the 4 and 5. It is 4:30.

2:00   3:30   1:00   5:30   8:00

10:30   12:00   9:30   2:30   3:00

Page 280

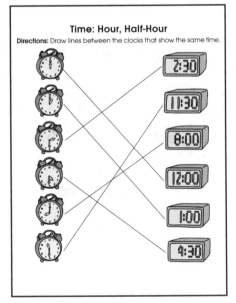

Time: Hour, Half-Hour

Directions: Draw lines between the clocks that show the same time.

2:30

11:30

8:00

12:00

1:00

4:30

Page 281

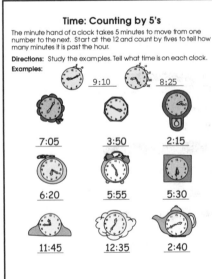

Time: Counting by 5's

The minute hand of a clock takes 5 minutes to move from one number to the next. Start at the 12 and count by fives to tell how many minutes it is past the hour.

Directions: Study the examples. Tell what time is on each clock.

Examples:

__9:10__   __8:25__

7:05   3:50   2:15

6:20   5:55   5:30

11:45   12:35   2:40

Page 282

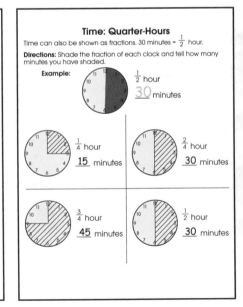

Time: Quarter-Hours

Time can also be shown as fractions. 30 minutes = $\frac{1}{2}$ hour.

Directions: Shade the fraction of each clock and tell how many minutes you have shaded.

Example:

$\frac{1}{2}$ hour
__30__ minutes

$\frac{1}{4}$ hour
__15__ minutes

$\frac{2}{4}$ hour
__30__ minutes

$\frac{3}{4}$ hour
__45__ minutes

$\frac{1}{2}$ hour
__30__ minutes

Page 283

Review
Counting

Directions: Write the number that is:

next	one less	one greater
68, 69, __70__	__56__, 57	12, __13__
786, 787, __788__	__649__, 650	843, __844__

Place Value: Tens & Ones

Directions: Draw a line to the correct number.

4 tens + 7 ones — 20
2 tens + 0 ones — 51
7 tens + 3 ones — 47
5 tens + 1 one — 73

Addition and Subtraction

Directions: Add or subtract.

15 + 5 20	14 - 4 10	7 + 3 10	8 - 6 2	10 + 7 17	14 - 5 9

Page 284

Review
2-Digit Addition and Subtraction

Directions: Add or subtract using regrouping, if needed.

66 - 37 29	38 + 18 56	87 - 69 18	52 - 15 37	40 + 17 57
84 + 17 101	65 + 14 79	99 - 48 51	61 - 36 25	56 + 46 102

Place Value: Hundreds and Thousands

Directions: Draw a line to the correct number.

4 hundreds + 3 tens + 2 ones — 7,201
6 hundreds + 7 tens + 6 ones — 290
5 thousands + 3 hundreds + 7 tens + 2 ones — 432
2 hundreds + 9 tens + 0 ones — 676
7 thousands + 2 hundreds + 0 tens + 1 one — 5,372

3-Digit Addition and Subtraction

Directions: Add or subtract, remembering to regroup, if needed.

458 - 248 210	793 - 414 379	822 - 460 362	528 + 319 847	697 + 108 805	569 + 288 857

Page 285

Review
Multiplication

Directions: Solve the problems. Draw groups if necessary.

2 x 8 16	6 x 4 24	3 x 2 6	8 x 4 32	5 x 3 15	2 x 2 4

Fractions

Directions: Circle the correct fraction of each shape's white part.

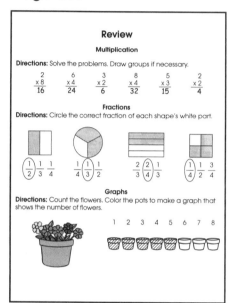

Graphs

Directions: Count the flowers. Color the pots to make a graph that shows the number of flowers.

1 2 3 4 5 6 7 8

Page 286

Review
Geometry

Directions: Match the shapes.

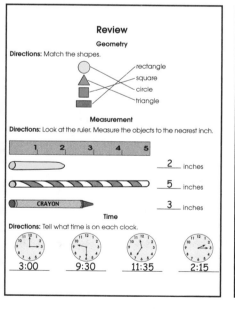

rectangle
square
circle
triangle

Measurement

Directions: Look at the ruler. Measure the objects to the nearest inch.

__2__ inches
__5__ inches
__3__ inches

Time

Directions: Tell what time is on each clock.

3:00   9:30   11:35   2:15

Page 287

Money: Penny, Nickel

Penny 1¢   Nickel 5¢

Directions: Count the coins and write the amount.

Example:

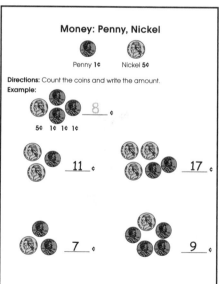

__8__ ¢
5¢ 1¢ 1¢ 1¢

__11__ ¢
__17__ ¢
__7__ ¢
__9__ ¢

Page 288

Money: Penny, Nickel, Dime

Penny 1¢   Nickel 5¢   Dime 10¢

Directions: Count the coins and write the amount.

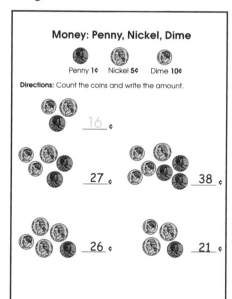

__16__ ¢
__27__ ¢
__38__ ¢
__26__ ¢
__21__ ¢

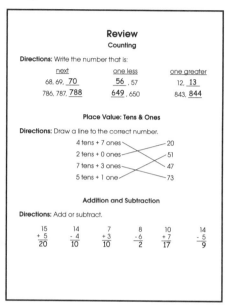
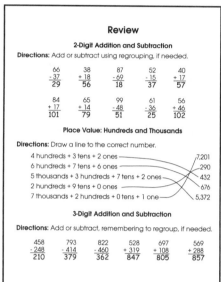

Page 289

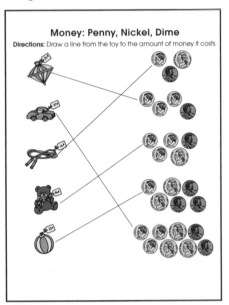

Money: Penny, Nickel, Dime

Directions: Draw a line from the toy to the amount of money it costs.

Page 290

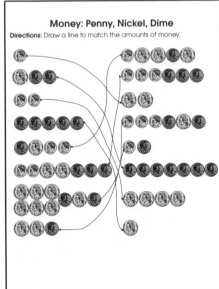

Money: Penny, Nickel, Dime

Directions: Draw a line to match the amounts of money.

Page 291

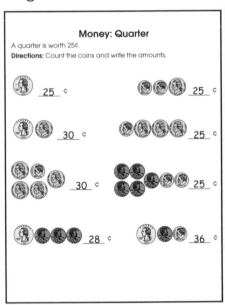

Money: Quarter

A quarter is worth 25¢.

Directions: Count the coins and write the amounts.

25 ¢   25 ¢

30 ¢   25 ¢

30 ¢   25 ¢

28 ¢   36 ¢

Page 292

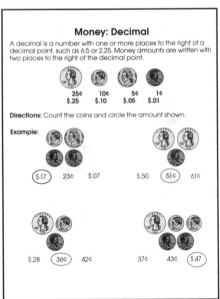

Money: Decimal

A decimal is a number with one or more places to the right of a decimal point, such as 6.5 or 2.25. Money amounts are written with two places to the right of the decimal point.

25¢   10¢   5¢   1¢
$.25 $.10 $.05 $.01

Directions: Count the coins and circle the amount shown.

Example:

($.17)   23¢ $.07 $.50   (51¢)   61¢

$.28   (36¢)   42¢   37¢   43¢   ($.47)

Page 293

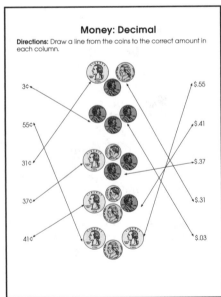

Money: Decimal

Directions: Draw a line from the coins to the correct amount in each column.

3¢ $.55

55¢ $.41

31¢ $.37

37¢ $.31

41¢ $.03

Page 294

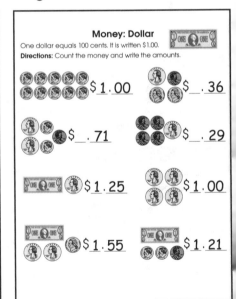

Money: Dollar

One dollar equals 100 cents. It is written $1.00.

Directions: Count the money and write the amounts.

$1.00 $ .36

$ .71 $ .29

$1.25 $1.00

$1.55 $1.21

Page 295

Adding Money

Directions: Write the amount of money using decimals. Then add to find the total amount.

Example:
$$\begin{array}{r} \$1.00 \\ .05 \\ +\ .02 \\ \hline \$1.07 \end{array}$$

$$\begin{array}{r} \$3.00 \\ \$.50 \\ \$.20 \\ +\$.01 \\ \hline 3.71 \end{array}$$

$$\begin{array}{r} \$1.00 \\ \$.75 \\ \$.20 \\ +\$.05 \\ \hline 2.00 \end{array}$$

$$\begin{array}{r} \$2.00 \\ \$.25 \\ +\$.40 \\ \hline 2.65 \end{array}$$

$$\begin{array}{r} \$1.00 \\ \$.25 \\ \$.30 \\ +\$.15 \\ \hline 1.70 \end{array}$$

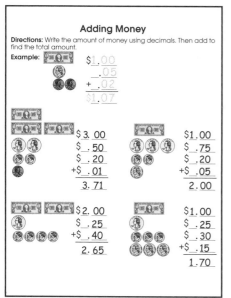

Page 296

Money: Practice

Directions: Draw a line from each food item to the correct amount of money.

$1.59
$.89
$1.27
$1.09
$.77
$1.95

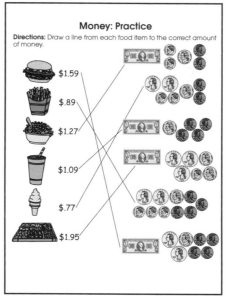

Page 297

Review

Directions: Add the money and write the total.

_41_ ¢

_35_ ¢

$ _1.32_

_76_ ¢

$ _2.63_

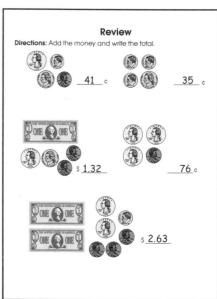

Page 298

Problem-Solving

Directions: Tell whether you should add or subtract. "In all" is a clue to add. "Left" is a clue to subtract. Draw pictures to help you.

Example:
Jane's dog has 5 bones. He ate 3 bones. How many bones are left?

subtract

$$\begin{array}{r} 5 \\ -\ 3 \\ \hline 2 \end{array}$$ bones

Lucky the cat had 5 mice. She got 4 more for her birthday. How many mice did she have in all?

add

$$\begin{array}{r} 5 \\ +\ 4 \\ \hline 9 \end{array}$$ mice

Sam bought 6 fish. She gave 2 fish to a friend. How many fish does she have left?

subtract

$$\begin{array}{r} 6 \\ -\ 2 \\ \hline 4 \end{array}$$ fish

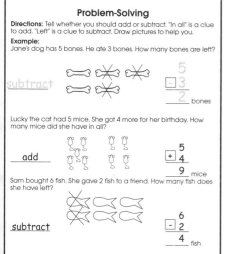

Page 299

Problem-Solving: Addition, Subtraction, Multiplication

Directions: Tell if you add, subtract or multiply. Then write the answer.

Example:
There were 12 frogs sitting on a log by a pond, but 3 frogs hopped away. How many frogs are left?

Subtract _9_ frogs

There are 9 flowers growing by the pond. Each flower has 2 leaves. How many leaves are there?

multiply _18_ leaves

A tree had 7 squirrels playing in it. Then 8 more came along. How many squirrels are there in all?

add _15_ squirrels

There were 27 birds living in the trees around the pond, but 9 flew away. How many birds are left?

subtract _18_ birds

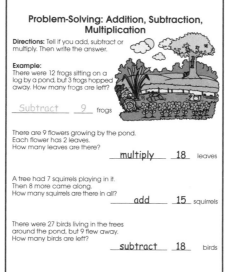

Page 300

Problem-Solving: Fractions

A fraction is a number that names part of a whole, such as $\frac{1}{2}$ or $\frac{1}{3}$.
Directions: Read each problem. Use the pictures to help you solve the problem. Write the fraction that answers the question.

Simon and Jessie shared a pizza. Together they ate $\frac{3}{4}$ of the pizza. How much of the pizza is left?

$\frac{1}{4}$

Sylvia baked a cherry pie. She gave $\frac{1}{3}$ to her grandmother and $\frac{1}{3}$ to a friend. How much of the pie did she keep?

$\frac{1}{3}$

Timmy erased $\frac{1}{2}$ of the blackboard before the bell rang for recess. How much of the blackboard does he have left to erase?

$\frac{1}{2}$

Directions: Read the problem. Draw your own picture to help you solve the problem. Write the fraction that answers the question.

Sarah mowed $\frac{1}{4}$ of the yard before lunch. How much does she have left to mow?

$\frac{3}{4}$

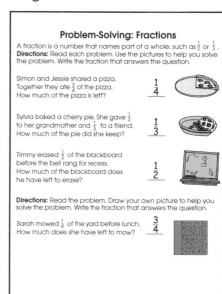

Page 301

Problem-Solving: Time

Directions: Solve each problem.

Tracy wakes up at 7:00. She has 30 minutes before her bus comes. What time does her bus come?

7 : 30

Vera walks her dog for 15 minutes after supper. She finishes supper at 6:30. When does she get home from walking her dog?

6 : 45

Chip practices the piano for 30 minutes when he gets home from school. He gets home at 3:30. When does he stop practicing?

4 : 00

Tanya starts mowing the grass at 4:30. She finishes at 5:00. For how many minutes does she mow the lawn?

30 minutes

Don does his homework for 45 minutes. He starts his work at 7:15. When does he stop working?

8 : 00

Page 302

Problem-Solving: Money

Directions: Read each problem. Use the pictures to help you solve the problems.

Ben bought a ball. He had 11¢ left. How much money did he have at the start?

40 ¢

Tara has 75¢. She buys a car. How much money does she have left?

30 ¢

Leah wants to buy a doll and a ball. She has 80¢. How much more money does she need?

8 ¢

Jacob has 95¢. He buys the car and the ball. How much more money does he need to buy a doll for his sister?

38 ¢

Kim paid three quarters, one dime and three pennies for a hat. How much did it cost?

88 ¢

Directions: Cut out the squares below. Match them to the pictures that are missing these letter-sound combinations.

ai	ea	ee
ie	ou	oo
aw	ow	oa

p__nt	l__f	sh__p
p__	h__se	b__ts
p__	sn__	b__t

Directions: Cut out the squares below. Match them to the pictures that are missing these letter-sound combinations.

mb	au	ph
dge	stle	ight
ew	spl	kn

co___	s___cer	dol___in
bri___	whi_____	n_____
scr___	___ash	___ock